The War Has Brought Peace to Mexico

The War Has Brought Peace to Mexico

World War II and the Consolidation of the Post-Revolutionary State

HALBERT JONES

UNIVERSITY OF NEW MEXICO PRESS • ALBUQUERQUE

Library of Congress Cataloging-in-Publication Data

Jones, Halbert, 1977–
  The war has brought peace to Mexico : World War II and the
consolidation of the post-revolutionary state / Halbert Jones.
      pages cm
  Includes bibliographical references and index.
  ISBN 978-0-8263-5130-2 (cloth : alk. paper) — ISBN 978-0-8263-5132-6
(electronic)
    1. World War, 1939–1945—Mexico. 2. Avila Camacho, Manuel, 1897–1955.
3. Mexico—Politics and government—1910–1946. 4. Mexico—Foreign relations—1910–1946. I. Title.
  F1234.J8 2014
  972.08'16—dc23

                    2013041225

This book was designed by Lisa Tremaine and is set in Janson Text and
Univers 67 display. Janson was designed in the late seventeenth century by
Miklos Kis, a Hungarian punch cutter. It is a favorite of book designers for its
strong design and elegant legibility. Univers was designed by Adrain Frutiger
under strict Swiss design and discipline standards and released in 1957.

For my parents, and for Irene and Gemma

CONTENTS

I fear that over the long lifetime of this project, I have accumulated many more scholarly and personal debts than I can properly acknowledge. Though I must therefore apologize in advance to colleagues and friends whose contributions I might fail to mention, I would like to assure all those who have played a part in making this study possible of my tremendous gratitude.

First of all, I am grateful to the institutions that provided the generous financial support that enabled me to undertake this project. Travel grants from the Department of History and the David Rockefeller Center for Latin American Studies (DRCLAS) at Harvard University allowed me to carry out preliminary visits to archives in Mexico City and Washington, and a Sheldon Traveling Fellowship from Harvard's Graduate School of Arts and Sciences funded the bulk of my research in Mexico. A grant from the Mexican government's Instituto Nacional de Estudios Históricos de la Revolución Mexicana helped me to extend my stay there. Finally, Mellon fellowships in Latin American history, administered by DRCLAS, were of great assistance after my return from the field.

I am indebted, too, to the administration and staff of the archives and libraries at which I worked. I would like to express special appreciation to Sofía Valdés and Alejandro Padilla of Mexico's Secretaría de Relaciones Exteriores for helping me identify collections relevant to my project and to Angélica Oliver of the Instituto Tecnológico Autónomo de México's

Biblioteca Manuel Gómez Morín for allowing me to consult the collections of that library during the ITAM's summer vacation. Finally, I must thank Norma Mereles de Ogarrio, Amalia Torreblanca, and the entire staff of the Fideicomiso Archivos Plutarco Elías Calles y Fernando Torreblanca for creating a real home away from home for me while I was in Mexico City.

Outside of the archives, a number of Mexican scholars were kind enough to share their time and expertise with me. At different points during the course of my work in Mexico, Eugenia Meyer, Alicia Hernández, Javier Garciadiego, Margarita Carbó, Blanca Torres, Luis Garfias, and Arturo Grunstein helped me to locate and gain access to valuable sources of information on Mexican politics during the 1940s. I also enjoyed and benefited from conversations with José Luis Martínez, who served as private secretary to Education Minister Jaime Torres Bodet during the Ávila Camacho administration, and with Miguel Moreno Arreola, who had been a member of the Mexican Expeditionary Air Force during World War II.

I also owe a debt of gratitude to the Harvard faculty members who assisted me with this project as it took shape. John Coatsworth provided me with a supportive institutional home at DRCLAS, and Akira Iriye helped me to think about the connections between my work and the field of international history. Jorge Domínguez, Jane Mangan, and the late William Gienapp also made important contributions to my development as a scholar. I am especially grateful to John Womack. Over many years now, through many hours of conversations on Mexican history, he has been unfailingly generous with his time, unfailingly encouraging when I have encountered frustrations in my research, and unfailingly impressive in his vast knowledge of modern Mexico and of many other subjects besides.

In closing, I would like to thank my friends, colleagues, and family for their many contributions to this endeavor. My fellow graduate students at Harvard and the fellow researchers who became friends during my months in the field provided much-appreciated companionship, helpful feedback, and invaluable moral support. Here I really do have many more debts than I could possibly acknowledge, but I would particularly like to thank Alison Adams, Robert Alegre, Stephanie Ballenger, Ingrid Bleynat, Isaac Campos, Amilcar Challú, Evan Dawley, Brian DeLay, Oliver Dinius, Carrie Endries, Daniel Gutiérrez, Sarah

Jackson, Robert Karl, Gladys McCormick, Aaron Navarro, Andrew Paxman, Sergio Silva Castañeda, Bill Suárez-Potts, Monica Rankin, Mónica Ricketts, Laura Serna, and Louise Walker. I am also grateful to colleagues at the Office of the Historian of the U.S. Department of State, the Instituto Tecnológico Autónomo de México, DRCLAS, the Latin American Centre at the University of Oxford, and St Antony's College for their interest and input over the past several years. Closer to home, my grandparents Millie Green and the late John Green and my sisters, Lydia Chastain and Catherine Miller, have taken a much-appreciated interest in this project. My parents, Halbert and Ann Jones, were patient and understanding providers of logistical support as I shuttled between Cambridge, Washington, Mexico City, and their home in North Carolina during the course of my research. Finally, my wife, Irene Gándara Jones, has provided encouragement and inspiration as she has accompanied me through my work on this book, and though our daughter, Gemma, has not yet shown much of an interest in Mexican political history, I very much hope this is a book she will want to read someday.

Text

CGT	Confederación General de Trabajadores
CNC	Confederación Nacional Campesina
CNO	Consejo Nacional Obrero
CNOP	Confederación Nacional de Organizaciones Populares
COCM	Confederación de Obreros y Campesinos de México
CPN	Confederación Proletaria Nacional
CROM	Confederación Regional Obrera Mexicana
CTAL	Confederación de Trabajadores de América Latina
CTM	Confederación de Trabajadores de México
DGIPS	Dirección General de Investigaciones Políticas y Sociales
EMP	Estado Mayor Presidencial
FAEM	Fuerza Aérea Expedicionaria Mexicana
FBI	Federal Bureau of Investigation
FSTSE	Federación de Sindicatos de Trabajadores al Servicio del Estado
OSS	Office of Strategic Services
PAM	Partido Autonomista Mexicano
PAN	Partido Acción Nacional
PCM	Partido Comunista Mexicano
PNR	Partido Nacional Revolucionario
PRI	Partido Revolucionario Institucional
PRM	Partido de la Revolución Mexicana

RMP	Región Militar del Pacífico
SNTE	Sindicato Nacional de Trabajadores de la Educación
UNS	Unión Nacional Sinarquista
USSR	Union of Soviet Socialist Republics

Notes

AEMEUA	Archivo de la Embajada de México en los Estados Unidos de América, Fondo Embamex Washington II (SRE)
AGN	Archivo General de la Nación
AHUNAM	Archivo Histórico de la Universidad Nacional Autónoma de México
AMGM	Archivo Manuel Gómez Morín
CERMLC	Centro de Estudios de la Revolución Mexicana "Lázaro Cárdenas"
Colmex	Archivo Histórico de El Colegio de México
DGIPS	Ramo Gobernación, Dirección General de Investigaciones Políticas y Sociales (AGN)
FAPEC	Fideicomiso Archivos Plutarco Elías Calles y Fernando Torreblanca
GSM	George S. Messersmith Papers
LC	Ramo Presidentes, Lázaro Cárdenas del Río (AGN)
MAC	Ramo Presidentes, Manuel Ávila Camacho (AGN)
NARA	National Archives and Records Administration
RG	Record Group (NARA)
SDN	Secretaría de la Defensa Nacional, Dirección General de Archivo e Historia
SRE	Secretaría de Relaciones Exteriores, Dirección General del Acervo Histórico Diplomático

On the eve of Mexico's Independence Day in September 1942, the large crowd gathered in the Zócalo, the capital's main square, witnessed a remarkable sight. Above them, on a platform erected in front of the National Palace, the country's six living ex-presidents stood shoulder to shoulder with President Manuel Ávila Camacho in an unprecedented display of unity. Bitter rivalries between several of these men had deeply marked the history of the two preceding decades, making this show of common purpose by the surviving members of Mexico's post-Revolutionary leadership all the more striking. Taking place as it did against the backdrop of a world at war, the scene reflected Ávila Camacho's policy of promoting national unity during a period of international crisis. Significantly, this Acercamiento Nacional, or National Coming-Together, as it was billed, was staged shortly after Mexico had itself become a belligerent in the Second World War; the government had responded to the sinking of two Mexican tankers by German submarines some four months earlier by declaring the existence of a "state of war" with the Axis powers. In his speech to those assembled for the event, former president Abelardo L. Rodríguez explicitly linked the solidarity that was on display to Mexico's entry into the war as a member of the Allied coalition. "If the war has been the cause that unites and makes a single unit of the Mexican people," Rodríguez said, "the war is welcome."[1] As he spoke, the men on the platform stood together, putting aside past differences and embodying the political unity that the war had brought about. Marveling at this impressive—and until recently unimaginable—sight, a commentator for the Mexico City daily *El Universal* published a column in the newspaper's Independence Day edition entitled, "The War Has Brought Peace to Mexico."[2]

A little more than three years later, on the eve of another patriotic holiday, large crowds again lined the streets of Mexico City and filled the Zócalo, this time to receive the Mexican Expeditionary Air Force, a unit that had seen action in the Pacific theater during the closing weeks of World War II. Though the exploits of Squadron 201 in the Philippines were largely forgotten during the decades that followed, its members were enthusiastically received by an admiring and grateful nation at the time of their return to Mexico in November 1945. Tributes to the servicemen poured in from around the republic, and tens of thousands of citizens turned out to welcome them home as their train made its way across the country. The arrival of the aviators in the capital coincided with the celebration of the thirty-fifth anniversary of the Mexican Revolution, and officials took advantage of the opportunity to stage another spectacle designed to inspire pride and a sense of national unity, while affirming the strength and legitimacy of the "Revolutionary" regime. As the unit's commander ceremonially returned its flag to President Ávila Camacho, political and military figures invoked the example set by the members of the squadron to exhort the Mexican people to maintain the levels of solidarity they had achieved during wartime.[3]

Because the battlefields of World War II lay thousands of miles from Mexican shores, and because the country's direct military involvement was limited to the essentially symbolic contribution made by a single air force unit, the war's impact on Mexico can easily be underestimated. As the Acercamiento Nacional and the triumphal return of Squadron 201 showed, however, there was a high degree of consciousness of the war in Mexico, and the conflict had a real and significant influence on events there. In Mexico as elsewhere during these years, reports from the fronts dominated newspaper headlines, newsreels, and radio bulletins. In the major cities, war news from Europe, North Africa, Asia, and the Pacific was practically inescapable, and word of developments overseas reached even remote rural regions, along with sometimes alarming rumors about how those events would affect Mexico. Certainly, the economic impact of the war was felt in every part of the country, as patterns of production were substantially reordered to meet the demands of the war economy in the United States and to fulfill domestic needs that could no longer be met from abroad due to the unavailability of many imports.[4] Mexican industry expanded, even as the difficulty of obtaining equipment and spare parts hampered its growth. Meanwhile, wartime inflation eroded the purchasing power of Mexican wage earners, and a shortage of manpower in the United States drew tens of thousands of Mexicans across the border as guest workers, or braceros.[5]

The conflict also had important political consequences. As in other belligerent nations, the crisis atmosphere created by the war served to strengthen the hand of the chief executive, to drive an expansion of the role of the state, and to make open opposition to the sitting government more difficult. International conditions thus enabled Ávila Camacho to incorporate into his administration figures from competing factions of the ruling Partido de la Revolución Mexicana (PRM) and to insist that rivalries between them be suspended, or at least tamped down, for the duration of the hostilities. By casting himself as a wartime leader, the president was also able to obtain a degree of support from organizations on the left and the right that would otherwise have been inclined to be more sharply critical of the government and many of its policies. In addition, the war helped to accelerate the professionalization of the Mexican armed forces by focusing the minds of ambitious young officers on military, rather than political, matters and by making it possible for Mexico to obtain modern defense equipment on favorable terms. The war also provided the Mexican state with an opportunity to assert a wider role for itself in a variety of areas. The introduction of conscription, the development of a larger and more active intelligence service, and the launching of a nationwide literacy campaign, to name just three examples, were all justified with reference to the demands of wartime.[6] Moreover, World War II played an important part in the reshaping of the country's foreign relations, allowing Mexico to repair ties that had been strained in the 1930s and to claim a leading place among Latin American nations in the forums of the postwar world.

At the same time, the war presented the Mexican government with significant challenges. In addition to managing the economic dislocations caused by the conflict, the Ávila Camacho administration had to confront threats to national sovereignty arising from U.S. pressure for security cooperation, to contend with competing demands from the left and the right for more or less involvement in the war, and to overcome the ambivalent feelings of many Mexicans about any kind of participation in the struggle. Because the idea of taking part in a distant conflict did not appeal in the least to a large part of the Mexican population, the decision to enter the war was not easy or popular, making the president's success in bringing a greater degree of political peace to the country through participation in the war all the more remarkable.

Proceeding from a recognition that Mexico's involvement in the Second World War had a significant effect on the country's politics and that Mexican participation in the conflict was by no means inevitable, this study will assess how the Ávila Camacho administration handled the potentially explosive question of Mexico's role in the war. Though Mexico's economic contributions to the Allied war effort were almost certainly more consequential than its diplomatic stance or the symbolic contribution of Squadron 201, the focus here will be upon the debates over formal entry into the war and over direct military participation, as those were especially emotional and delicate questions over which the regime was especially likely to face resistance. This account will show that by insisting on national unity during a period of worldwide crisis, by cautiously taking his country into the war, and then by gradually deepening Mexican involvement in the conflict, Ávila Camacho and his collaborators were able to build and hold together a broad political coalition during a difficult, ideologically charged period. Though this coalition was unwieldy and the country's wartime unity was perhaps superficial, it was nonetheless sufficient to create a political situation at the national level in which opposition groups found it difficult to criticize the president, in which influential figures within the ruling establishment found it necessary to make public shows of support for the administration, in which the ruling party's powerful left wing could be held in line even as the regime began a turn to the right, and in which the armed forces could be brought increasingly under civilian control. The war and the international conditions it created thus played a significant part in facilitating the consolidation of the post-Revolutionary state.

Though that process of consolidation was by no means complete by 1945, and though Mexico's dominant-party regime was perhaps never as centralized and effective as was once thought, a comparison of the political conditions in Mexico at the time that the Second World War broke out with those that prevailed at the end of the conflict helps to make clear the scale of the war's impact. To be sure, when German forces invaded Poland in September 1939, there were few immediate repercussions in far-off Mexico. Despite a strongly anti-fascist ideological orientation, the administration of President Lázaro Cárdenas announced that the country would remain neutral in the conflict. Mexicans were, in any event, far more preoccupied with internal political questions than with the fighting in Europe. Since taking office in 1934, Cárdenas had built a strong constituency by implementing land reform and supporting organized labor, and he had accumulated considerable political clout by isolating more conservative opponents, by transferring powerful generals, and by restructuring the governing PRM.[7] However, wealthy businessmen and landowners bitterly opposed the president, and many devout Catholics saw his efforts to impart "socialist" education to the nation's youth as diabolical.[8] Moreover, relations with the United States had been tested, and relations with Great Britain had been broken off, as a result of the Mexican government's March 1938 expropriation of the holdings of foreign oil companies.[9] With elections due in July 1940, Mexicans anxiously awaited indications of the country's future political direction, wondering if Cárdenas would seek to impose a successor who would press ahead with ever more radical reforms or if the regime would move more cautiously, seeking to consolidate its gains or perhaps to change course.

By the end of World War II in September 1945, as the country anticipated another presidential election in 1946, the Mexican political landscape looked quite different. The moderate administration of Manuel Ávila Camacho included not just *cardenistas*—including the former president himself—but also more conservative figures who had been marginalized and even exiled in the 1930s. Labor leaders continued to profess their loyalty to the "Revolutionary" state, and they joined with Mexican officialdom in celebrating the defeat of fascism overseas, but by 1945 the government's relationships with the Roman Catholic Church and the industrial elite were also quite cordial. The country was preparing to elect a civilian candidate to the presidency for the first time since the Revolution of 1910, and at a convention in January 1946, the ruling PRM would reconstitute itself as the Partido Revolucionario Institucional (PRI), which would go on to dominate Mexican politics for the rest of the twentieth century. In contrast to the situation in the 1930s, the military lacked formal representation in the restructured party, and a new, largely middle-class "popular sector" took on a prominent role, often eclipsing the influence of the peasant and labor confederations that had previously provided the regime with its firmest bases of support.[10] Furthermore, not only had relations with the United Kingdom been restored by 1945, but diplomatic ties with the Soviet Union had been reestablished (a step that not even the "radical" Cárdenas had taken), and relations with Washington were arguably warmer and closer than at any time since Mexican independence. All of these shifts attest to the importance of the war years as a time of change in Mexico. This narrative will make clear that many of these important changes came about, in whole or in part, because of Mexico's participation in World War II.

The picture that emerges from this account is one of a state that was stronger and more centralized at the end of—and as a result of—the war than it was at the beginning, one that had new and improved tools at its disposal that would help it to meet the political challenges of the postwar years. This is not to say that World War II turned the Mexican state into a leviathan, a juggernaut, or a ruthlessly efficient "perfect dictatorship." Recent studies have shown that the Mexican regime was not so firmly established as that in the 1940s, if it ever was, and it certainly continued to face major challenges at the dawn of the Cold War era.[11] Indeed, by highlighting the constraints imposed upon Ávila Camacho by public opinion, by strong demands from both ends of the ideological spectrum, and by pressure from abroad, this story of Mexican participation in World War II helps to make clear the limits of presidential power in mid-twentieth-century Mexico. Nonetheless, wartime conditions, as managed by the Ávila Camacho administration, did serve to augment presidential authority, to stimulate the development of state institutions, and to impose a degree of stability on Mexican politics as the regime underwent what otherwise might have been a much more difficult transition from the *cardenista* period to the postwar years.

Understanding how the Mexican administration was able to bring the country into the war as a belligerent and later as an active participant is important not just because of the direct political effects of involvement in the conflict, but also because Ávila Camacho's success in implementing controversial and even unpopular policies related to participation in the war without triggering a significant backlash is itself indicative of the manner in which he was able to steer the regime away from the political framework of the cardenista period while avoiding damaging internal conflicts. The Ávila Camacho administration's cautious, deliberate handling of explosive issues meant that his term in office saw few dramatic political confrontations or major reforms that would win attention from future generations of historians, but the relatively quiet shifts that were taking place in a variety of policy areas during the war years had a significant impact on the course of the country's history over the decades that followed.

This study joins a growing body of work that highlights the 1940s as a pivotal period in Mexico's twentieth-century political development. In both popular memory and the scholarly literature, this period was long overshadowed by the more radical cardenista reforms that preceded it and by the more pronounced turn to the right that followed during the administration of Miguel Alemán (1946–1952), whose presidency coincided with the early years of the Cold War. Indeed, the historiography of twentieth-century Mexico has, until recently, been dominated by studies of the Revolution of 1910 and its immediate aftermath, with much less historical work done on the decades after the end of Cárdenas's presidency. Reviewing the literature in 1985, one historian observed that the year 1940 "seems to have served as a historiographical watershed dividing the Mexican past into its 'historic' and 'contemporaneous' epochs, inviting historians to study the former and neglect the latter."[12] At the end of the century, another scholar still found that even "venerable academic journals treat 1940 as an absolute divide, beyond which they do not tread."[13]

For many years, to the extent that they did seek to explain Mexico's political development after 1940, historians and other analysts tended to focus less on the period of the war and more on the so-called "Mexican miracle," an era of rapid economic growth and apparent political stability that stretched from the late 1940s through the 1960s. In these narratives, the Ávila Camacho *sexenio* generally appeared, if at all, not as a significant period in its own right but rather as the tail end of the cardenista era or, at best, as a vaguely defined transitional period between the redistributive economic nationalism of the mid- to late 1930s and the more conservative authoritarianism of the postwar regime.[14] The most sophisticated analyses of these years recognized the importance of the role played by Ávila Camacho as an arbiter between left and right as the Revolution took a more moderate course, and they noted that the war created new conditions that were propitious for the consolidation of the state, offering "superb terrain on which to build the national consensus to which the regime was committed," but on the whole the early 1940s and the impact of World War II on Mexico received relatively little serious attention.[15]

Fortunately, if Mexico's "contemporary" history was once neglected, it is now receiving the close examination that it deserves. Since the late 1990s, and particularly since the democratic transition of 2000, the period after 1940 in general and the 1940s in particular have attracted much more attention from scholars, with historians entering the field more fully and with greater confidence. With the era of the PRI's political dominance at an end (or so it seemed at the time), the decades following Cárdenas's presidency could more easily be claimed and analyzed as part of a historical past. Moreover, that task has been facilitated by new freedom of information laws in Mexico that have made many archival materials available to researchers for the first time.[16] The resulting scholarship has added depth and nuance to traditional narratives of Mexico's mid-twentieth-century political history, with several authors shedding additional light on the significance of the country's involvement in World War II. For example, María Emilia Paz has focused on the U.S.-Mexican security relationship during the war, concluding that the crisis atmosphere of the war years gave Mexico a remarkable degree of leverage in its dealings with its more powerful neighbor to the north.[17] Monica Rankin has examined wartime propaganda in Mexico, showing how officials capitalized upon the conflict to promote industrialization, and in his extensive work on politics, society, and U.S.-Mexican relations during the 1940s, Stephen Niblo has concluded that Mexican "participation in World War II became absolutely critical in the process of shifting the revolution away from Cárdenas's populism and onto a more conservative course."[18]

While these valuable contributions to our understanding of Mexican politics during the war are generally consistent with the traditional view that the post-Revolutionary state was achieving a high degree of consolidation at midcentury, other recent works have called this premise into question, challenging the idea that the PRI regime attained the degree of dominance and control that has been attributed to it. These studies have highlighted the persistence of regional strong men and military chieftains, the chaotic and often violent nature of local politics, and the extent of popular resistance during a period that was previously thought to have been characterized by the establishment of an imperial presidency, the subordination of once-powerful generals to civilian authority, and the docility of a population that was enjoying the benefits of rapid economic growth. In addition to works on national politics that focus on the electoral challenges that the regime continued to face into the 1950s, regional studies have shown that the Mexican state was shaped in this period not just by the will of the president but by complex interactions between the center and the periphery and between political elites and popular movements. They show, too, that while the state could deploy its ample capacity for repression when necessary, its vaunted political stability often looked less impressive from below.[19]

These new insights into the complexity of the Mexican political land-scape during and after World War II serve to reinforce the importance of examining the period more closely. To that end, this study aims to contribute to a better understanding of how international conditions during the war years intersected with a dynamic internal political situa-tion, providing the administration with an opportunity to insist on unity even as it faced daunting challenges. The chapters that follow provide an account of Mexico's deepening involvement in World War II between Ávila Camacho's inauguration in December 1940 and the return of the Mexican Expeditionary Air Force from the front in November 1945, high-lighting how at every stage the administration was able to capitalize upon the international situation to strengthen its position. Chapter 1 notes the precariousness of the president's authority during his first year in office and describes how his government took advantage of the crisis atmo-sphere to win support for itself during those difficult months. Chapter 2 outlines Mexico's response to the Japanese attack on Pearl Harbor, show-ing how the government found a middle ground between pressures com-ing from Washington and much of the Mexican left for a firm response to Axis aggression and the desire of most Mexicans to avoid direct par-ticipation in the war. Chapter 3 explains how Ávila Camacho was able to lead a reluctant nation into a formal state of war in May 1942, after the sinking of two Mexican ships by German U-boats. Here again, by deep-ening Mexico's role in the war while insisting that its role would remain limited, the government was able to win the backing of virtually every political faction and much of Mexican society. Chapter 4 describes the administration's efforts to rally the nation around it during Mexico's first full year as a belligerent, when, for a time, mass meetings, military train-ing, and other measures succeeded in convincing much of the country's population of the need for unity behind the president during a period of worldwide crisis. Chapter 5 details the government's subsequent steps toward direct military participation in the war. With the danger of an attack on Mexican territory receding, a cautious movement toward the deployment of a military unit overseas served to remind Mexicans that their country was at war while also addressing the growing desire of some elements of the armed forces for an active role in the conflict. The sixth and final chapter reviews the final year of the Second World War, when the Mexican Expeditionary Air Force went into action, relating how even a symbolic military role in the war helped the government to minimize the disruptive and potentially destabilizing effect of political maneuvering in advance of the 1946 presidential elections. Finally, an epilogue reviews the critical role played by events many thousands of miles away in the political transformation that took place during the early 1940s and reflects on how the impact of World War II on Mexico came to be largely forgotten during the decades that followed.

Ávila Camacho's Difficult First Year

DECEMBER 1940–DECEMBER 1941

During the first year after his inauguration on December 1, 1940, President Manuel Ávila Camacho faced considerable challenges as he sought to establish his authority as the head of the Mexican state and as the leading figure in Mexican public life. Many of the conservative elements that had backed opposition candidate General Juan Andreu Almazán in the bitterly contested election of July 1940 continued to grumble that fraud and violence had deprived their man of victory, and they demanded revisions to the radical policies of the 1930s that they found most objectionable. At the same time, those who had most actively supported Ávila Camacho's candidacy also looked upon the new president with suspicion. Though they pledged unstinting loyalty to him, labor unions, peasant groups, and other left-leaning organizations watched his every move, worrying that Lázaro Cárdenas's chosen successor might prove to be insufficiently committed to his predecessor's "revolutionary" project of redistribution and economic nationalism. In this polarized political environment, Ávila Camacho sought to steer a middle course. He endeavored to appease both radicals and reactionaries by pledging that his administration would focus on consolidating the gains of the Mexican Revolution rather than pushing ahead with new reforms, and he ensured that his cabinet represented a broad range of viewpoints. Though this approach was generally successful in preventing explosive confrontations between competing factions, it led some observers to conclude that the president was a weak, vacillating figure.

Confronted with these domestic political difficulties, Ávila Camacho took advantage of the international situation to augment his clout and to enhance his prestige. Though Mexicans were not eager to play an active part in the war that had raged in Europe since 1939, the global repercussions of the fighting there meant that the Mexican president's preeminent role in the formation of foreign policy took on added significance. To be sure, moving too quickly toward a more active role in the war might have led to deepened dissatisfaction with the government, inasmuch as most Mexicans favored neutrality and had ambivalent feelings (at best) about the prospect of close cooperation with the United States in hemispheric defense efforts. But by gradually adopting a more stridently anti-Axis position and by emphasizing Mexico's vulnerability to foreign infiltration and economic disruption during a period of worldwide crisis, the Ávila Camacho administration made more credible its insistence that national unity behind the president was necessary.

After the German invasion of the Soviet Union in June 1941, Ávila Camacho derived even greater political benefits from his efforts to lead Mexico toward a position of more open support for the anti-fascist cause. With much of the Mexican left suddenly enthusiastic about the Allied war effort, the president found it possible to move to the right in some domestic policy areas without losing the backing of the groups that had formed his electoral base. The left's redoubled support for Ávila Camacho's foreign policy gave the president some additional room for maneuver in other fields. At the same time, the assertion that spies and saboteurs posed a clear and present danger to the security of nonbelligerent countries allowed the Mexican regime to craft for itself new tools that would help it to stamp out what it saw as subversion and preserve its brand of order long after World War II came to an end.

★ ★ ★

When Ávila Camacho assumed the presidency, Mexico maintained a policy of neutrality with respect to the war in Europe. Fifteen months earlier, on September 4, 1939, President Cárdenas had responded to the German invasion of Poland and to the subsequent British and French declarations of war on the Third Reich by issuing a statement expressing his regret that a number of states had "resorted to armed struggle to seek the solution of their differences" and conveying his government's decision that Mexico would remain neutral in the conflict.[1] Though the president's statement was more a lamentation that war had broken out than a denunciation of the German violation of Polish sovereignty, the Mexican declaration of neutrality certainly did not reflect any official sympathy for fascism. Indeed, during the years leading up to the outbreak of World War II, the Cárdenas administration had taken a leading role in denouncing the Italian conquest of Ethiopia (1935) and in supporting the cause of the Republicans in the Spanish Civil War (1936–1939) as they waged an ultimately unsuccessful struggle against General Francisco Franco's German- and Italian-backed forces. Mexico had even stood alone in denouncing Germany's annexation of Austria in 1938.[2] However, in September 1939, with the United States and most Latin American nations seeking to keep the war in Europe from reaching the Western Hemisphere, the Mexican government chose to join its neighbors in distancing itself from the conflict by announcing a policy of neutrality.

Moreover, Cárdenas recognized that there was little domestic support for an activist Mexican stance in response to the events overseas. Through much of the 1930s, leftist groups had been the most vocal critics of the Nazi regime, but in the wake of the August 1939 nonaggression pact between Germany and the Soviet Union, the leadership of most of these organizations adjusted their positions to reflect the new party line emanating from Moscow, characterizing World War II as a struggle between competing imperialist blocs. The national teachers' union, for example, praised Cárdenas's declaration of neutrality, claiming that the only people who could be interested in "the continuation of the imperialist war" were "those who wish to carry out a new carving up of the world" that would threaten Mexico's "independent and sovereign existence."[3] In the state of Michoacán, a regional convention of the Partido Comunista Mexicano (PCM) similarly lauded the president for his stance "in the face of the imperialist war."[4]

While many rank and file members of groups like these recognized the cynicism with which their leaders had changed their positions after the signing of the Molotov-Ribbentrop Pact, Cárdenas had little incentive to take sides in the European conflict as long as the interest groups that had previously advocated a staunchly anti-fascist foreign policy remained on the sidelines.[5] Meanwhile, other Mexicans simply appreciated the president's calls for peace and his efforts to keep the war from reaching the country's shores. One local chamber of commerce thanked Cárdenas for making the nation less vulnerable to foreign attack, and a civic association made up of members of the 1917 convention that had written the national Constitution applauded the president for keeping Mexico out of the fighting overseas, condemning warfare in general as "a crime against humanity and a demonstration of backwardness, barbarity, and savagery."[6]

In the months that followed, the Cárdenas administration moved slowly and deliberately toward a policy that was more critical of Germany and its allies as it denounced their acts of aggression against smaller countries, but the Mexican government steadfastly maintained its status as a nonbelligerent. As the leader of a relatively weak country that had once lost half of its territory to its northern neighbor, Cárdenas felt it was important to speak out against violations of national sovereignty when they occurred. Therefore, at the Pan-American foreign ministers' conference held in Panama in September–October 1939 in response to the outbreak of the war, the Mexican representative, Eduardo Hay, denounced the German attack on Poland and Czechoslovakia.[7] A foreign ministry bulletin issued around the same time made clear that Mexico would continue to maintain relations with the deposed Polish government and that the Cárdenas administration would "not recognize, for any reason, conquests obtained by force."[8] The Mexican president subsequently protested the May 1940 assault on Belgium and the Netherlands by the forces of "militarist imperialism," and just days before German forces marched into Paris in June 1940, he sent a message of solidarity to the French president, expressing his government's disgust at the clearly opportunistic Italian declaration of war against France.[9]

Despite these denunciations of fascist aggression, however, Mexican authorities did not move away from their policy of neutrality. Indeed, in his May 1940 statement on the plight of the Low Countries, Cárdenas was almost as harsh in his criticism of the Allied countries that had failed to contest the German occupation of those nations as he was in his condemnation of the invasion itself, and shortly thereafter he reiterated to the Mexican press that his government's policy was one of "absolute neutrality in the European conflict, a position that has been sustained and approved in the various Pan-American conferences."[10] Nor did Cárdenas limit his protests against infringements of sovereignty to situations in which Germany and Italy were the aggressors. Much to the

consternation of the leftist leaders who were praising the "peace policies" of the USSR, the Mexican president also issued a statement on
December 5, 1939, denouncing the Soviet attack on Finland.[11] Rather
than taking an ideologically anti-fascist position that would have placed
Mexico squarely in opposition to Germany and Italy in the European
war, the Cárdenas administration limited itself to objecting to individual
acts of aggression while emphasizing its neutrality.

The Mexican government also reacted to developments overseas in
1939 and 1940 by quietly stepping up diplomatic and military cooperation
with the United States. Cárdenas privately recognized that "our proxim-
ity to the United States situates us—whether we like it or not—within
the field of [possible future] military operations," and since U.S. strate-
gists would be making plans to defend their southern flank with or without the help of the local authorities, the president judged it necessary to
establish a basis for bilateral collaboration that would safeguard Mexican
sovereignty.[12] The Mexican government therefore aimed to prevent the
establishment of U.S. bases on Mexican soil and U.S. incursions in the
name of self-defense by stressing that Mexico would be a dependable,
self-sufficient partner in the defense of the hemisphere. To demonstrate
Mexican reliability on the diplomatic front, the Cárdenas administration participated not just in the 1939 Panama meeting of foreign ministers but also in a July 1940 Pan-American conference in Havana, where
the Mexican delegation supported a resolution establishing the princi-
ple that an attack on any country in the Americas by an outside power
would be considered as an act of aggression against the entire region.[13]
This agreement would later play an important role in bringing about a
deepening of Mexican involvement in the war.

The Cárdenas administration also entered into secret military talks
with the United States beginning in the summer of 1940. Mexican
ambassador Francisco Castillo Nájera and the military officers who
participated in the meetings insisted that their country would be able
to respond effectively to any invasion from overseas without assistance
from the United States, and they steadfastly resisted their American
counterparts' suggestions that Mexico allow the U.S. Navy to establish
bases at Bahía Magdalena and Acapulco.[14] Though little headway was
made in the talks, the establishment of direct contact between military representatives from both countries gave Washington an indication that the Mexican government took its responsibility for the defense

of the country's territory seriously. At a time when the government of Franklin D. Roosevelt was desperately concerned about its preparedness for war and its possible vulnerability to attack, signals such as these helped to protect Mexico from overt U.S. interference in its internal affairs without compromising the country's neutrality or its sovereignty.

Mexican officials recognized that Washington's preoccupation with the tumultuous international situation offered not just challenges but also opportunities for their country to improve relations that had been strained as a result of the Cárdenas administration's 1938 expropriation of foreign-owned oil interests. The two governments continued to discuss ways to resolve the claims that had arisen in connection with the nationalization of the petroleum industry, as well as older claims relating to the expropriation of land owned by U.S. citizens and companies.[15] As these talks continued, some within the Cárdenas administration saw that the war provided a chance for Mexico to obtain a more favorable settlement on those fronts and in other negotiations with the United States. As Undersecretary of the Treasury Eduardo Villaseñor observed in advocating Mexican participation in the Havana Conference during a June 19, 1940, meeting of Cárdenas's advisers, "The moment in which the United States has such a great interest, is an opportunity to negotiate with the United States. It is an opportunity to resolve the greater part of the problems that we now have."[16] The generally sympathetic and favorable attitude toward hemispheric defense initiatives adopted by Mexico in light of considerations such as these may well have played a role in the Roosevelt administration's decision to send a strong signal of support to incoming President Manuel Ávila Camacho as the date of his investiture approached. While Cárdenas's nationalist economic policies had enraged U.S. business interests, he had been a helpful partner in the effort to build up an American bloc of nonbelligerent nations, and therefore Roosevelt sent his vice president elect, Henry Wallace, to attend the inauguration of Cárdenas's successor on December 1, 1940. This unequivocal demonstration of U.S. support for the new administration thwarted the *almazanistas*' dwindling hopes that they might succeed in installing their defeated candidate as president by launching a rebellion with U.S. backing.[17]

As Ávila Camacho began his term in office, he confronted a political landscape marked by deep divisions, and he struggled to win the support of competing factions that were often bitterly at odds with one another.

To reassure the generally conservative Catholic faithful that he would not pursue the anticlerical policies implemented by previous administrations in the 1920s and 1930s, Ávila Camacho publicly revealed before his inauguration that he himself was a "believer."[18] Such a statement from a post-Revolutionary president of Mexico was unprecedented; indeed, the archbishop of Mexico City stated that he had great confidence in Ávila Camacho, inasmuch as he was "the only President of Mexico in the passage of many years who has declared publicly and categorically that he is Catholic."[19] At the same time, though, the incoming chief executive sought to foster political reconciliation by allowing two of the church's most ferocious persecutors to return from exile. Former Tabasco governor Tomás Garrido Canabal and former president Plutaco Elías Calles, both of whom had left the country in the mid-1930s after falling out with Cárdenas, came back to Mexico in March and May of 1941, respectively.[20]

Meanwhile, to calm fears among labor and peasant organizations that the new administration would abandon their interests and move to the right, Ávila Camacho told the February 1941 congress of the powerful official labor bloc, the Confederación de Trabajadores de México (CTM), that he remained committed to his predecessor's goal of social justice, and he named cardenistas to head the ministries that mattered most to Mexican workers and to leftist ideologues. Cárdenas's former private secretary and interior minister Ignacio García Téllez received the post of labor minister, and Luis Sánchez Pontón was put in charge of the education ministry. Ávila Camacho was careful to ensure that other political groups were also represented in the cabinet, however. A former *callista*, Ezequiel Padilla, was named foreign minister. Padilla also had close ties with conservative former president Emilio Portes Gil, as did the new agriculture minister, Marte R. Gómez, who hailed from Portes Gil's home state of Tamaulipas. For his part, the new economy minister, Francisco Javier Gaxiola, was clearly the personal representative in the cabinet of the wealthy businessman and former president Abelardo L. Rodríguez, whom he had served as private secretary.[21] In short, the incoming government represented a broad cross section of the ruling Partido de la Revolución Mexicana (PRM), leaving many observers to wonder what Ávila Camacho's true intentions were.

Without any clear, deeply committed constituency of his own, Ávila Camacho called for a program of national unity that would bring the

Figure 1: President Manuel Ávila Camacho and his cabinet, drawn from many factions of the fractious "revolutionary family." (Fototeca Nacional, Instituto Nacional de Antropología e Historia; © 641611 CONACULTA.INAH.SINAFO. FN.MÉXICO)

country's disparate and fractious social and political groups together under his leadership. Emphasizing the need for solidarity in the face of the unsettled international situation therefore served the new president well. Cautiously but steadily, Ávila Camacho went beyond the steps taken by Cárdenas to involve Mexico more deeply in the global conflagration and to place the country in a more clearly anti-Axis position. In early March 1941, for example, the government publicly acknowledged the military discussions that had been going on between representatives of the Mexican and U.S. armed forces. The talks had previously been carried out in secret, though rumors that negotiations were under way had circulated for some time.[22] A few days later, on March 7, Foreign Minister Padilla appeared before the Mexican Senate to lay out the administration's position with respect to the war. With subversive propaganda then claiming that Ávila Camacho had pledged to provide naval bases and fighting men to the United States in exchange for recognition of his electoral victory, Padilla stressed that the government had signed no secret agreements with Washington.[23]

In an effort to prepare the population for the possibility of more extensive participation in hemispheric defense efforts, however, the foreign minister added that the administration would consider entering into a formal military alliance with the United States in the future "if the exigencies of the current conflict were to require it," and he reiterated that the government would consider an attack on any American nation as an attack on Mexico. When one skeptical senator asked Padilla if it would not be best for Mexico to continue following its "policy of strict neutrality" rather than pursuing bilateral military arrangements with the United States, the foreign minister replied that "neutrality is a word that cannot be heard in these moments in which the destinies and the liberty of the Continent are demanding a positive, effective, and bold action for the defense of America."[24] Though Padilla stopped short of explicitly taking sides in the European conflict, his rhetorical references to the cause of "democracy" and his offhand dismissal of the importance of observing strict neutrality suggested that a significant shift was under way in Mexican policy, with the Ávila Camacho administration moving as quickly as it prudently could toward putting the country on a war footing.

Prudence and caution were necessary, to be sure, especially since many groups on the left continued to describe the war as a meaningless struggle between rival camps of capitalist imperialists. Indeed, when CTM-affiliated workers gathered two weeks prior to Padilla's appearance before the Senate for an assembly organized by one of the labor confederation's constituent unions, a leader of the national journalists' union denounced "the imperialist and rapacious character of the present war," asserting that while the Mexican people would be willing to give their lives "in a just and holy war for their liberty," they were "not disposed to sacrifice even a single one of their men . . . in defense of the bankers of Wall Street."[25] Predictably, then, after the foreign minister's March 7 speech, a PCM member in Mexico City wrote to Ávila Camacho to inform him of the "alarm" with which he had read the declarations of the "reactionary" Padilla, who seemed to be trying to involve Mexico "in a war that is outside the scope of our interests."[26] For its part, the CTM's official newspaper, *El Popular*, managed to find praiseworthy aspects of the policy outlined by the foreign minister—an editorial lauded the administration for maintaining friendly relations with the United States while steadfastly defending Mexican sovereignty—but the mouthpiece of the CTM's former secretary-general, Vicente Lombardo Toledano, also insisted that the ultimate aim of the government should be to keep the country "out of the terrible imperialist conflict whose painful consequences weigh upon humankind."[27] Thus, while *El Popular* joined much of the mainstream press in praising Padilla's exposition of Mexican foreign policy, moving too far, too quickly toward an active role in the war still threatened to alienate influential organizations on the left end of the political spectrum.[28]

Nonetheless, the Ávila Camacho administration continued to push ahead with its policy of building up the Western Hemisphere's defenses in cooperation with the United States and of taking an increasingly strong stand against Axis aggression. On April 1, 1941, the Mexican and U.S. governments announced that they had concluded an agreement that would allow military planes from each of the two nations to use specific airfields in the other country while in transit to other destinations. The accord made it possible for the U.S. armed forces to move warplanes easily between the United States and its bases around the strategically vital Panama Canal while relieving pressure on Mexico to grant more extensive base rights to its northern neighbor. To counter possible claims that the treaty violated Mexican sovereignty, the pact was framed as a reciprocal agreement, though it was unclear where planes from Mexico's tiny air force would go if they ever made use of their right under the accord to land on American airfields while passing through the United States.[29]

At the same time, the Mexican government came closer to taking a clear position against Germany and Italy when it seized merchant ships from those two countries that had been in Mexican harbors since the outbreak of the war. On April 8, noting that the crews of Axis-owned vessels had carried out acts of sabotage in the ports of other American countries and that sailors on the Italian craft *Atlas* had apparently sought to blow up their ship in Tampico harbor, the Mexican government asserted its right to take possession of the nine Italian and three German ships that were then in Gulf coast ports, promising that compensation would be paid at the conclusion of the war. Despite protests from the German and Italian ministers, the Mexican government confined the ships' crewmen to the city of Guadalajara and later detained them in Perote, Veracruz. Most of the vessels were turned over to the national oil company for its use.[30]

Even as the Mexican government moved to seize the Axis ships, thereby expanding its own merchant fleet, the foreign ministry issued another condemnation of German attacks on neutral countries in Europe, further confirming the administration's increasingly pronounced anti-Axis tilt. On April 7, Padilla noted that "once again the German armies have invaded the territory of a neutral country," in this case Yugoslavia, and that the Reich had also expanded its campaign against Greece. The foreign minister pointedly referred to the unhappy experience of these countries as an instructive example for "those who continue believing that neutrality is a guarantee of peace and salvation."[31] The message was clear: Mexico would have to be prepared for deeper involvement in the war, even if it intended to maintain its neutrality.

However, some on the left remained uncomfortable with the administration's moves toward more direct involvement in a war that it had been denouncing as an "inter-imperialist" conflict. A May 29, 1941, open letter to Ávila Camacho from Vicente Lombardo Toledano gave the president an opportunity to address these concerns. The message from the still-influential former head of the CTM posed a number of questions about Mexico's international position.[32] Probably by pre-arrangement with Lombardo Toledano, Ávila Camacho released his May 30 reply to the questionnaire to the press, taking advantage of the opportunity to reiterate that no secret agreement with the United States existed, that the nation's sovereignty was being jealously guarded, and that Mexico's commitments at the conferences of Panama and Havana would not oblige the country to take part in any fighting outside of the Western Hemisphere. The president stressed that the "collaboration of Mexico and the United States is not the result of a military alliance, but rather the product of a regional understanding of a defensive nature." Therefore, he said, "if the North American [U.S.] Government were to declare war upon some Asian or European power, that fact alone would not compel Mexico automatically to adopt the same attitude."[33]

Ávila Camacho was quick to add, though, that "it would be erroneous to think that, in the present state of things, the destiny of one of the American nations can indefinitely remain isolated from the destiny of the rest." The "dictatorial forces" overseas would almost certainly seek to subvert and undermine the "democratic unit" formed by the American republics, the president explained, so Mexico would take whatever future steps might be necessary to uphold the country's honor and to guarantee its independence.[34] Thus, even as he endeavored to assuage the fears of leftist and other critics that Mexico was becoming too involved in World War II by committing his government to a purely defensive policy, Ávila Camacho sought to prepare the public for further steps that might be taken in the name of resisting foreign "dictatorial forces."

Leftist publications and organizations hailed Ávila Camacho's reply to Lombardo Toledano while continuing to stand firmly against more active Mexican participation in the conflict overseas. Highlighting the president's statement that Mexico was under no obligation to take part in an "extra-continental" war, *El Popular* celebrated the fact that the country would not be forced to participate in "a struggle in which its interests have not been attacked nor are they threatened."[35] For its part, the PCM also praised Ávila Camacho's explanation that a U.S. declaration of war would not necessarily require Mexico to become a belligerent, and party leaders restated their view that "the only patriotic attitude is that of not giving moral or material support to either of the imperialist bands at war" with one another, pledging that Mexican communists would continue fighting "against those who try to involve the country in the war."[36] Similarly, the Union of Graphic Arts Workers chose to interpret Ávila Camacho's letter as a repudiation of a bellicose foreign policy. The group released a statement lauding the president's declaration "precisely because the peoples [of Mexico and other countries] have no interest in this war, which is a new struggle for the redistribution of the world."[37] At the same time, the most powerful institution in the world of Mexican organized labor, the CTM, declared its support for Ávila Camacho's foreign policy "strongly and with real enthusiasm." While the official labor confederation restated its opposition to "nazi-fascism" and called for unity against it, the CTM also "energetically" condemned "the inter-imperialist war."[38] Because of their views on the international situation, these groups all read Ávila Camacho's May 30 message selectively, framing their praise for his remarks in such a way that he would seem to be committed to a policy of keeping Mexico out of World War II.

Just a few weeks later, though, after Germany invaded the Soviet Union on June 21, the leadership of Mexican leftist groups became markedly more willing to take sides in the fighting in Europe. Even noncommunist groups on the left tended to admire the Soviet Union as a nation that was ostensibly guided by socialist ideals, so when Hitler violated the nonaggression pact he had concluded with Moscow by sending German armies into Soviet territory, many labor leaders and leftist activists in Mexico and elsewhere abruptly revised their view that the war was a meaningless clash between imperialist forces. Suddenly, it became important to contribute all available resources to the fight against fascism. Lombardo

Toledano called upon Latin American nations "to contribute with efficacy to the defeat of fascism . . . through the expropriation of the goods
of the fascists and the dissolution of the political parties and groups of
creole fascists behind which international fascism is found."[39] *El Popular*
similarly responded to the new geopolitical situation by advocating the
formation of a broad front made up of all anti-fascist groups, affirming
that the right-wing ideology posed a danger to the whole world and not
just to Europe.[40] The left's sudden discovery of the danger of fascism
worked greatly to the advantage of Ávila Camacho, who could now count
on the enthusiastic backing of leftist organizations that had previously
given only lukewarm and conditional support to his efforts to move the
country toward a more strongly anti-Axis position.

For the benefit of those who continued to believe that Mexico could
enjoy security and avoid the effects of the war by remaining neutral,
Foreign Minister Padilla pointed to the German attack on Russia
as evidence that a policy of "abstention—[and] even assistance to the
nazi-fascist powers" would not be taken into account by the "totalitarians" as they pursued "a policy that does not recognize any brake
but that of force."[41] The following month, an exchange of diplomatic
notes between the German minister in Mexico and the Mexican foreign
ministry added to the growing tensions between the two countries. In
response to the U.S. government's decision to block the assets of various German individuals and businesses whose names were included on
a blacklist it had drawn up, the top German diplomat in Mexico City,
F. H. Rüdt von Collenberg, wrote to Padilla on July 28 to encourage
him not to accede to U.S. pressure to take action against the businesses
on the list that were based in Mexico. The German minister suggested
that the Mexican government might wish to protest the U.S. government's actions against companies "protected by Mexican sovereignty,"
and he menacingly hinted that Mexican acceptance of the U.S. blacklist
"could not fail to influence the resolutions of the German Government
upon reopening commercial relations with Mexico after the war." In an
unusually strong reply, Padilla pointedly told Rüdt von Collenberg that
Mexico would respond to the U.S. list in the manner "that it might deem
most adequate, without the need to receive or to follow insinuations of
other authorities." In reply to the veiled threat at the end of the minister's note, Padilla said that his government found it necessary "to reject
this premature warning that reveals . . . a position of imperious and

unacceptable pressure."[42] The administration then proceeded to release the German note and the Mexican reply to the public, thereby holding itself up as a staunch defender of the country's dignity and sovereignty while laying the groundwork for a harder line against the Axis by casting Germany in a negative light.

With the left firmly committed to his increasingly anti-fascist foreign policy, Ávila Camacho felt free to make a significant move to the right in September 1941. On September 11, the president announced that a conservative politician, Octavio Véjar Vázquez, would replace Luis Sánchez Pontón as education minister. Anticommunist groups and individuals congratulated Ávila Camacho on the move, hoping it would be a first step toward the elimination of the extensive leftist influence that existed in the nation's schools, where a Cárdenas-era constitutional provision required that students receive "socialist" instruction.[43] Within weeks, the new education minister was actively investigating financial improprieties involving communist sympathizers within his ministry and pushing for the consolidation of several rival teachers' unions, which would serve to diminish the influence of the most radical organization. These moves provided what U.S. embassy officials described as "the first hard blow that the 'left-wing' movement has received from the Administration of President Ávila Camacho."[44]

A few days after Véjar Vázquez's appointment, on September 29, there was another sign that the administration was making a turn to the right, as the president's older brother, Maximino Ávila Camacho, was named to head the communications and public works ministry. Maximino had just completed his term as governor of Puebla, where he had clashed, sometimes violently, with CTM-affiliated labor organizations. Known as a volatile, colorful individual, Maximino lived up to his reputation by striding into his ministry's grand edifice on Calle Tacuba accompanied by a large entourage and flanked by armed gunmen, taking possession of his new office there in dramatic fashion.[45]

In some circles, the appointment of Maximino to the cabinet was taken as a sign of the president's weakness.[46] Indeed, the appointment appeared to confirm some analysts' long-standing suspicions that the president's more dynamic, better-known brother would be the real power behind the throne during Manuel's term in office. Officials in Washington had apparently operated on that assumption when they lavishly entertained Maximino during an April 1941 visit to the United States, and in August,

Manuel had felt compelled to issue a statement indicating that "neither my relatives nor any other person have been allowed or will be allowed to interfere in the resolutions I have dictated or will dictate in the exercise of the powers vested in me." [47] His naming of Maximino to head the communications ministry just a few weeks later seemed to contradict this statement. In fact, the president was navigating treacherous waters fairly successfully: giving his famously corrupt brother a lucrative position from which he would oversee the government's public works projects meant that Maximino would have access to the spoils of office without necessarily being able to exert much influence on the making of policy.

These personnel changes in the president's cabinet caused consternation among leftists, as did an unfortunate incident that occurred outside Ávila Camacho's official residence on September 23. That day, an army detachment stationed at Los Pinos fired upon a group of striking workers from the government's war materials factory that had approached the presidential palace to seek an audience. Initial reports indicated that at least seven workers were killed, though rumors suggested that the death toll might well have been considerably higher. [48] Union leaders and leftist press outlets naturally denounced the use of force against the workers, but rather than withdraw their support from the government, they blamed the incident on the machinations of fascist elements within Mexico and called for even stronger unity around the president. The CTM's *El Popular* was quick to distance Ávila Camacho from the incident outside his home, reporting that the president had promised "to work with all energy to punish those responsible for the unfortunate event." [49] The PCM's *La Voz de México* cited the "massacre" as "an example of what the reactionaries and nazi-fascism will be capable of in Mexico, if the people, and particularly all the forces of the left of the Mexican Revolution, do not organize themselves rapidly, putting aside their differences, and form an unbreakable anti-fascist bloc." [50] To be sure, the CTM, the PCM, and other leftist organizations were deeply worried about the apparent rightward drift of the Ávila Camacho administration, and in public manifestos pointedly reminding the president that they were responsible for his election, these groups called upon him to reconfigure his cabinet and to take stronger action against "the nazi-fascist fifth column," which apparently included all conservative elements in Mexico. [51] Nonetheless, the left stopped well short of directly criticizing Ávila Camacho, who, after all, had clearly moved the country toward a harder line against fascism in the international arena.

Meanwhile, the government moved to use the international situation to strengthen its hand in its dealings with groups and individuals that it judged as subversive. Ostensibly to prevent foreign agents from laying the groundwork in Mexico for the invasion or infiltration of the country, as they had done in various European countries before those nations were conquered by the Axis, the Ávila Camacho administration sent a proposal to the legislature in September 1941 that would revise the federal penal code, stiffening penalties for espionage during wartime and establishing the crime of "social dissolution." The new offense was defined as disseminating propaganda "spreading ideas, programs, or norms of action of foreign governments that disrupt public order or affect the sovereignty of the Mexican state" or as committing acts "that prepare materially or morally [for] the invasion of the national territory or the submission of the country to any foreign power."[52]

The left welcomed the proposed legislation, which would later be used extensively against troublesome union leaders and other activists. *El Popular* assured its readers that "the reforms to the Penal Code do not diminish the principles of liberty and democracy that inspire the form of Government that presides over us, and they do, on the other hand, provide for the conservation of the internal and external peace of the country in the present circumstances." The CTM newspaper also cited a deputy who soothingly pledged that "the spirit of the initiative was preventive, defensive, and that there would not be false interpretations [of the new law] at the hour of applying it."[53] For its part, the government newspaper *El Nacional* dismissed worries that the proposed changes might be used to prevent "the free manifestation of ideas in general" and against "those who disagree with the official opinion at a given moment." Indeed, the editorial went on, "Unless they are thinking of deliberately exceeding the fixed constitutional limits on the freedom of expression to the point of committing the grave crimes of treason that are now being defined, we do not see why some writers and political activists would have to worry themselves about the inclusion of [these crimes] in the Penal Code."[54] The Chamber of Deputies and the Senate both approved the bill unanimously, giving the Mexican state a powerful tool that it would use for decades to come against those whose actions, in its judgment, tended to disturb public order or affect national sovereignty.[55]

As Ávila Camacho approached the end of his first year in office, he found his political strength very much enhanced as a result of his adept use of the international situation to increase his stature and to consolidate his authority at home. The gathering war clouds also gave his administration additional leverage as it managed the country's foreign relations. For example, the fighting overseas and the pro-Allied policies that Ávila Camacho adopted in response to the war made it possible for the Mexican government to reestablish diplomatic relations with Great Britain. The United Kingdom had severed ties with Mexico in 1938, after Cárdenas expropriated the oil industry, which was then largely in British hands. Although officials in London had repeatedly stated that relations with Mexico would not be restored until the claims of British oil companies were addressed, Foreign Secretary Anthony Eden told the House of Commons on October 22, 1941, that His Majesty's Government would send a minister to Mexico City in recognition of the "declarations and actions by which President Camacho and the Mexican Government have shown their clear-sighted appreciation of the issues raised by the aggressive actions of the Axis Powers."[56]

Moreover, the increasing likelihood that the United States would be pulled into the conflict no doubt helped the Mexican administration to conclude an agreement with Washington on November 19, 1941, that settled all outstanding oil and property claims. The Roosevelt administration's need for Mexican military and diplomatic cooperation was so great that it was willing to ignore the protests of U.S. oil companies and other interested parties that would have preferred to have held out for a more favorable settlement. Through much of Ávila Camacho's first year as president, his government sought to push discussions on the subject forward by pointing out to U.S. officials that failure to resolve the existing disputes would constitute "a material obstacle to the complete [mutual] understanding of two friendly countries and [would] deplorably weaken the firmness of all future Pan-American action." Citing "the convenience of coordinated action, for the defense of Democracy, with the rest of the American republics, and in particular, with the United States of North America," Mexican officials sought "an effective, rapid, and just arrangement of the pending matters between the two nations."[57] For his part, U.S. secretary of state Cordell Hull made clear in his conversations with Mexican diplomats that his own eagerness to reach a settlement was based on "world conditions and especially those of our Hemisphere," which made "friendship and cooperation between American countries and, particularly, between

Mexico and the United States" more important than ever.[58]

While the recalcitrance of American oil companies delayed a settlement for many months, the Roosevelt administration moved quickly to seal an agreement in the fall of 1941, as the danger posed to the United States by World War II grew. The resulting accord was widely seen as highly favorable to Mexico; some U.S. newspapers criticized State Department negotiators for being too generous. These editorials convinced Mexican officials that the international situation had allowed them to conclude an unusually good deal. "When commentaries like these are read, the conviction, among us, is strengthened that the agreements . . . are definitely good for our country," wrote Ambassador Castillo Nájera.[59]

Despite his skillful manipulation of an international environment that worked in his favor, however, the Mexican president's position remained somewhat precarious. At the end of November 1941, the U.S. Federal Bureau of Investigation (FBI) expressed concern that Ávila Camacho's alleged weakness was causing consternation among the responsible sectors of Mexican society that resented the apparent influence of "demagogues" like Lombardo Toledano. FBI director J. Edgar Hoover wrote that the president "is in for a difficult situation unless he shows more determined strength than he has in the past six months of his administration." While the president personally was "considered a clean, sincere man, very conservative, and slightly inclined to the right," he had "so far failed to clean up known crookedness and disloyalty in some of his Governmental departments," and "some conservative elements in Mexico are wondering if he is strong enough to handle 'the situation' . . . which is steadily becoming more acute."[60] Similarly, at the end of 1941 an analyst at the U.S. Office of Strategic Services (OSS, the forerunner of the Central Intelligence Agency) called the Ávila Camacho administration "weak and divided." The president's program of "unifying the warring elements in Mexican politics" was "ill-advised," he said, inasmuch as the result was a "cabinet made up of weak personages with reactionary tendencies."[61]

But if Ávila Camacho's failure to take a strong stand against either the left or the right caused some observers to perceive him as a weak executive, his practice of balancing the two extremes of the political spectrum against each other in fact left him free to move cautiously toward the establishment of a more moderate regime. The president retained the rhetoric of the Mexican Revolution to rally popular support while laying the foundations for a state that would place more emphasis on the creation of wealth than on its equitable distribution. During his first year in the presidency, Ávila Camacho faced harsh criticism at various times from both conservatives and members of the official "revolutionary" coalition, but the fact that a war was raging beyond the country's borders sharply limited the scope of possible opposition to the president, particularly after the left came to identify itself with Ávila Camacho's pro-Allied foreign policy. The geographic expansion of World War II that occurred in dramatic fashion at the end of 1941 made it even easier for Ávila Camacho to hold the middle ground in Mexican politics and to demand national unity behind his program.

TWO

Increasingly Tenuous "Neutrality"

DECEMBER 1941–MAY 1942

Although Pearl Harbor lies more than 2,500 miles from the nearest point on the Mexican coast, the December 7, 1941, Japanese attack on the U.S. naval base there brought World War II much closer to Mexico. Indeed, the fact that the country's powerful neighbor to the north had finally been drawn into the global conflict presented the Ávila Camacho administration with a significant challenge. In the days after the strike on Hawaii, Mexican authorities suddenly faced intense U.S. pressure for a deepening of military cooperation. Top officials in Washington even hinted that Mexico would do well to join several smaller Latin American countries in declaring war on the Axis. Within Mexico, however, nationalist sentiment rejected U.S. involvement in the country's defense, and most Mexicans were against full participation in the war. While a few leftist leaders had become active in lobbying for greater Mexican contributions to the fight against fascism since the German invasion of the Soviet Union six months earlier, most of their compatriots failed to see why their country should become involved. Mexico had not been attacked, they reasoned, and the war's battlefields were very far away. Thus, the expansion of the war to the Western Hemisphere gave rise to a situation in which it would be difficult for President Ávila Camacho to meet U.S. demands for a stronger stand against the Axis without upsetting the many Mexicans who opposed participation in the Second World War. Having just completed a year in office during which his hold on power had at times appeared tenuous, the president could ill afford to adopt policies that would alienate much of the population.

around the government of the "flag bearer" of national unity, Manuel Ávila Camacho, which was "demonstrating palpably that its international position is correct, firm, and patriotic."[4]

At the same time, the executive committee of the CTM issued a statement echoing the stance taken by *El Popular*, calling on Mexicans "to forget our small or large differences that might have existed in order to form with all the People of Mexico a single front of struggle in favor of the democracies and against nazi-fascism." This kind of unity would be necessary, the official labor confederation said, in order to reinforce "the Government led by General of Division Manuel Ávila Camacho, to whom all Mexicans owe solidarity and support so that, as Chief of the Mexican Nation, he might be the one who leads and directs the entire population, in this tragic hour that humanity is living."[5] Separately, the main federation of public employees' unions issued a manifesto calling for the severance of relations with the Axis, the seizure of Axis-owned properties, and the reestablishment of diplomatic ties with the Soviet Union, and it staged a large parade in support of the president on December 9.[6] However much Lombardo Toledano, the CTM, and others in the labor sector might have been concerned about the rightward drift of the Ávila Camacho administration during its first year in power, the international situation prompted them to pledge their full support to the president at this pivotal moment in December 1941. With the left putting the global fight against fascism and the heroic cause of the Soviet Union above all other considerations as the war spread to the Americas, the administration gained much greater freedom of maneuver in all policy areas.

Like their allies in the labor movement, senators and deputies known as leading representatives of the PRM's left wing were also quick to demand stern action against Japan and its allies. Deputies César Garizurieta of Veracruz and Carlos Zapata Vela of the Federal District hailed Padilla's initial declarations condemning the strike on Pearl Harbor and offering Mexican support to the United States as being "those of the greatest transcendence that have been made in the history of Mexico." Arguing that "the aggression that the United States just suffered at the hands of Japan is also an aggression upon Mexico," the lawmakers said they would issue a call on the floor of the Chamber of Deputies for the expulsion of the Japanese and German ministers in Mexico (the breaking of diplomatic relations with Japan had not yet been announced) and for the detention of Japanese and German citizens in Mexico in concentration camps.[7] Garizurieta reportedly indicated, too, that he would support a declaration of war upon Japan.[8]

In their anti-fascist zeal, these left-leaning lawmakers offered their unconditional loyalty to the president. A prominent labor-sector senator, Vidal Díaz Muñoz of Veracruz, called first and foremost for "national unity around the President of the Republic" and said that the country's workers in particular should be "closely linked, today more than ever" with Ávila Camacho. Another labor representative in the Senate, Alfonso Sánchez Madariaga of the Federal District, agreed, saying that "the unification of all Mexicans around General Manuel Ávila Camacho" was essential, as the president "interprets faithfully the national feeling in favor of continental solidarity for the defense of liberty."[9] A group of deputies led by Garizurieta and Zapata Vela even proposed legislation that would give President Ávila Camacho practically unlimited "extraordinary powers" over the functions of the ministries of national defense, the navy, the treasury, communications, and foreign relations, so that he would be able to meet any unforeseen contingencies arising from the situation in the Pacific.[10]

From beyond the capital, too, powerful political figures across the ideological spectrum rushed to register their support for the president in the face of the international crisis precipitated by the attack on Pearl Harbor. In addition to the hundreds of *adhesiones* (messages of support) that poured into the president's office from governors, generals, state legislatures, lesser officials, and local organizations, Ávila Camacho received assurances of loyalty from several of his predecessors, each of whom commanded a significant political following.[11] From Michoacán, former president Lázaro Cárdenas sent an "extra-urgent" telegram to his successor informing him that because of the outbreak of war between the United States and Japan, he wished to place himself "at the disposition of the government worthily led by you."[12] At the same time, from Baja California a more conservative former president, Abelardo Rodríguez, sent word to Ávila Camacho that "in view [of the fact that the] international situation is becoming more complicated," he wished to offer his services to the government, "in order that it might take advantage of them in the form that you judge convenient."[13] And Cárdenas's mentor-turned-archrival Plutarco Elías Calles visited Ávila Camacho at the National Palace on December 11 to pledge his support. After meeting with the president, Calles told the press that "as a soldier and a citizen" he was "at the disposition of the Government of Mexico," and he advised his countrymen "to rally around the Government, for I am sure that the serene patriotism of the President will resolve such [international] problems, in accordance with the highest national interests and without dishonor for our dignity as a free and sovereign people."[14] Just as the expansion of World War II to the Western Hemisphere prompted left-ist groups to back the president despite any misgivings they might have had about his domestic policies, so, too, did the spread of the conflict help Ávila Camacho in his efforts to limit the disruptive effects of the factional infighting that had weakened the regime during the preced-ing decades. With the towering figures of Mexican politics lining up squarely behind his leadership during a time of international crisis— despite the often deep divisions between them—the president's hand was strengthened as he sought to capitalize on the international situation by pushing ahead with his program of national unity.

But while the statements of support and offers of assistance that arrived in Ávila Camacho's office during the days after December 7 were certainly very welcome to him, the president recognized that much of the general public was less than enthusiastic about the pros-pect of deeper involvement in a far-off war. He realized, too, that many Mexicans remained suspicious of the United States and were reluctant to see their country cast its lot with its historic enemy, the rapacious "colossus of the north." To be sure, the fact that Japan's strike on Pearl Harbor was clearly an unprovoked, aggressive act undermined much of the sympathy and admiration for the Axis that had existed in some circles in Mexico. A U.S. consular official in Veracruz reported that the "treacherous attack aroused universal indignation, and solidified pro-American opinion as no other event could have done," while his counterpart in Mazatlán wrote that the attack "greatly shocked a large majority of the population," giving rise to unprecedented support in the region for the United States and for a policy of "continental solidarity."[15] Nonetheless, observers in other parts of the country noted that "dislike for Americans" remained "inbred," that Japanese victories in the Pacific were "undoubtedly finding praise among certain classes," and that even in cases in which the assault on Pearl Harbor had caused "great surprise and some indignation," "it did not lead to a popular desire to enter the war."[16] In Mexico City, a newspaper reported that the prospect that the country might enter the war at any moment had provoked "great nervous tension" on the streets of the capital.[17] One newspaper vendor there told a reporter for the afternoon daily *Últimas Noticias* that the latest developments overseas would increase his sales, but he nonetheless expressed his hope that the authorities would "not take us into the war."[18]

Moreover, right-leaning conservative groups made no secret of their hostility to the idea of direct participation in the war. The rapidly growing Unión Nacional Sinarquista (UNS), in particular, had stressed in the months leading up to Pearl Harbor its opposition to Mexican involvement in the conflict and to cooperation with the United States in the name of hemispheric defense.[19] Founded in 1937, the fervently Catholic, intensely anticommunist organization attracted hundreds of thousands of devout small farmers and village dwellers to its ranks by presenting itself as a nationalist movement that would bring order to a country that had been plagued by chaos. The group's name was meant to suggest that it stood in diametrical opposition to anarchy, and to impose the discipline it claimed was lacking in Mexican society, the UNS set up a rigid hierarchy of jefes (chiefs) that functioned throughout much of the republic, especially in the countryside of west-central Mexico. The organization was dogged by accusations of secret links with the fascist parties of Europe and with the Spanish Falange, but the UNS leadership always insisted that the movement was apolitical and purely Mexican.[20]

In the aftermath of the December 7 attacks, the staunchly nationalist, proclerical organization blamed "Communist agitators" for spreading the "false news" that "the time has come to recruit Mexicans and send them to 'fight the Japanese.'" Calling these "extremists" "inveterate enemies of the Nation," the Sinarquista leadership pledged to "fight to keep our Homeland out of the war" and suggested that members of the UNS "pray to God that He may guide our Government to keep Mexico out of the war."[21] Given the large following that the movement enjoyed among hundreds of thousands of deeply religious peasants in the Mexican countryside, the administration might well have hesitated to move too far toward active participation in the Second World War for fear of provoking unrest in the regions where the Sinarquista organization was strongest.[22]

With prominent politicians rallying around him even as much public sentiment remained opposed to active involvement in the war, Ávila Camacho moved to define with greater precision the position that his administration would adopt in response to the attack on Pearl Harbor.

In a December 9 speech, the president sought both to take a strong anti-Axis stance in order to assure himself of the continued support of the prowar left and to convince Mexicans who were more skeptical about the desirability of participation in the war that the country's role in the conflict would remain limited. Explaining that the war "now threatens, in a direct manner, the security of our territory and the inviolability of our destinies," Ávila Camacho declared that Mexico would stand against the dictatorships that sought "to destroy the moral equilibrium of democracy" and with "those nations that do not admit that the international order can remain indefinitely subject to the arbitrariness of the strongest." Mexico joined with the rest of the hemisphere in its solidarity with the United States, he said, noting the special significance of U.S.-Mexican cooperation in light of past conflicts between the two countries.[23]

Ávila Camacho assured those Mexicans who might still harbor anti-American sentiments that the two nations could work together to defend their common "democratic ideals," inasmuch as Roosevelt's Good Neighbor Policy reflected the recent "spiritual evolution of the North American people." Though he expressed his confidence that the Mexican armed forces would "do honor to their traditions" in the event of an attack on the country, the chief executive hastened to add that, for the moment, at least, Mexico's principal contribution to the defense of the Americas would be economic rather than military. Therefore, while the government had broken off its relations with Japan, there would be no immediate declaration of war. "Our fight will not take place in the trenches," Ávila Camacho told his countrymen, "but rather in the factories and in the fields, in order to increase the capacity of our economy, to strengthen the productivity of our commerce, and in order that all efforts might be directed to the same end: to contribute to the security of America."[24]

The president's speech won praise both from enthusiastic anti-fascists on the left and from more conservative press outlets. After Ávila Camacho delivered his December 9 address, a number of prominent left-leaning labor and peasant-sector representatives joined in promoting a resolution in the Senate that expressed the upper chamber's strong backing for the "patriotic, firm, thoughtful, and brave attitude of the President."[25] Meanwhile, in the legislature's lower house, *cetemista* deputy Alberto Trueba Urbina announced that "the labor movement sincerely praises the President's recent message and will loyally cooperate with him." The

Figure 2: Both before and after Mexico formally entered the war, officials stressed that the country's primary contribution to the war effort would be economic. This wartime poster, issued by the interior ministry, associates production with patriotism. (National Archives and Records Administration)

CTM would "willingly forget all past animosities and differences and place themselves at the orders of the President," the legislator said.[26] *El Popular* also lauded Ávila Camacho's "serene and firm conduct" in support of "continental solidarity," and the newspaper hailed the "dignity and frankness" of his explanation for the administration's strongly pro-U.S. position.[27] If some on the left regretted that the government had not joined the nine Central American and Caribbean republics in immediately declaring war on the Axis, they hid their disappointment as they pronounced themselves well pleased with Ávila Camacho's unequivocally pro-Allied policy and with his call for active Mexican support for the democratic cause.

At the same time, less radical voices stressed their appreciation for the calm and measured tenor of the president's address. *Excélsior*, a relatively conservative newspaper that was often at odds with Lombardo Toledano and his leftist allies, praised the "just, dignified, and carefully thought out policy" outlined by Ávila Camacho in his speech, lauding the president for his decision to keep the country formally out of the war. In announcing that Mexico would not fight "if an unjustified and fallacious aggression did not oblige it do so," Ávila Camacho was adopting an "attitude perfectly congruent with our old international doctrine of defense, of peace, but energetically opposed to all acts that offend against our sovereignty and territory," *Excélsior*'s editorialist wrote. While some centrist to conservative Mexicans had worried in the months before Pearl Harbor that Ávila Camacho lacked the ability to stand up to the left, *Excélsior* now celebrated the fact that the president had shown himself capable of acting on his moderate inclinations. "The country now knows that at its head is found a leader whose serenity does not exclude firmness and who never will work in opposition to the national interests or divorced from the wishes of the people," the editorial concluded.[28]

A second moderate, mainstream broadsheet, *El Universal*, agreed that the "tone and the content of the presidential speech . . . were exactly those that are appropriate to the gravity of the moment." Indeed, Ávila Camacho had shown himself to be "a statesman equal to the situation" in "the present critical moments," the Mexico City daily said, and the "just and tranquil presidential evaluation of the situation will find a broad echo, without any doubt, in the public conscience." *El Universal*'s editorial stressed, apparently with some sense of relief, that Mexico was not formally at war with Japan, but it backed Ávila Camacho's contention that the country would have to be ready for any eventuality, calling for the nation "to proceed, starting immediately, as if hostilities with Japanese totalitarianism had broken out and to render up to the last fiber of its muscles in a firm effort to contribute, in the exact measure of its possibilities, to the defeat of the global totalitarian confabulation." To achieve that goal, the newspaper concluded, the population should "group itself, as a single man, around the chief of its government, who with such precise judgment signaled to it last night the road to follow."[29] Elsewhere in the pages of *El Universal*, another moderate commentator, one-time industry minister Miguel Alessio Robles, called the president's December 9 speech "an example of measured thoughtfulness" that raised Ávila Camacho "to a higher plane, as a Mexican, as a governor, and as a statesman."[30] Certainly, the president's ability to take a firm stand against the Axis while resisting calls for Mexican entry into the war raised his stature in the eyes of moderate Mexicans, including many who might have entertained doubts about his personal and political strength during his first year in office.

Ávila Camacho's call for unity was even embraced by generally critical conservative groups. No doubt encouraged by the emphasis that the president placed on the importance of production and economic growth in his post–Pearl Harbor statements, the wealthy industrialists of Monterrey, who had frequently clashed with Cárdenas and who had strongly backed Ávila Camacho's opponent in the 1940 presidential elections, sent a delegation to Mexico City to inform the president that he had their full support.[31] According to one member of the delegation, the president was initially so "flabbergasted" that the group had come just to offer its services that he was "almost speechless," but he was reportedly able to regain his composure sufficiently to thank the visiting executives and to invite them to dine with him. The U.S. consul in Monterrey noted the significance of the fact that the powerful business community in that northern city, "which for years has been opposed to the President in office on account of his labor policies, has now placed itself openly in the camp of President Ávila Camacho."[32]

For its part, the UNS, grateful that the administration had rejected leftist proposals for a declaration of war, made a statement praising Ávila Camacho's post–Pearl Harbor speech. "Sinarquismo believes that the President's statement of December 9th to the effect that the country must defend itself through abundant production is patriotic," the organization declared. Sinarquista leaders also pledged that the group's members would heed the president's appeal for greater production by directing "all our energies toward work, thus demonstrating our love for Mexico." The UNS statement closed with words that Ávila Camacho himself might have uttered in support of his appeals for unity: "We hope that the danger of war may bring in Mexico, as a healthy consequence, a Government for all, in order that we may have civil peace, and bring about conditions which will permit all Mexicans to work."[33]

Similarly, the new Partido Acción Nacional (PAN) echoed the president's call for solidarity. That conservative group, founded by prominent attorney and former national university rector Manuel Gómez Morín in 1939 and backed primarily by urban Catholics and industrialists, declared on December 16 that "this is the proper time to express and strengthen national unity and that the Government should carry out these purposes."[34] There were signs, too, that the general public in many parts of Mexico appreciated the president's measured response to the crisis brought on by the attack on Pearl Harbor. The U.S. consul in Tampico reported that among the population there, the president's declaration that Mexico would formally remain a nonbelligerent "was welcomed by many as at least a temporary escape from the active involvement in hostilities which had been feared."[35]

The president won additional admiration and support from moderate to conservative Mexicans who were wary of the left's enthusiasm for full-scale participation in the war when he announced on December 12 that he did not want the extraordinary emergency powers that would have been bestowed upon him under a proposal made by members of Congress.[36] *Excélsior*'s afternoon edition, *Últimas Noticias*, noted that past Mexican leaders would have taken the opportunity presented by a worldwide conflict "to assume the dictatorial powers that our submissive, docile, and often servile idiosyncrasy is always ready to grant" but that Ávila Camacho had "declined outright to diminish our liberties, while that was not strictly indispensable." The newspaper praised the president for his refusal to be seduced by the prospect of "hyper-inflated power" and for attempting to follow, "as far as humanly possible, the ideals of a true democratic regime."[37] By showing restraint in refusing the emergency powers that were offered to him, Ávila Camacho thus gained greater respect from many of his countrymen, allowing him to lead and to govern more easily, even without recourse to any extraconstitutional faculties.

In the aftermath of the strike on Pearl Harbor, then, Ávila Camacho was able to enhance his stature and to gain commitments of support from a broad cross section of the Mexican population. His calm but firm response to the Japanese attack, his calls for heightened production and anti-Axis measures short of war, and his appeals for unity won praise from Mexicans of all political stripes, quickly dampening rumblings of discontent. Indeed, following up on scattered pre–Pearl Harbor reports that dissatisfaction with the Ávila Camacho administration could give rise to unrest, a U.S. embassy official reported that "this situation has changed to a great extent since the United States entered the war." Since then, he wrote, "all walks of life in Mexico have indicated their solidarity with President Avila Camacho and his international policy."[38]

Having rallied Mexicans behind him by announcing that their father-land was in danger of attack, Ávila Camacho moved to strengthen the government's capacity to respond to an assault on Mexican shores and to the danger of sabotage and subversion within the country's borders. As the president reorganized the armed forces and police services to meet those threats, he expanded the reach of the Mexican state and enhanced the level of executive control over many of its key components. Citing the need for "a more efficient coordination between the Chief Executive and the different Ministries" "in view of the international situation," for example, the president issued a decree on December 10 transforming the small group of military aides attached to his office into a more powerful general staff, the Estado Mayor Presidencial (EMP), which was charged with a broad range of military planning and command functions.[39] After Congress approved a revision of the organic law of the armed forces on December 31 to provide for the functioning of the EMP, its chief, General J. Salvador S. Sánchez, explained that the new institution would operate "in the name and in representation of the President of the Republic, as the element coordinating and directing all activities that in the future will govern the military policy of the country."[40] The EMP assumed responsibility for many tasks that had previously been carried out by the defense ministry—its Military Technical Directorate was abolished on February 1, 1942, because its functions had been transferred to the presidency—and, as an organization that reported directly to Ávila Camacho, the general staff organization had new powers to manage the activities of other ministries and agencies.[41] Although the EMP subsequently lost much of its clout as a result of further reorganizations that took place through 1942 and 1943, its creation marked a significant step toward the consolidation of presidential authority over the armed forces.

In another December 10 decree that served to strengthen his control over the Mexican political landscape, Ávila Camacho placed all of the military and naval zones along Mexico's western coast under the jurisdiction of a new Región Militar del Pacífico (RMP). The move represented an effort to coordinate defensive efforts in a vast area suddenly seen as being vulnerable to Japanese attack, but more important than the creation of the new military command was the appointment of Lázaro Cárdenas to take charge of the armed forces in the region.[42] By accepting the influential former president's offer of his services, Ávila Camacho gained a greater degree of control over his predecessor's activities and tapped into his large political base. Though Cárdenas had avoided active involvement in politics since his departure from office in 1940, many officials and a great many workers and peasants still looked to him as their natural leader. With Cárdenas accepting a key role in the national defense effort led by Ávila Camacho and actively calling for unity behind his successor, the incumbent president gained a greater degree of confidence from cardenista bureaucrats and military officers and from the cardenista masses that might otherwise have begun to doubt that he was a true heir of his predecessor's legacy.[43]

Moreover, by placing a staunch nationalist in charge of the country's Pacific defenses, Ávila Camacho sent a reassuring signal to those Mexicans who might have been wary of the prospect of military cooperation with the United States. Given Cárdenas's reputation as a tireless defender of the nation's sovereignty, his appointment to command the RMP meant that many Mexicans would be less concerned about the possibility that U.S. forces would take advantage of the international situation to set up bases or otherwise to establish a military presence on Mexican soil. Indeed, as he took up his new duties Cárdenas did place a high priority on keeping American soldiers out of Mexican territory. Just after taking his post, upon hearing reports that the U.S. military was carrying out reconnaissance and conducting patrols in Baja California, Cárdenas told a member of his staff that his primary task was "to expel the American troops who, with the pretext of defending us, had entered our territory without the authorization of the Mexican government."[44] Later, in March 1942, a U.S. intelligence report quoted him as saying that his forces were prepared to "repel any attempt at invasion, whether such enemy force came from the west . . . *or from the north.*"[45] While U.S. officers were often frustrated with the obstacles that Cárdenas placed in the way of their efforts to conduct patrols or to install radar equipment south of the border, even when they had received authorization for such actions from Mexico City, the former president's presence at the head of Mexican forces on the Pacific coast and the fact that he had publicly committed himself to the government's international policies served to enhance Ávila Camacho's authority. Inasmuch as it was the crisis triggered by the attack on Pearl Harbor that allowed Ávila Camacho to place Cárdenas in a role in which his predecessor was clearly subordinate to him, the war greatly helped the president to strengthen his political position.[46]

With fears widespread that Axis agents might carry out acts of espionage and spread dangerous propaganda, the administration moved not just to strengthen its coastal defenses and to reorganize its armed forces but also to build a more effective intelligence-gathering and internal security apparatus. Almost immediately after the attack on Pearl Harbor, for example, the Mexican government sought U.S. assistance in its efforts to establish an office that could intercept and decipher coded communications.[47] The U.S. government responded by sending, at its own expense, a Spanish-speaking cryptographer from the FBI to assist the communications ministry in setting up such an operation.[48] Separately, after the rupture in relations between Mexico and the nations of the Axis, the interior ministry, the Secretaría de Gobernación, established a special corps of investigators to monitor the activities of the Japanese, German, and Italian diplomatic personnel who remained in Mexico.[49]

Shortly thereafter, on December 29, a presidential ruling confirmed the authority of the Gobernación over all investigations into subversive activities related to the international situation. A special section within its office of political and social investigations was assigned to monitor the activities of foreigners in the country, and existing police forces were instructed to cooperate with and to provide relevant information to the ministry. Acting on instructions from the interior minister, future president Miguel Alemán, the secretariat's third-ranking official, Adolfo Ruiz Cortines (also a future president), met with the chiefs of the Federal District police, the Federal District investigative police, and the military investigative police on January 9, 1942, to set up procedures for collaboration and information sharing.[50] The war thus provided the impetus for greatly expanded domestic intelligence-gathering operations at Gobernación, which helped to make the holder of that cabinet portfolio a particularly powerful political figure in the decades that followed. On a more general level, the ministry's increased monitoring of potentially disruptive activities in various parts of the country represented an expansion of the capacities of the executive branch, one that allowed the president to grasp the reins of power more firmly, both during the war and afterward.

Even as he managed the complicated political landscape within Mexico and strengthened his control over the institutions of the Mexican state, however, Ávila Camacho had to contend with increased pressure from the United States for new forms of military cooperation. Given the fear that Japan might follow up on its raid on Pearl Harbor with an attack on the American mainland, possibly via the undefended shores of Baja California, U.S. requests for Mexican assistance in the defense of the Pacific coast were not entirely unreasonable. Indeed, early rumors and intelligence reports suggested that a second Japanese task force was on its way to strike military facilities and war industries around San Diego, and the Mexican military attaché in Washington, Cristóbal Guzmán Cárdenas, later recalled that he was summoned to the office of U.S. Army chief of staff George Marshall within an hour after bombs started to fall on Hawaii to discuss the apparent danger of an attack on California.[51] But even if cooperation and coordination were necessary, granting U.S. requests for an active role in patrolling and monitoring Mexican territory threatened to inflame nationalist sentiment in Mexico and to undermine the careful work that the administration had done to rally the country around the president and to lead it toward a deeper (though still limited) role in the war. Ávila Camacho therefore moved quickly to convey to U.S. officials that his government would take any steps that might be necessary to safeguard the coasts of northwestern Mexico, while assuring his countrymen that the task of defending the nation's territory would remain in Mexican hands.

During the first unsettled hours after the attack on Pearl Harbor, Mexican authorities sought to be as accommodating as possible when approached by U.S. officials seeking permission to investigate the possibility of a Japanese threat to their country's western flank. A December 8 request for authorization to carry out reconnaissance flights over Baja California and Sonora was granted immediately, after Military Attaché Guzmán Cárdenas received clearance over the phone from General Salvador Sánchez in Mexico City.[52] Army officers in Washington were pleased that they had been able to obtain "blanket permission" for these flights "without difficulty."[53] In another telephone conversation with Guzmán Cárdenas less than forty-eight hours after the strike on Hawaii, Sánchez also authorized the placement in northwestern Mexico of radio detector equipment that might provide an early warning of Japanese movements toward the region.[54] In addition, U.S. officials sought and received permission to send ground patrols into Mexican territory in search of clandestine Japanese landing fields and to lay the groundwork for the establishment of an aircraft warning service. Though they were unable to receive immediate clearance for these patrols through Guzmán Cárdenas, a U.S. colonel telephoned Maximino Ávila Camacho, "a personal friend of his," who reportedly "promptly secured permission from the President."[55] Through various channels, the Mexican government thus signaled its willingness to cooperate fully with the United States at a moment when the possibility of an attack on both countries seemed very real.

It soon became clear, however, that allowing U.S. forces to operate openly on Mexican territory could severely undermine popular support for the pro-Allied policy that the Ávila Camacho administration had laid out for the country. Indeed, when a group of U.S. troops arrived at the border crossing separating San Isidro, California, from Tijuana on the morning of December 9, the rumor that the unit intended to cross into Mexico to carry out a patrol "provoked cries of protest and of patriotic fervor" from a large crowd that gathered on the Mexican side of the frontier. The U.S. troops withdrew from the border at the request of the local Mexican military authorities, but the Mexican consul in San Diego reported that negative feelings toward the U.S. military persisted in Tijuana.[56]

Mexican officials might also have been unnerved by a December 10 memorandum received from a U.S. Army Air Corps official seeking guidance on the action that should be taken by the aerial reconnaissance patrols operating over Baja California and Sonora in the event that they should encounter evidence of secret Japanese bases in the area. The note indicated that U.S. forces "would be pleased to cooperate with, and assist with your air force in taking the necessary action against any such bases" and that they would even "be willing to conduct these operations ourselves."[57] Though the tone of the general's note was polite, the idea of American forces taking military action against a point in Mexican territory must have sent chills through the officials in Mexico City who read his message. Realizing that direct U.S. participation in the defense of Mexico could breed resentment, the Ávila Camacho administration adjusted its responses to American requests for cooperation and assistance in the days that followed.

In an effort to avoid the development of a visible U.S. military presence on its soil, the Mexican government began to insist that it was capable of guarding its own territory without extensive outside assistance, while it continued to stress that it was fully committed to the cause of hemispheric defense. In accordance with new instructions he received on December 12, Military Attaché Guzmán Cárdenas conveyed this very message to U.S. military officials, telling them that Mexico "guaranteed [that its] western coasts would not be used by the Japanese for operations against the United States." He then asked that "American planes not take direct action against possible objectives on Mexican soil," a request that was granted by the officers with whom he spoke, who ordered the U.S. air command "to abstain from bombing Mexican soil and to limit themselves to informing Mexican military authorities of the presence of enemy activities."[58]

When Ambassador Castillo Nájera returned to Washington after spending much of the first part of December consulting with officials in Mexico City, he brought with him Ávila Camacho's personal assurances that Mexico fully supported the Allied war effort and that it would adequately defend the shores of Baja California. In a December 16 meeting at the White House, Castillo Nájera told President Roosevelt that the Mexican government, "faithful to its policy of good neighborliness and to its conviction that Pan-American solidarity is necessary, will make all possible efforts to cooperate in the defense of the continent and to contribute to the triumph of the democracies," and he briefed the U.S. chief executive on the disposition of Mexican forces along the country's Pacific coast. Realizing that Washington's preoccupation with the security of southern California presented a good opportunity for Mexico to gain new military equipment on favorable terms, the ambassador added that his country needed machine guns, antiaircraft batteries, coastal artillery, and at least a hundred airplanes.[59] One clear implication of this request for supplies was that his country desired material aid that would enhance its capacity to defend itself rather than the deployment of U.S. troops on its territory.

Even as Mexican officials became more concerned about the scale and visibility of American military activities in their country, they generally continued to respond favorably to U.S. requests for permission to carry out various small operations south of the border. However, they began to place significant conditions on the authorizations they gave in an effort to minimize the potential nationalist backlash that might result from the discovery of an overt U.S. presence on Mexican soil. For example, on December 15 the Mexican government granted a U.S. request for authorization to place up to four mobile detector stations in the northern Mexican states of Coahuila, Nuevo León, and Tamaulipas, but it stipulated that the detachments operating the equipment would have to remain in civilian dress while in Mexico.[60] Similarly, the Ávila Camacho administration agreed to the establishment of small units of U.S. maintenance personnel at the airports in Tampico, Veracruz, and Tapachula, where they would service American planes passing through en route to Panama, but these soldiers, too, would have to leave their uniforms at home.[61]

After the Mexican military attaché informed a U.S. official on December 16 of his government's new general requirement that U.S. servicemen wear civilian clothes when in Mexico, the American staff officer lamented that the "tide of Mexican military cooperation with the United States is beginning to recede." Guzmán Cárdenas himself reportedly expressed regret that politicians had stepped in to place restrictions on the military cooperation that, in his view, had been going smoothly "as long as it was left to military men."[62] Nonetheless, his superiors in Mexico City clearly recognized that opponents of the Ávila Camacho administration and of its international policy could potentially capitalize on a situation in which foreign troops were stationed on Mexican soil, technically in violation of the country's Constitution. Therefore, although it made American military leaders unhappy, the ruling that any U.S. soldiers entering Mexico would have to do so unarmed and without uniforms stood.[63]

The Ávila Camacho administration also found ways to ignore or dodge other U.S. requests that could have caused political difficulties in Mexico. Though both Undersecretary of State Sumner Welles and President Roosevelt hinted to Castillo Nájera in meetings on December 15 and 16 that it would be in Mexico's best interests to declare war on the Axis—Roosevelt told him that such a move "would greatly facilitate mutual aid"—the Mexican ambassador simply replied that "this suggestion is known by my Government."[64] Another unsettling U.S. proposal came in a December 17 conversation between Welles and Castillo Nájera, in which the State Department official raised the possibility of entering into a bilateral agreement that would give the United States access to naval bases at Acapulco and Bahía Magdalena.[65] In response to the ambassador's report on the meeting, Foreign Minister Padilla advised Castillo Nájera confidentially that the Mexican government would not be able to enter into such an arrangement unless "important modifications" were made, including changes to the text that would provide "indispensable guarantees for the safeguarding of the inalienable interests of our Fatherland." In short, any pact remotely resembling the one proposed by Welles would be unacceptable, inasmuch as such an agreement would appear to compromise Mexican sovereignty. Nonetheless, Padilla indicated to Castillo Nájera that he should tell Welles "that our Government is studying [the proposal] with great interest," while drawing the undersecretary's attention to a December 16 bill proposed by Ávila Camacho that would grant the ships of all American republics free access to Mexican ports for the duration of the war. Though that measure would not give the United States all the rights and privileges sought by Welles at Acapulco and Bahía Magdalena—under the terms of the proposed Mexican legislation, foreign warships would still have to contact port authorities before entering Mexican harbors, and no foreign nation would be able to establish anything resembling a base on Mexican territory—Padilla expressed his hope that the administration's initiative would be accepted by the U.S. government as a sign of good faith, making it easier to put off further discussion of Washington's desire for naval bases in Mexico. He asked Castillo Nájera to use his characteristic "tact and patriotism" to make State Department officials see that Mexico's hesitance to accede to their wishes was not "an unfriendly act," and he suggested that the bill on access to Mexican ports could be presented as strong evidence of their country's good intentions.[66] Thus, the Ávila Camacho administration was able to avoid adopting policies advocated by the United States that would have been deeply unpopular in Mexico while still presenting itself to officials in Washington as a loyal and dependable partner worthy of political and material support.

Mexico further ingratiated itself with the United States by standing firmly and unequivocally with its neighbor when its own sovereignty was not obviously at stake. For example, just as it had moved quickly to sever its ties with Japan after the attack on Pearl Harbor, the Mexican government immediately broke off relations with Germany and Italy in response to those countries' declarations of war on the United States on December 11, again referring to the accords reached in Havana in 1940 as the basis for its display of solidarity with Washington.[67] The Ávila Camacho administration also readily agreed to the suggestion made by Welles and Roosevelt in their meetings with Castillo Nájera on December 15 and 16 that Mexico and the United States form a bilateral commission that would coordinate military cooperation between the two countries. Perhaps recognizing that the creation of such a body could potentially facilitate the flow of military and other aid to his country, Padilla quickly sent word that Mexico had no objection to the proposal, and the two governments announced the establishment of the Joint Mexican–United States Defense Commission on January 12, 1942.[68]

The Mexican government also had an opportunity to demonstrate its loyalty and usefulness to the United States at the Pan-American foreign ministers' conference that convened in Rio de Janeiro during the latter half of January 1942. U.S. secretary of state Cordell Hull had called for the meeting just after the attack on Pearl Harbor so that the American republics could coordinate their response to the act of aggression against his country, and within a few days Ambassador Castillo Nájera had learned from his contacts in Washington that the U.S. government hoped to use the conference to convince all of the nations of Latin America to join the United States in declaring war on Germany, Italy, and Japan.[69] As the date of the meeting approached, reports began to appear indicating that various Central American and Caribbean countries that had already declared their belligerency would support a Dominican resolution calling for a hemisphere-wide declaration of war, but it also began to become clear that the Argentine government would resist any move away from its policy of strict neutrality.[70]

Thus, as the conference began on January 15, Mexico took on a key role as a cosponsor, along with Colombia and Venezuela, of a compromise resolution that called for the entire region to break off its relations with the Axis powers. Abandoning its hope of achieving unanimous support for formal entry into the war by all of the American republics, the U.S. delegation supported the call for the severance of diplomatic ties with the Axis, and Foreign Minister Padilla emerged as the resolution's champion. As the Mexican delegate to the conference, Padilla attracted immediate attention in the meeting's opening session with a speech calling for Pan-American solidarity in the fight against fascism that was hailed "as one of the most notable oratorical pieces that has been heard in this city."[71] Throughout the conference, Padilla distinguished himself as a leading advocate of regionwide cooperation in the struggle against the Axis, and in the end, despite the resistance of the Argentine government, the assembled delegates unanimously approved a modified version of the Mexican proposal calling for the cutting of ties with the totalitarian powers. Though in its

Figure 3: Foreign Minister Ezequiel Padilla, shown here at the 1945 Chapultepec Conference in Mexico City, was the leading proponent within the administration of the Allied cause and of close cooperation with the United States. (National Archives and Records Administration)

final form the resolution was framed only as a "recommendation" that the nations of the hemisphere break off relations with the Axis in accordance with their own procedures for taking such an action, the fact that a consensus was reached when the danger of a deadlock had seemed so real was a great relief to the U.S. government.[72] Undersecretary Welles, who served as the U.S. delegate at the meeting, and officials back in Washington were therefore very grateful to Padilla and the Mexican government for the leadership and support that they had provided during the conference.

Mexican support for the United States paid dividends for the Ávila Camacho administration in the months that followed. Having proved itself a loyal and dependable partner in hemispheric defense efforts, the Mexican government was allowed to enter into a Lend-Lease accord with the United States on March 27, 1942. The pact made it possible for Mexico to obtain much-needed modern military hardware from the U.S. government on favorable terms. According to the agreement, Mexico was eligible to receive up to ten million dollars worth of equipment to be used for the defense of the country, and it would receive a 52 percent discount on the materiel thus acquired.[73] The benefits of close cooperation with the United States were also on display during late March and early April 1942, when Ezequiel Padilla received an unusually warm reception during an official visit to Washington. Welles publicly lauded the Mexican foreign minister as a "champion of democracy," and his trip to the U.S. capital was the subject of a cover story in *Time*.[74] Meanwhile, in his talks with State Department officials Padilla received a sympathetic hearing for his request for twenty million dollars in U.S. aid to rehabilitate the Mexican rail network, and he made progress toward the conclusion of a commercial treaty between the two countries.[75] In the international arena as well as domestically, the Mexican government thus found itself in a stronger, more advantageous position after December 7, 1941, because of the policies that it adopted in response to the Japanese attack on Pearl Harbor.

Within Mexico, however, the national unity for which Ávila Camacho called and to which all factions had pledged themselves was not a reality during the early months of 1942. While the president's strength was enhanced in the crisis atmosphere that existed immediately after the war spread to the Western Hemisphere, leftist and conservative elements continued to denounce and attack one another in the months that followed, limiting the ability of the administration to define and manage the national political agenda.

An incident in February 1942 highlighted the danger that ideological conflicts could undermine efforts to unify the country to meet the challenges posed by the international situation. When the governor of Sinaloa, Rodolfo Loaiza, called for a meeting of the governors of Pacific coast states to discuss defense measures, suspicions arose among conservatives that the gathering was being engineered by former president Cárdenas for political rather than military purposes.[76] As Mexico City newspapers charged that the meeting was intended to usurp presidential authority and to build up a regional power base for Cárdenas, Ávila Camacho tried to defuse the situation by announcing that he "did not consider the governors' meeting dangerous" and that "he believed in the work the governors are carrying on."[77] For his part, the commander of the RMP stayed away from Mazatlán when the conference took place from February 18 to 20. The meeting still caused an outcry, however, because Governor Silviano Barba González of Jalisco, a left-leaning cardenista, used the occasion to charge that priests in his state were spreading pro-Axis propaganda from their pulpits. *El Popular* and other leftist media outlets applauded Barba González's strong stand against the "reactionary" clergy, while conservatives who were sympathetic to the church howled in protest that the governor was making unfounded accusations against priests.[78] Rather than bringing Mexicans together in the name of national defense, the Pacific governors' meeting deepened the divisions between the left and the right.

Meanwhile, the CTM and other leftist organizations did not let their strong professions of support for Ávila Camacho's international policy prevent them from carrying out disruptive strikes and demonstrations in protest against other Mexican officials to whose actions they objected. As part of an ongoing feud with Veracruz governor Jorge Cerdán, the CTM called for a series of nationwide work stoppages in mid-February.[79] Bitter divisions between rival teachers' unions persisted, too, and several stood stridently in opposition to the education minister, Octavio Véjar Vázquez, who was then engaged in a purge of ministry employees with communist or other radical ties. Anti–Véjar Vázquez sentiment threatened to reach a boiling point after a March 6 protest against him by students from the National Polytechnic Institute was violently broken up by police and firefighters in downtown Mexico City, resulting in the death of a policeman and a bystander.[80]

The CTM's newspaper even joined right-leaning publications in criticizing Padilla during his visit to Washington in early April. Having praised and congratulated the foreign minister for his successful mission in Rio de Janeiro in January, *El Popular* now aired complaints that Padilla was engaging in undignified self-promotion as he received accolades from U.S. officialdom and the North American press.[81] Similar denunciations of Padilla appeared in the conservative press; *El Hombre Libre*, a little-read newspaper espousing anti-U.S. and often anti-Semitic views, charged the foreign minister with seeking prematurely to advance his presidential aspirations, and the PAN's weekly magazine, *La Nación*, referred sarcastically to Padilla's publicity-seeking behavior.[82] Such criticisms of the government's foreign-policy spokesman at a time of international crisis provided a strong indication that the ideal of national unity had not been achieved to the extent that President Ávila Camacho would have liked.

In the midst of these internal conflicts and clashes, the war was all but forgotten. Moderate newspapers lamented that the president's call for unity was not being heeded. "It does not cease to be astonishing that the more the Government of the Republic insists on recommending union, peace, and work, the number of disagreements, conflicts, and uncertainties of the different groups and social tendencies seems to increase," *El Universal* proclaimed.[83] Nonetheless, most Mexicans showed little interest in the fighting that was taking place in Europe and the Pacific. The new U.S. ambassador, George S. Messersmith, who had arrived in Mexico in February, reported between March and early May 1942 that Ávila Camacho was "far ahead of the people" in his support for the Allies, that the pro-U.S. foreign minister Padilla had practically no strength "among the masses," and that the public had an "apathetic" attitude toward the global conflict.[84] With his drive to rally all factions behind him stalled, the president perhaps realized that deepening the country's role in the war might allow him to bring a greater degree of order to the fractious world of Mexican politics. Before such a step would be politically feasible, however, the war would have to come closer to Mexico.

THREE

Mexico Enters the Global Conflict

MAY–JUNE 1942

Just before midnight on May 13, 1942, a torpedo launched by a German U-boat struck the bridge of the Mexican oil tanker *Potrero del Llano* as it steamed northward off the Atlantic coast of Florida. Thirteen men, including the ship's captain and most of its officers, perished in the explosion. Rescuers later pulled the twenty-two surviving members of the crew from the burning waters around the crippled vessel, but one, a machinist named Rodolfo Chacón, subsequently died of his injuries in a Miami hospital. The attack, and the loss of life, shocked and saddened many in Mexico, but it was by no means clear how the government would react to the incident. Labor leaders and others on the left, whose enthusiasm for the Allied cause had been growing ever since the German invasion of the Soviet Union in June 1941, insisted on an immediate declaration of war on the Axis powers, but other voices suggested that a less extreme response would be sufficient. In any event, it was clear that the vast majority of Mexicans still did not wish to see their country embroiled in the world war.

When President Manuel Ávila Camacho responded to the attack on the *Potrero del Llano* by dispatching a forceful ultimatum to Berlin, Rome, and Tokyo, and by calling for the declaration of "a state of war" after Mexico's protest was answered only by the sinking of another ship, the *Faja de Oro*, on May 20, the president was not following the lead of public opinion. Rather, he sensed that deepening Mexico's involvement in the war—taking the nation beyond the awkward policy of pro-Allied "neutrality" that it had followed since Pearl Harbor—would provide new opportunities for him to foster a climate of national unity within Mexico and to gain benefits for the country in the international arena. Because there was little popular support for participation in the war, Ávila Camacho had to proceed with great caution, but his gamble paid off in the months ahead, as groups and individuals from across the political spectrum found that they had little choice but to rally behind his "patriotic" policies in defense of the national honor and as improved relations with Mexico's new partners among the Allied "United Nations" bore fruit.

★ ★ ★

When news of the sinking of the *Potrero del Llano* began to reach Mexico on May 14, reactions varied widely. Legislators and government officials expressed outrage but were generally noncommittal when asked how Mexico should respond, saying only that they would support whatever measures the president might recommend. The tone of declarations on the subject by other political figures and by popular organizations tended to depend on their ideological orientation, with those on the left generally advocating a declaration of war against the Axis and those on the right calling for calm and a more measured response. In between the anti-fascist war hawks and the more cautious conservatives, most Mexicans simply felt unenthusiastic about the prospect of entering the war and uneasy about the sacrifices they might be called upon to make. Mistrust of the United States played a part in shaping the public's lukewarm feelings about the possibility of formally joining the Allies, as did a strong fear that Mexican soldiers would be sent abroad to fight and die on distant battlefields. These concerns surfaced occasionally in letters written to government officials, but more often the prevailing ambivalence was recorded only as an apparent apathy that worried many observers. Ávila Camacho did not lead a united country into the war, but by making Mexico a belligerent—with appeals to patriotism and reassurances for those who feared the consequences of such a momentous step—he succeeded, at least temporarily, in rallying the nation behind him and in strengthening his authority.

The initial reaction to the sinking of the *Potrero del Llano* in official circles was cautious. In public statements made in the immediate aftermath of the attack, members of Congress and prominent functionaries expressed different ideas about how Mexico should respond. Whatever their personal views might have been, however, they generally took great pains to emphasize that it was up to the president to define the country's foreign policy. Senator León García of San Luis Potosí took an unusually definitive position when he declared it to be "absolutely indispensable that our country declare war upon the Nazi-fascist powers," and he announced to journalists that he himself would call a special congressional session to take that step.[1] García toned down his comments just a few hours later, however, reportedly after a meeting with the president. Stating that he had been misquoted and acknowledging that it was up to the president to convene the legislature, the senator made no further reference to a declaration of war, saying only that "we ought to have faith that the First Magistrate will know how to demand with all dignity the respect which our Nation deserves as a nonbelligerent country."[2]

Other legislators betrayed a lack of enthusiasm for war. In a statement that might have reflected the views of Maximino Ávila Camacho, his conservative patron, Senator Noé Lecona of Puebla suggested that going to war would not be in the country's best interests.[3] And Senator Alfonso Flores M. of México state, often a maverick and always a critic of pro-Allied foreign minister Ezequiel Padilla, said that "there are other means of preserving the honor and the dignity of Mexico."[4] Like García, however, Flores showed a willingness to make adjustments to his position; speaking a few days later, when it seemed clear that Mexico would formally enter the global conflict, he enthusiastically stated that "we will declare war on those who have provoked a wave of savagery in the world."[5]

Perhaps in an effort to avoid having to make such retractions, most congressmen and officials spoke in vaguer terms as they waited to see what approach the administration would adopt. Deputy Mariano Samayoa of Chiapas denounced "the Nazi practices that do not respect nonbelligerent countries," but he left the issue of Mexico's response entirely in Ávila Camacho's hands, saying only that "we will know how to respond with dignity to this aggression, always according to the line of conduct which the President of the Republic, as the standard-bearer of the Nation, might indicate." Deputy Alberto Betancourt Pérez of Yucatán stated that he would be an advocate of war "if the honor of Mexico continues to be outraged," but he quickly added that such a step would naturally have to be made "under the direction of the President of the Republic, who is he to whom it falls to adopt the appropriate measures in this situation."[6] A cabinet member, Agriculture Minister Marte R. Gómez, went no further than saying that he was, naturally, "completely committed to [Ávila Camacho's] domestic and international policies," and the head of the official party, PRM National Executive Committee president Antonio Villalobos, said simply that the sinking of the *Potrero del Llano* should serve as a chastening blow to those who had sympathized with the Axis and argued against an alliance with the United States.[7] The willingness of all of these political actors to defer to the judgment of the president suggests that even if the *Potrero del Llano* incident did not create a clear consensus on what Mexican policy toward the war should be, it did create a crisis atmosphere in which Ávila Camacho's position was strengthened. The initiative was left entirely in his hands.

Recognizing the decisive role that the president would play in determining Mexico's response to the May 13 attack, both advocates and opponents of a declaration of war sent their appeals directly to the National Palace, sometimes seeking to bring pressure to bear on Ávila Camacho by publishing their letters and by organizing demonstrations. Impassioned arguments in favor of Mexican entry into the war came primarily from the leadership of left-leaning labor organizations and from communists and other admirers of the Soviet Union. Former CTM leader Vicente Lombardo Toledano was among the first to write to the president with a call for Mexico formally to join the fight against the Axis. Although he had stepped down as the head of the official labor federation in February 1941, Lombardo Toledano maintained a high profile in leftist circles by traveling and speaking extensively. He spent the war years trying to extend his influence even beyond the borders of Mexico by promoting the Confederación de Trabajadores de América Latina (CTAL), a regionwide labor organization that he had helped to establish in 1938. As president of the CTAL, he sent an open letter to Ávila Camacho on May 14, 1942, arguing that in the face of the attack on the *Potrero del Llano*, "there is no fitting response . . . other than the declaration of war against Nazi Germany." "The hour has arrived," he wrote, "for Mexico to do honor with supreme decisiveness to its traditions as a country that fights for its own liberty and for respect for the liberty of all the men and all the nations of the earth."[8] In an effort to build greater momentum behind his appeal for a declaration of war, Lombardo Toledano gave wide publicity to his letter, drawing criticism from the right. The PAN's weekly magazine, *La Nación*, blasted the self-proclaimed leader of the hemisphere's workers for publishing this document "without the least preoccupation about a sounding out of public opinion, without even the lightest consideration of the consequences," and for irresponsibly pressuring the government in a bid to win prestige for himself and his "phantom continental organizations."[9] The head of the CTAL had succeeded, nonetheless, in drawing attention to his call for war.

Another prominent leftist, Narciso Bassols, directed a similar message to Ávila Camacho. Bassols, a respected intellectual who had served in key cabinet and diplomatic posts during the 1930s, wrote to the president in the name of the Liga de Acción Política, a group that he had established. His letter reminded Ávila Camacho that his organization had called for a declaration of war immediately after the attack on Pearl Harbor and asserted that "with the first physical aggression against us having been consummated today," the government should enter the fight against the Axis without further hesitation. Repeating an argument he had made the previous December, Bassols stressed that a declaration of war would be an important political statement, even if the country was not in a position to send a large number of soldiers into battle. While it was the sinking of the *Potrero del Llano* that prompted Bassols to renew his call for Mexican participation in World War II, his letter makes it clear that for many on the left, sympathy for the Soviet Union was a key factor that dictated strong support for the global fight against fascism. Citing another passage from his organization's post–Pearl Harbor letter to the president, Bassols suggested that it was only "after the 22nd of June [1941], on which Hitler assaulted the Soviet Union," that "the true interests of the people [began to] demand that we add our forces to those of all the countries that fight against Nazi-fascist barbarity." And even before he reiterated his call for a declaration of war, Bassols insisted upon the reestablishment of diplomatic relations with the USSR, which had been broken off in 1930.[10]

Lombardo Toledano's former colleagues in the leadership of the CTM added their voices to the leftist chorus that demanded war against the Axis. On May 15, the federation's national committee, chaired by Secretary General Fidel Velázquez, adopted resolutions calling for a declaration of war and for a crackdown on the subversive activities of German, Italian, and Japanese citizens in Mexico. Sensing an opportunity to increase its own clout at the expense of conservative groups

Figure 4: After the sinking of the *Potrero del Llano* in May 1942, labor unions were among the leading proponents of a declaration of war. Here, members of the CTM call for Mexicans to take up arms. (Fototeca Nacional, Instituto Nacional de Antropología e Historia; © 615003 CONACULTA.INAH.SINAFO.FN.MÉXICO)

that might find themselves on the wrong side of the ideological divide, the CTM declarations went on to propose that "the existence of anti-democratic organizations," like the UNS, the PAN, and the Spanish Falange, should not be permitted and that publications favoring the Axis should be banned. "Henceforth," the CTM said, "no attack by the reactionary press on the organizations or persons who fight in favor of the democracies should be tolerated, for this is another of the methods that the fifth columnists use to favor the interests of Hitler, Mussolini, and Hirohito."[11] These proposals suggest that the left saw in a declaration of war the prospect of silencing their bitter enemies on the right and of dominating the political landscape in a wartime Mexico. Seeking to press what they perceived as their advantage, the CTM joined other groups in planning a massive protest meeting to be held in the Zócalo, on Sunday, May 24, to demand a forceful response to Axis aggression.[12]

But leftist sentiment was not unanimously in favor of Mexican involvement in the war. Indeed, the left's most prominent figure, former president Lázaro Cárdenas, privately expressed his misgivings about the possibility of a declaration of war in a May 18 letter to his successor. The commander of the RMP told Ávila Camacho that the sinking of the *Potrero del Llano* "could induce our people, through sentimentality and lack of reflection, to an inclination toward a declaration of war," though he was no doubt aware that it was the administration, more than the populace, that was showing such an inclination. Cárdenas expressed confidence that the president, with his "recognized capacity and serenity," would "know how to resolve this and other problems that might present themselves to the country," but his letter made it abundantly clear that he thought that entering the war would be a mistake. Cárdenas stressed the fact that Mexico was not in a position "to obtain by means of arms reparation for the aggression suffered," lacking, as it did, sufficient military strength to wage a modern war. Assuming that the president and his advisers might be viewing a declaration of war as a way to gain additional access to U.S. materiel and equipment, he cautioned that Washington "will always find reasons to put off the provision [of supplies and ammunition] on the pretext of the demand for armament in Europe, Asia, and in their own territory." He also pointedly noted the need to take into account "the mission that the ship was carrying out when the sinking occurred, in waters outside of our jurisdiction."[13] Though he did not say so directly in his letter, Cárdenas wrote in his diary that by carrying fuel to a country at war, the ship, in his view, "was exposed to every contingency of the war itself." He stated that Mexico should not fail to respond to the incident in some way but that he that he did not wish to see the country act without sound legal and moral justification.[14]

Nor was Cárdenas alone as a leftist leader who opposed Mexican entry into the conflict. His former communications minister, Francisco J. Múgica, also voiced reservations about a war declaration to the president. Though he spent most of the Ávila Camacho administration in a kind of semi-exile as governor of the isolated territory of Baja California Sur, Múgica was an important figure. He had played a key role in the drafting of the socially progressive Constitution of 1917, he had worked closely with Cárdenas on the 1938 oil expropriation and on other radical policies, and he had been the leading left-wing contender to succeed Cárdenas until he was passed over for the official candidacy in favor of the more moderate Ávila Camacho. In a May 20 letter to the president, Múgica asked if it was not at least possible "that the Allied Powers might be using some trick like the sinking of a ship to stir up our patriotism and to obligate us to enter definitively into the war." He suggested that this would be logical, as U.S. authorities likely viewed Mexico's formal neutrality as an obstacle to the permanent stationing of troops, planes, and ships south of the border. Therefore, he wrote, they would "surely think of seeking psychological means that would change our attitude," and obviously, "those [means] that are hidden and difficult to identify, like the treacherous attack on our merchant ships and even the sabotage of our poor industry, could be [for them] the most adequate."[15] While suspicions that the United States was responsible for the attack on the *Potrero del Llano* were widespread among many Mexicans, Múgica was perhaps the only prominent official to suggest that possibility directly to the president.

But even if Axis responsibility for the attack could be established, Múgica doubted that Mexico was prepared to be an active participant in a conflict like World War II. "What war is it that Mexico can declare?" he asked. "We have no preparation whatsoever for defensive war, much less for an offensive one," and he refused to believe that the government was seriously considering the shameful step of declaring a war that it did not intend to wage, as the smaller countries of Central America and the Caribbean had done. "I do not want even to imagine that we are going to declare a war like that of Cuba, like that of Puerto Rico, or that of Honduras, because in the moments in which all of humanity writes entire pages of gallantry defending its own convictions, it is more than ridiculous to declare a war of pure hot air," he wrote. Múgica worried that by proclaiming Mexican solidarity with the "Continental" cause so loudly and so often, without making it clear to Washington that additional time was necessary to erase memories of old injuries received at the hands of the United States before an "Anglo-Saxon alliance" could be established, the foreign ministry had left the country "in an alley so narrow that soon we will have no way out." Nonetheless, he suggested that, rather than declaring war, the government should focus on strengthening the military, boosting production, and building up infrastructure, so that the country would be ready to meet future challenges.[16]

The staunch nationalism of Cárdenas and Múgica, along with the fact that both men were based on the strategically important Baja California peninsula in the spring of 1942, may help to explain their opposition to a Mexican declaration of war. As men of the left, they despised fascism, but for Cárdenas, who had spoken out against the Italian invasion of

Ethiopia in 1935 and against the conquest of Europe's smaller, weaker nations at the beginning of World War II, defending national sovereignty was a top priority. Having battled since his appointment as commander of the RMP in December 1941 to keep American forces off of Mexican territory (and, especially, out of Baja California, the region with which U.S. officials were most concerned), he no doubt feared that Mexico's entry into the war would make it more difficult to decline "friendly" U.S. offers to assist in defending the country by establishing bases and patrols. Múgica, too, from his vantage point in La Paz, had seen the interest shown by U.S. officials in the establishment of a naval station at Bahía Magdalena, on the Pacific coast of his territory. As his May 20 letter to Ávila Camacho shows, he believed that interest to be so great that it was at least conceivable that the United States had carried out the attack on the *Potrero del Llano* in an effort to draw Mexico into the war and thus to gain access to the Mexican bases it had not theretofore been able to obtain. While anti-fascist convictions, sympathy for the Soviet Union, and calculations centering on possible political gains prompted others on the left to support a declaration of war, worries about the implications of co-belligerency with the United States apparently led nationalist leftists like Cárdenas and Múgica to take a position on the issue that was closer to that adopted by some of the more conservative forces in Mexican politics.

The right-leaning PAN, for example, also wrote to Ávila Camacho seeking to convince him not to take the country to war. Because the organization was sharply critical of Cárdenas-era policies that promoted socialist education and the redistribution of private property, PRM functionaries and leftist leaders often labeled PAN leader Manuel Gómez Morín and his followers as "reactionaries" and called for the suppression of their party. In foreign affairs, the group did not take a virulently anti-American position, but it was wary of rising Protestant influence in Mexico and generally unenthusiastic about the closer ties that were being forged with Washington.[17] In the wake of the attack on the Mexican tanker, the party's central committee told Ávila Camacho that "Mexico should not consider as a casus belli [*caso de guerra*] the sinking of the 'Potrero del Llano.'" In the view of the committee, formal entry into the war would be justified only in the event of an assault on Mexican territory. "For reasons of justice, of true dignity, and of the supreme national interest," the committee members wrote, "a declaration of war would only be called for to reject by force a violent, actual attack against the honor or the integrity of the Nation." The PAN believed that the government should adopt measures short of war to uphold Mexican honor in the case of the *Potrero del Llano* and argued that such a policy would "strengthen the international situation of Mexico" while enjoying "the unanimous and resolved support of the Mexican people," thus contributing to the "realization of the national unity which is absolutely indispensable in the face of decisions with irrevocable consequences for the Fatherland."[18]

In contrast to the approach adopted by Lombardo Toledano, the PAN did not publicize its May 21 letter to Ávila Camacho, perhaps because, in the volatile political environment that existed after the sinking of the *Potrero del Llano*, the party leadership wished to avoid the left-wing charges of fifth columnism that inevitably would have followed its publication. In explaining why they were making their appeal privately, the authors of the letter cited a desire not "to contribute to a divisive climate of political discord."[19] However, the PAN did provide the public with a slightly more subtle statement of its position in its weekly magazine. According to an analysis of the situation that appeared in *La Nación*, Mexican public opinion "condemns without vacillation the sinking of the 'Potrero del Llano'" and "laments with deep sincerity the loss of Mexican lives," but it also "denounces and condemns the attitude of the political operatives who want to capitalize upon this painful and grave matter for their own gain or to advance the interests of particular groups," and it "hopes, above all, that the Government of the Republic [would] not consent to being coerced by non-national forces or interests."[20] The clear implication was that Lombardo Toledano and groups like the CTM were pushing for war in a bid to gain a political advantage and that the Ávila Camacho administration should resist external pressures to go to war, whether those pressures were coming from Washington or, indirectly through Mexican communists and their sympathizers, from Moscow. The PAN, aware of the difficulties it might well face as an opposition group in a country at war, suggested that what the Mexican people fundamentally desired was "the realization of an authentic program of national unity in which the Government establishes the Common Good as its supreme goal."[21] Unlike the CTM and its allies, which saw in the war an opportunity to wipe out their ideological enemies, the PAN could discern no advantage to be gained from Mexican participation in the war and could hope only for the implementation of a program of "unity" that would allow for its survival.

Another group on the right, the Sinarquistas, also expressed opposition to a declaration of war. Throughout the war, the UNS had criticized the government for its ever closer ties with the United States and had argued in favor of Mexican neutrality. In the wake of the sinking of the *Potrero del Llano*, the organization held a rally in León, Guanajuato, its birthplace, which attracted forty thousand people and at which Sinarquista orators openly opposed Mexican participation in the war.[22] Ambassador Messersmith commented that the speeches at the León rally had "definitely taken the mask from Sinarquism, so that it is now clear that there is nothing friendly to us in the Movement nor to the democracies, but that it is a thinly veiled antidemocratic movement into which many thousands of unsuspecting and good Catholics have been drawn."[23]

Another much smaller force on the right, the tiny Partido Autonomista Mexicano (PAM), took a similar position. The former *almazanista* activists who made up the PAM had remained harshly critical of the Mexican regime since their candidate's defeat in the fraud-ridden July 1940 presidential elections, and one of their favorite charges was that the Ávila Camacho administration had consistently demonstrated servility to the United States. While the party attracted only a small following, the government was sufficiently concerned about its subversive potential that it sent an interior ministry agent to observe the group's sparsely attended meetings. This investigator reported to his superiors that at a May 20, 1942, gathering of about forty PAM members, a leader of the party's youth organization, a Señor Sánchez, argued that "what is now happening because of the sinking of the steamship 'Potrero del Llano' is a result of the ineptitude of the Government, to its lack of foresight," because it had put Mexican sailors in harm's way. As for the propaganda effort that was under way to bring Mexico into the war, it was being "fomented by the United States, which has always considered Mexicans as inferior beings and wants them to go to war to serve as cannon fodder [*carne de cañon*], while their armies remain intact," he said. But despite the appeals for war being made to "the putrid and nauseating Government of Ávila Camacho" by legislators and the CTM, Sánchez asserted that "the people will not allow themselves to be fooled."[24]

Another speaker at the PAM meeting claimed that the U.S. government was pressuring Mexico to enter the war to fulfill the terms of an apocryphal December 1940 pact in which Ávila Camacho had allegedly agreed that the Mexican people would "be at the disposal of the United

States and serve as cannon fodder" in exchange for U.S. recognition of his legitimacy as president. And the presiding officer spoke of widespread rumors that "a belligerent nation"—in this context, clearly a reference to the United States—"sank the ship to oblige Mexico to enter the war."[25] The accusations that were leveled at Washington throughout the meeting perhaps reflected the bitterness that almazanistas still felt over the Roosevelt administration's failure to back their cause in 1940. In any event, with all of their enemies, foreign and domestic, lining up behind the Allied war effort, many of these die-hard conservative critics of the regime were determined to resist the movement that called for a declaration of war.

Either because it lacked the resources to get its message out, or because it wished to be cautious in a highly charged and highly changeable political environment, the PAM did not make a high-profile statement of its views on the *Potrero del Llano* incident in the days after the attack. But some far-right publications did take a public stand against Mexican entry into the war. Staunchly anticommunist and frequently anti-Semitic newspapers like *Omega* and *El Hombre Libre* wielded little influence over public opinion, but they reflected the point of view of a certain segment of recalcitrant ex-almazanistas and Germanophiles in Mexican society. In the pages of these publications, commentators expressed regret over the loss of Mexican lives in the attack on the *Potrero del Llano*, but they contended that the sinking of the ship was a natural consequence of the government's failure to observe its formal commitment to neutrality. "If Mexico had preserved the neutrality to which it was obligated, because the Anglo-German dispute, in which our 'Good Neighbor' out of ambition voluntarily involved itself, implied no offense, no threat, no danger to the country . . . we would have a right to demand respect for our flag protecting a national ship," *El Hombre Libre* argued. "But the ship that was torpedoed was not even Mexican," the editorialist went on, reminding readers that the *Potrero del Llano* had formerly been the Italian vessel *Lucifero*, one of the Axis ships that had been impounded by the Ávila Camacho administration in April 1941. "Nor were we in any way neutral," he said, "since we broke our diplomatic relations with the Axis powers to ingratiate ourselves with Roosevelt, putting ourselves under his command."[26]

Columnists in both *Omega* and *El Hombre Libre*, which were run by the same editor, also advanced the argument that the use of submarines to disrupt shipping along the U.S. coastline was a legitimate war measure. While *Omega* acknowledged the rumors that were circulating, to the effect that the United States had attacked the Mexican tanker to draw their country into the war, the newspaper's staff admired the brazen effectiveness of the German war machine too much to allow for that possibility. With barely concealed glee, an editorialist noted the ability of the German navy to humble Mexico's powerful North American neighbors, pointing out that in recent days U-boats had "attacked the ships of the powerful Allies even in the Saint Lawrence River, within the boundaries of Canada, and at the mouth of the Mississippi." *Omega* asserted that in legal terms "the blockade is justified because it constitutes, now more than ever, a great imperative necessity of marine warfare" and that "legal scholars accept almost without any disagreement that neutral states must accept the consequences however disastrous they might be" when they allow their ships to operate in a war zone. [27] An *El Hombre Libre* article noted that Argentine and Brazilian ships had been sunk without those countries threatening a declaration of war, and it denounced those in Mexico who advocated such a step.[28]

Groups like the PAM and press outlets like the right-wing publications cited previously may have represented only a tiny fringe of Mexican public opinion, but it seems probable that a majority of Mexicans shared their opposition to a declaration of war. In a survey of 11,464 Mexico City residents carried out by the newsweekly *Tiempo* on May 21 and 22, after the sinking of the *Potrero del Llano* but before news of the loss of the *Faja de Oro* was widely known and before Ávila Camacho had announced his intention to declare war, 59.3 percent of the respondents said that Mexico should not enter the conflict. What support there was for Mexican entry into the war was largely limited to those who identified themselves as members of "groups of the left"; fully 92.2 percent of the 2,144 anti-fascists, communists, and oil and railway workers who were surveyed backed a declaration of war. By contrast, 78.4 percent of the presumably less ideological "men on the street" who were polled opposed Mexican participation in the conflict. The sampling techniques used in the execution of this survey would almost certainly fail to satisfy modern pollsters, but the substantial number of respondents and the effort that was made to identify the background of those who took different positions make this survey a valuable snapshot of public opinion in the capital toward the possibility of a declaration of war during the days immediately after the *Potrero del Llano* incident.[29]

Letters from Mexican citizens urging government officials not to take the country to war and anxious reports from foreign diplomats suggest that lingering suspicion of the United States played an important role in stimulating resistance to the idea of entering the war on the Allied side. Particularly damaging to efforts to build support for a declaration of war were widespread, and widely accepted, rumors that it had been a U.S. submarine that had torpedoed the Mexican tankers, with the intention of forcing Mexico into the global conflict. One Mexico City resident expressed this belief in a letter to Ávila Camacho written shortly after the attack on the *Potrero del Llano*, saying,

> With respect to the sinking of the petroleum ship, you need to show
> a little more responsibility and not to be tricking the people by
> saying that it was sunk by submarines of the totalitarian powers; you
> and all Mexicans know perfectly well that this act was committed by
> the brutal yankees in order to oblige us to enter the war and in this
> manner to have our nation always under their domination, which
> those disgraceful gringos have always wanted, and they are accom-
> plishing it through the act of casting the blame on others.

He went on to tell the president that "we Mexicans are not disposed to defend the gringos and cooperate with them in acts of war."[30]

A few days later, another resident of the capital wrote to the president to suggest that the United States might have sunk the ships "in order to fire up the spirits of the Mexicans and to oblige Mexico to enter the fight, which is what the Americans want." He added that Americans were not to be trusted, given that "they live constantly thinking about how they might gain control over our territory, since they have already taken part of it." To support this hypothesis, he asserted that the Americans had blown up their own battleship in Havana Harbor in 1898 in order to create a pretext for war with Spain and the occupation of Cuba. The letter writer also suggested that Americans were responsible for the death of the pioneering Mexican aviator Francisco Sarabia, who had perished in a 1939 plane crash in the Potomac River near Washington; they sabotaged his engine, he claimed, "because the Americans don't want anyone to outdo them."[31] Even two years later, another correspondent clung to this interpretation of the events of May 1942 in a letter to the president protesting against deepening Mexican involvement in the war. "We all know that the affair of the ships was just a plan set up so that Mexico would enter the war," he or she wrote.[32]

U.S. officials and other observers were shocked by the broad acceptance of this version of events. Ambassador Messersmith noted the circulation of such rumors as early as May 15, and according to an account delivered privately to the U.S. embassy by a Mexican newspaperman, even some of the surviving officers of the *Faja de Oro* believed that an American submarine had attacked their ship.[33] Even after Ávila Camacho presented his war message to the legislature on May 28, the assistant naval attaché at the embassy reported that "one of the most surprising features of the present situation is the incredibly general belief that the Potrero del Llano was sunk by a United States submarine." He wrote that "all classes of people all over the country are convinced that this is so and that it was done to draw Mexico into the war."[34] From the Pacific port city of Mazatlán, where General Cárdenas was establishing his headquarters, the U.S. consul confirmed that "Nazi propaganda that the aggressor submarine was an American one . . . is persuasive to a large section of the local public."[35] A U.S. naval officer based in the same region reported that in the nearby mining town of Compostela, Nayarit, many of the locals were also "anti-American and think that the sinking of Mexican vessels in the Gulf of Mexico was engineered by the United States for the purpose of drawing Mexico into the war on our side," and that in Puerto Vallarta, Jalisco, "many people feel that the U.S. is doing everything to drag Mexico into war."[36] The American consul in the important northern industrial center of Monterrey added that many people there believed that the sinking of the *Potrero del Llano* had in fact been the result of a conspiracy between the U.S. government and Foreign Minister Ezequiel Padilla so that Mexico would enter the war and so that it would be possible to send Mexicans into combat in the place of Americans. He suggested that "thinking people know that [this] is fifth column propaganda, but the man and the woman in the street are easily affected by a whispering campaign of this kind."[37]

While Axis agents might well have been partially responsible for the spread of this rumor, it is likely that many Mexicans did not need to be exposed to foreign propaganda to draw the conclusion that the United States had been involved in the attacks. Roosevelt's "Good Neighbor" policy might have convinced some that the "colossus of the north" posed less of a threat to Mexican sovereignty than it had in the past, but most Mexicans remained acutely conscious of the fact that their country had lost almost half of its territory to the United States in the mid-nineteenth century and that U.S. forces had occupied Veracruz and crossed the border in pursuit of Pancho Villa just a few decades earlier, during the Mexican Revolution. In light of what was seen as a pattern of disregard for the rights and dignity of Mexico, the natural inclination of many Mexicans was to blame the United States for this latest outrage, especially since it had taken place so close to U.S. shores. One American citizen living in the small town of Jacala, Hidalgo, told an acquaintance at the U.S. embassy in Mexico City that his neighbors had independently "decided that the U.S. is doing the sinkings in order to force Mexico and other Latin countries into the war." Indeed, he reported that he was "astounded at the unanimity" of the people there in their belief that the United States was trying to push Mexico into the war by attacking Mexican ships. "They are convinced," he said, "that the U.S. wants Mexicans as cannon fodder." His letter stressed that since there was practically no other foreign presence in the town (only one other American lived there), and because he figured it was too small to be a target for Mexican agitators, the reaction of the residents of Jacala was apparently a "spontaneous" one.[38]

Even those who believed that Germany probably had been responsible for the attacks on Mexican shipping did not necessarily favor war if it would mean an alliance with the United States. In a protest against a possible declaration of war, one group of Mexico City residents who identified themselves as "heads of households who find themselves in misfortune as a result of the bad faith of the Ungrateful Gringos" accused Ávila Camacho of leading the nation into the conflict "only to please the Neighbors [*los Srs Vecinos*], who are those who instead of giving us aid have harmed us in whatever way they have been able."[39] And a correspondent from the small town of Nogales, Veracruz, informed the president that popular opposition to a declaration of war was based largely on hostility to the United States. "That which most wounds the soul," he said, "is having to favor the side of those who have always made fun of us, of those who have fomented our revolutions in order to have us plunged into the most abject misery."[40] Despite the efforts of both the U.S. government and the Ávila Camacho administration to foster friendlier feelings toward the United States, the anti-American sentiment that persisted in Mexico in 1942 significantly dampened any enthusiasm that might have been felt for active Mexican participation in the Allied war effort.

And regardless of their feelings about their powerful neighbors to the north, many Mexicans feared that going to war would result in the needless sacrifice of many Mexican lives on distant battlefields. One Mexican father no doubt spoke for many when he wrote to Ávila Camacho with a plea for him to "think carefully" before taking the country to war. "There is no need for such an extreme measure," he wrote. To highlight the point that Mexico's lack of military preparedness would make its participation in the war disastrous, he added that "we do not have anything with which to wage war," and he suggested that Mexico would gain nothing from taking part in a conflict "that in the end will only benefit the great powers, whichever ones they might be, that win on the battlefield or diplomatically." He asked the president to "think of the suffering of your people, [and] of the Mexican families that would lose their sons, brothers, and fathers" in the war, and he expressed hope that he, his military-age sons, and the rest of the Mexican people would be able to "live under your Presidency in relative tranquility in the midst of the destruction that consumes the world."[41] Feelings such as these, coupled with the anti-American sentiment described previously, greatly limited the spread of "war fever" in Mexico in the days after the sinking of the *Potrero del Llano* and the *Faja de Oro*.

Although Ambassador Messersmith initially judged that "the sinking of the Potrero del Llano has made a tremendous change in the public attitude" by "bringing the war closer [to] home to a good number of the masses," reports from American diplomats stationed around the country attested to the largely apathetic response of the Mexican people to the attacks on the tankers and to the lack of widespread enthusiasm for war.[42] The U.S. consul in the border town of Nuevo Laredo reported that while "feeling in the official community is extremely high, . . . the population in general seems rather apathetic." He noted, too, that "as might be expected," rumors attributing the sinking of the *Potrero del Llano* to a U.S. submarine were circulating in his district.[43] In Torreón, a commercial hub in the Laguna region of north-central Mexico, the American consul wrote that "there was no excitement or indignation manifested here" in response to the attack, which had not inspired editorial comment in either of the local newspapers. "So far as I have been able to observe or to learn from other observers, Mexicans have either shrugged or laughed it off," he reported.[44]

Figure 5: The coffin of Rodolfo Chacón, a crewman on the *Potrero del Llano*, is
carried through the streets as part of a May 1942 protest against Axis aggression.
(Fototeca Nacional, Instituto Nacional de Antropología e Historia; © 615026
CONACULTA.INAH.SINAFO.FN.MÉXICO)

In Tampico, an important center for the oil industry, a May 24 prowar demonstration attracted approximately ten thousand people, but the
U.S. consul observed that despite some indignation over the sinking of
Mexican ships, "war sentiment seems to be confined to the labor element" and that "the people as a whole are not enthusiastic for war." In
the port city of Tampico, especially, this lack of enthusiasm might have
been based partly on a sense of vulnerability, as its oil refineries and
shipping facilities could easily have been shelled by enemy submarines
firing from offshore.[45] But even in inland population centers, and even
when prowar officials and groups staged large demonstrations appealing
to the emotions and to the patriotism of their compatriots, a widespread
sense of outrage over the attacks failed to develop. When the surviving
crewmen of the *Potrero del Llano* passed through Monterrey en route to
Mexico City bearing the body of their shipmate Chacón on May 21, a
large crowd assembled to receive them. The U.S. consul noted, however,
that "it was a curious apathetic crowd, not one with any burning desire
for revenge or satisfaction." References by speakers to a possible declaration of war on the Axis "received rather scant applause," and "the crowd
as a whole seemed . . . more as if it were a circus parade than something
which might vitally affect every man, woman and child in the country."[46]

Figure 6: The May 24, 1942, demonstration in Mexico City's Zócalo, after two Mexican tankers were sunk by German submarines. (National Archives and Records Administration)

Nor did the CTM's May 24 prowar rally in the capital, which also featured the survivors of the *Potrero del Llano* and Chacón's corpse, convincingly demonstrate the existence of a massive popular desire for Mexican entry into the global conflict. To be sure, the labor confederation's newspaper, *El Popular*, hailed the demonstration as having the "characteristics of an apotheosis" and as being a sign of the unity of all classes behind Ávila Camacho's international policy.[47] The principal Mexico City dailies played up the protest's significance as well. *Excélsior* called it "the biggest demonstration that there has [ever] been in the capital," and *El Universal* described the crowd as "so numerous that in the entire Plaza of the Constitution there was no place to put any more people."[48]

Foreign observers were far less impressed with the anti-Axis mass meeting, however. The U.S. embassy's dispatch on the event noted that while "the speeches in general were calculated to inspire emotionalism, the orators," including Lombardo Toledano and others, "were listened to with apparent apathy." During the course of the rally, which was held in Mexico City's main square, with President Ávila Camacho looking on from the balcony of the National Palace, "there was considerable milling about in the crowd and not a few people were noticed sleeping peacefully in the shade of trees and bushes." The American embassy's

Figure 7: Signs identified many of those attending the May 24 demonstration as members of labor unions or of other left-leaning organizations. (National Archives and Records Administration)

observer came away with the impression "that attendance of most of the delegations was a duty performance in which the individual members possessed little heartfelt interest." Those who had not come under duress as representatives of their unions "seemed chiefly to be curious Sunday morning strollers who soon became bored with the speeches," he reported.[49] The U.S. assistant naval attaché also commented on the "very noticeable lack of enthusiasm" at the rally, and he said that the crowd, which he estimated as numbering between ten thousand and fifteen thousand people, was much smaller than those that ordinarily gathered for large-scale patriotic demonstrations.[50] Journalist Betty Kirk, a foreign correspondent with extensive experience in Mexico, also placed the attendance figure at fifteen thousand—"and hundreds of these were constantly drifting away."[51] Thus, even at an event that had been intended to demonstrate to the president and to the world at large the depth and intensity of the Mexican people's support for a declaration of war, it became apparent that the enthusiasm of certain union leaders and politicians for such a step was far from universally shared.

Figure 8: Members of the Partido Comunista Mexicano called for a Mexican declaration of war on the Axis. (National Archives and Records Administration)

Faced with all of this evidence of apathy, ambivalence, and even hostility toward the idea of Mexican participation in the war, Ávila Camacho must have recognized that the sinking of the *Potrero del Llano* had not created a consensus in Mexican society, nor even within his own administration, in favor of deeper involvement in the conflict. Nonetheless, the president moved almost immediately after the attack to lay the groundwork for a declaration of war.[52] The most decidedly prowar member of his cabinet, Foreign Minister Ezequiel Padilla, who had probably been waiting for just such an opportunity as this one, helped the president to do this. Padilla shared the left's desire to see Mexico more deeply involved in the fight against the Axis, but he was no leftist. He was more interested in closer, warmer relations with the United States than in the reestablishment of ties with the Soviet Union, and since taking office he had established himself as a leading advocate of the doctrine of continental solidarity that was promoted by Washington and embraced by the Ávila Camacho administration. Critics charged that Padilla was seeking personal credit for the Mexican government's increasingly pro-American policies in an effort to win U.S. support for a future bid for the presidency, but while the foreign minister was not averse to receiving publicity for himself, he always insisted that he was simply carrying out the wishes of his president.

It was Padilla who informed Ávila Camacho of the sinking of the *Potrero del Llano* on May 14. On that same day, with the president's approval, he sent a strongly worded protest to the governments of Germany, Italy, and Japan, in which he demanded reparations for the sinking of the Mexican tanker and assurances that such an attack would not be repeated. If an adequate reply were not received by May 21, the note said, the Mexican government would "take the measures that the national honor demands." The U.S. naval attaché's office later learned from the Swedish diplomat charged with transmitting the Mexican note to Berlin, Rome, and Tokyo that a deadline of May 28 had appeared in an earlier draft of the protest, but that the Mexican government had decided to give the Axis one week to respond, rather than two.[53] The Swedish chargé observed that the note "amounted to nothing short of an ultimatum" and said that due to the slowness of communications, it would be practically impossible for Germany to reply in such a short period of time. This "indicated to him that Mexico does not wish an answer."[54]

By sending such a message, Ávila Camacho and Padilla created a situation in which Mexico's honor would be seen as being at stake, making a Mexican declaration of war almost inevitable. Unless Germany made a full apology for its actions—which was exceedingly unlikely to happen—cabinet members and other political actors would find it difficult to argue against the adoption of a stronger anti-Axis stance. After the foreign ministry announced on May 21 that Germany had refused even to receive the Mexican protest and that Italy and Japan had not responded to the note, and after word reached Mexico that the *Faja de Oro* had been torpedoed and sunk in the Straits of Florida on the night of May 20, it would become even harder for opponents of war in the decision-making circles of the government to take an open stand against entering the conflict.

On Saturday, May 22, with the deadline for an Axis response to the Mexican protest having passed and news of the attack on the *Faja de Oro* appearing on the front pages of Mexican newspapers, Ávila Camacho called a cabinet meeting to discuss the action to be taken by his government. A detailed record of what transpired during the three-hour session that began at 6:45 p.m. has not come to light, but the limited accounts of the meeting that are available suggest that some of the assembled officials expressed significant misgivings about the possibility of active Mexican participation in World War II. Economy Minister Francisco Javier Gaxiola recorded in his memoirs that Ávila Camacho opened the meeting by explaining the object of the gathering "in a solemn tone" and that Padilla then proceeded to lay out the case for declaring a state of war against the Axis. The foreign minister's presentation was followed by "a momentary and tense silence," Gaxiola recalled.[55] In the course of the discussion that followed, Agriculture Minister Marte R. Gómez and Treasury Minister Eduardo Suárez expressed their hope that "Mexico would not carry out any act of hostility that could stain its clean international historic tradition," perhaps indicating a desire among some cabinet members to ensure that Mexican belligerency would not result in direct military involvement in the global conflict.[56] Gaxiola wrote, too, that Labor Minister Ignacio García Téllez, a close associate of Cárdenas, "made a long exposition that revealed his judgment about the situation presented by the secretary of Relations"; while the economy minister did not reveal what his colleague's "judgment" was, a report reached the U.S. embassy that García Téllez had followed his mentor's lead by opposing a declaration of war.[57]

While the nature and extent of the opposition to participation in the war voiced by García Téllez and others is unclear, José C. Valadés, who had served as Padilla's private secretary at the time, later told a U.S. embassy official that "practically every member of the Cabinet except Padilla" had been opposed to a declaration of war and that only with difficulty had the president and the foreign minister been able to convince them that Mexican participation in the conflict would be to the country's advantage.[58] Valadés's account might well have been designed to raise Padilla's prestige further in Washington, but Agriculture Minister Gómez confirmed that the discussion had been spirited. In a letter to a J. Rubén Romero, a literary figure and the Mexican ambassador to Cuba, who was troubled by Mexico's entry into the war, Gómez wrote that he and his colleagues "spoke, you can be sure, with our hearts in our hands. We examined the pros and the cons, the advantages and disadvantages. . . . In our expressions there was not reticence or dissembling, and the determination at which we arrived was the result of that which was expressed, considered, and weighed." The decision that they ultimately reached was based on "a firm desire to adjust ourselves to the tradition of our fatherland and to safeguard our most immediate interests," he said.[59]

In the end, the president's support for Mexican entry into the war was decisive. Indeed, Gaxiola wrote that the outcome of the meeting was not in doubt after Ávila Camacho had opened the session and Padilla had made his presentation. The awkward silence that followed that exposition was one in which the cabinet members meditated not upon "the final resolution, which was inevitable, but rather [upon] the personal reasons that would have to determine our votes."[60] At 9:37 p.m., the ministers finally emerged from the National Palace conference room in which they had been meeting, and the president's private secretary, J. Jesús González Gallo, then announced to the press that Ávila Camacho would be asking Congress's Permanent Commission to call the legislature into an extraordinary session for the purpose of conferring upon the president the power to declare a "state of war" against the Axis.[61]

The decision to demand not a "declaration of war" but rather the declaration of a "state of war" represented an important compromise, however. To overcome the objections of his associates in the government and to reassure those who feared Mexican troops would be sent to engage actively in the fighting of the war, Ávila Camacho agreed to this semantic distinction. According to Valadés, Padilla believed that it might well have been impossible to persuade some members of the cabinet to support anything more than the declaration of an intentionally passive-sounding "state of war."[62] But the antiwar position of one political figure who was not even in the cabinet might well have been a more important consideration than any resistance from government ministers. The decisive factor in Ávila Camacho's decision to call for a measure that would appear to fall short of a full-blown declaration of war, Valadés said, was General Cárdenas's "violent" opposition to the sending of Mexican troops abroad and the ex-president's "insistence . . . in conversations with the President and Padilla that there should be nothing more than a declaration of a state of war."[63]

Cárdenas recorded in his diary that when he met with his successor at the presidential residence on the evening of May 21 after flying to the capital for consultations, he told Ávila Camacho that while some within the administration might favor a declaration of war, he felt it his duty "to speak to him also, for my own part, regarding the inconveniences that such a declaration would represent."[64] Ávila Camacho might well have been able to assuage his predecessor's concerns by promising to declare only a state of war. Appeasing Cárdenas would have been important to the president not just because he still commanded a large following both in political circles and among the masses, but also because Ávila Camacho wished to bring him into his cabinet as defense minister.[65] By bringing Cárdenas into the government, Ávila Camacho would be able to assure himself of the support of leftists who still looked to the ex-president for leadership, and he would further limit the political independence of his predecessor. By taking Mexico into World War II, he created a situation in which this strategically important move would be possible.

If using the concept of a "state of war" proved to be an effective way for Ávila Camacho to break down the resistance of Cárdenas and other government officials to Mexican entry into the global conflict, it also functioned to reassure the public that entering the war would not result in the deployment of Mexican troops abroad. For several days immediately after the administration announced its intention to declare the existence of a state of war, government officials stressed this point in statements to the press in an effort to calm the fears of an apprehensive public. On May 22, the government-run daily *El Nacional* and other papers reported a declaration by General J. Salvador S. Sánchez, the chief of the Estado Mayor Presidencial, to the effect that Mexico would not send a single soldier abroad and that the government would not rely on "the immoral resource of impressment [*leva*]" to raise troops.[66] The conservative Mexico City newspaper *Novedades* hailed this pronouncement as "a sedative for the popular bitterness" surrounding the decision to go to war and said that the statement demonstrated "the extent to which the good sense and the serenity of the President have been able to withstand the test of a natural nervousness arising from the rapid succession of events."[67] The rest of the national press repeated the government's soothing message. In the May 24 edition of *El Universal*, the first boldfaced subheading under the banner headline announced that no Mexican fighting men would be sent outside of the country.[68] And *La Prensa*, a widely read tabloid with a penchant for sensationalism, assured its readers on May 23 that entry into the war "does not imply a fundamental alteration in the rhythm of our life," reminding the public that "Costa Rica and Cuba declared war on the Axis the day after they did so in the United States, and nevertheless, their soldiers have not gone to fight in Java or anywhere else."[69]

Reassurances such as these might not have generated much new enthusiasm for Mexican entry into the war, but they do appear to have dulled fears about the possible consequences of such a step, thereby limiting the amount of opposition that Ávila Camacho's plans would encounter. When *Tiempo* followed up on its earlier survey by asking Mexico City residents on May 23 and 24 if, in their view, it was "patriotic to support the policy which the President of the Republic has adopted in defense of the national interests and decorum," fully 81.65 percent of the 17,745 individuals polled answered affirmatively. Certainly, the question was phrased in such a way as to make a negative response unlikely, and the fact that at least some of the votes were collected among the crowds that gathered for the wake of the slain sailor Rodolfo Chacón can be said to have introduced a certain bias into the results. Nonetheless, the news that Mexico would be declaring only a "state of war" and that Mexican soldiers definitely would not be sent to the fronts almost certainly contributed to the positive response to the president's policy.[70] Indeed, the increasing emphasis placed by the press and by government spokesmen on the limited nature of any Mexican involvement in the war probably played at least as much of a part as the sinking of a second Mexican ship in generating more widespread acceptance of entry into the war as May 1942 came to a close. In its analysis, *Tiempo* noted that while the *Faja de Oro* incident and the German rejection of Mexico's diplomatic protest had "managed to change the dispositions" of many Mexicans who had initially felt "unease and discomfort" about a possible declaration of war, the announcement that there would be no impressment and government assurances that the war would not have an adverse economic impact had also played a significant role in "dissipating many doubts" among the unorganized masses of Mexican society that had been disconcerted by the wave of rumors that had circulated in the wake of the sinking of the *Potrero del Llano*.[71]

On May 28, with the legislature gathered for its extraordinary session to act upon the president's request for authority to declare a state of war, Ávila Camacho made his way to the congressional chamber, passing through Mexico City streets lined with large crowds. On this occasion, the U.S. assistant naval attaché observed that the people at least "showed a little more enthusiasm than they did" at the demonstration that had taken place on May 24.[72] In the speech he made to a joint session of the Congress, the president made clear that "the 'state

Figure 9: Surveys showed that "the man on the street" was unenthusiastic about participation in the war, but many Mexicans were reassured by presidential statements indicating that the country's role in the conflict would be limited. (Fototeca Nacional, Instituto Nacional de Antropología e Historia; © 54076 CONACULTA. INAH.SINAFO.FN.MÉXICO)

of war' is war . . . with all its consequences," but he again stressed that Mexico would not send its troops outside of the country to take part in combat. "We well know the limitations of our resources for war," he said, "and we realize that in view of the enormous magnitude of the struggle, our part in the present conflict will not consist in going into action outside our Continent, something for which we are not prepared." He explained his decision to use the phrase "state of war" by suggesting that a conventional declaration of war would make it appear that Mexico was becoming a belligerent by choice, in violation of the country's pacifist tradition. Declaring a state of war, he argued, would signify that the country was entering the conflict only because it had been compelled to do so "by the severity of the deeds and the violence of the aggression" carried out against it.[73] The Congress of the Union dutifully approved Ávila Camacho's proposal, with the Chamber of Deputies voting unanimously (138–0) on May 29 to grant the president the power to declare a state of war and the Senate passing the same measure, also without dissent (54–0), on May 30. Armed with legislative authorization, Ávila Camacho on June 1 signed a decree stating that Mexico was at war with Germany, Italy, and Japan, retroactive to May 22. The decree became official when it appeared in the *Diario Oficial* the next day.

The ambiguity of the meaning of "state of war" had served and would continue to serve Ávila Camacho's purposes. The adoption of the term had helped to squelch rumors that troops would be sent abroad, and in his speech to the legislature, the president had used it as a way of reaffirming Mexico's image of itself as a peace-loving country. At the same time, however, in announcing that "the 'state of war' is war"—because in legal terms, no such distinction existed—Ávila Camacho was subtly serving notice that the country would be entering a real conflict and that he would be taking on the role of a wartime leader. As such, he would be in a stronger position politically, and his calls for national unity, internal harmony, and increased production would carry greater moral authority. And his authority would be enhanced in more concrete ways, too. Along with his proposal for a declaration of a state of war, Ávila Camacho submitted an initiative that would give him the power to suspend a long list of constitutional rights for the duration of the emergency. This legislation also received swift, unanimous approval from both congressional chambers. Though the president promised to use his powers sparingly and only in cases of dire necessity, opposition groups or uncooperative politicians recognized that if they failed to heed his appeals for solidarity and unity, he would have the tools necessary to enforce his will.

Recognizing the shift in the balance of political power toward the presidency that was taking place as a result of Mexico's entry into the war, groups that had expressed opposition to that step hastened to assure the chief executive of their loyalty. The PAN, for example, issued a statement on June 2 affirming "the irrefutable duty and right" of all Mexicans "to share the immense common effort" demanded by the declaration of a state of war. Professing an "unbreakable resolution to strengthen national unity," the party pledged that it would subordinate all of its activities to that end.[74] The danger that the organization would be subjected to official harassment if it did not publicly back the government's international policy must have seemed real enough to the PAN's leaders. In correspondence between the party leadership and the attorney general's office during the summer of 1942, the federal official insisted that wartime rules issued in conjunction with the suspension of constitutional guarantees required the group to provide full information on the times and places at which internal party and committee meetings were held. PAN officials tried to argue that the law requiring advance notice of political meetings applied only to events that were open to the public, but Ávila Camacho's attorney general, José Aguilar y Maya, ruled that information on all political meetings was required so that it would be possible for the government "to dictate the measures of vigilance [that are] indispensable for the maintenance of order." Political freedom remained intact, Aguilar y Maya said, but he indirectly hinted that if the PAN was to continue enjoying its right of expression, it would have to live up to the "trust" that the president had placed in it and in other political organizations by allowing them to continue to operate. The president had not thought it necessary to restrict the freedom of all parties to express their political positions, the attorney general wrote to the PAN's leaders, "but he has judged it to be appropriate to monitor political activities, conscious of his grave responsibility in this critical period in the history of our Fatherland."[75] In this context, the PAN must have felt a need for a certain amount of circumspection in the positions that it took on the question of Mexican participation in the war and on other issues of interest to the administration.

The Sinarquistas also adapted their position on the war to the new realities. A June 1 statement by the UNS acknowledged the president "as the supreme authority charged with watching out for the common good" and asserted that in deciding to declare a state of war Ávila Camacho had "proceeded with the uprightness that is befitting a good citizen and a good governor." Therefore, even though "no Mexican, jealous of the good of his country, [had] desired to take part in the war," especially after the country had already lived through what the Sinarquistas described as "thirty years of strife, of misery, and of ruin" since the start of the Mexican Revolution, the UNS announced that it would support the president's policy.[76] Observers at the U.S. embassy had their doubts about the sincerity of this profession of loyalty, coming as it did from a group that they still regarded as potentially dangerous, but they acknowledged the possibility that "with continuing statements similar to [this one], the organization can be turned into an ally of the Mexican Government."[77] But even if an alliance between the right-wing Sinarquista movement and an ostensibly revolutionary administration proved impossible to establish and maintain, Ávila Camacho had succeeded in neutralizing the more conservative critics of his regime. He had drawn upon their favored vocabulary of patriotism and nationalism as he took Mexico into World War II, and now, as they faced a president armed with emergency powers to control "subversive" elements, they had little choice but to support his decision.

While pressure from the PAN and the UNS was at least momentarily neutralized by Mexico's entry into the war, the small threat posed to the regime by the Partido Autonomista Mexicano was eliminated entirely. During the days leading up to Ávila Camacho's May 28 speech to Congress, the PAM's leaders concluded that with constitutional guarantees to be suspended during wartime, it would be impossible for their organization to continue to function. According to an informant reporting back to the government, they feared, among other things, that the authorities would take advantage of the "emergency" by deputizing members of the official party as policemen and allowing them to sack the PAM's offices.[78] Therefore, the party leadership decided to suspend the group's operations. According to the party's public statement, this determination was adopted "out of a high sense of patriotic responsibility and in light of the latest national events."[79] After that, controlling the remnants of the ex-almazanista political organization proved to be a relatively simple matter for the administration. When, in September 1942, the president of the party, Pedro Julio Pedrero, wrote to Ávila Camacho asking that the PAM be allowed to reconstitute itself in advance of the 1943 congressional elections, his petition was forwarded to the interior ministry, where no action on it was taken.[80]

In January 1943, Pedrero wrote again to the president, reminding him that the PAM had been the only party willing to set aside its own interests completely when Mexico entered the war and asking for an audience so as to be able to explain to him the reasons for the discontent of the people and thus to help him achieve the national unity that he sought.[81] When he finally met with the president around the end of March or the beginning of April 1943, Ávila Camacho was able to co-opt the PAM leader by offering him a position in his government.[82] Much to Pedrero's disappointment, the position turned out to be in the customs office of Coatzacoalcos, Veracruz, an insalubrious backwater, but he held on there through 1946 in the hopes of eventually obtaining a more comfortable, more lucrative post.[83] Though he reemerged as an opposition figure in the 1946 election campaign, Pedrero and his party, never very important after the 1940 elections, were rendered utterly insignificant as a result of Mexico's entry into World War II.

Of much more significance than the reaction of the PAM to Mexico's entry into the war was the reaction of the Roman Catholic Church. A statement on the war by the church would be taken seriously by many millions of devout Mexicans, including the religious country folk who formed the base of the Sinarquista movement. Therefore, it was noteworthy when the archbishop of Mexico City, Luis María Martínez, affirmed on May 30 that "it falls to the Civil Government to define for a nation the attitude that it ought to adopt in international affairs and especially in conflicts with other nations" and that therefore "we Catholics ought to put aside our personal ideas, however well founded they might seem to us, in order to comply with the dispositions issued by the Civil Authority." Martínez added that "duty and patriotism" demanded cooperation with the war effort, calling patriotism "a profoundly Christian virtue that imposes unity and harmony in these moments which are so grave for our Fatherland."[84] These phrases hardly amounted to a ringing endorsement of Mexico's entry into the war, but they did clearly indicate that Mexico's Catholic faithful should accept the administration's decision to take the country into the conflict. An analyst at the U.S. embassy judged that the archbishop's call for support of the war effort would be helpful to the Allied cause; Martínez's words, which were featured prominently in all the major newspapers, would "have a great deal of effect in turning a number of Catholics from their pro-Axis leanings," he wrote.[85]

The cleric's statement might well have come at the urging of Ávila Camacho: the president later told Ambassador Messersmith that just prior to his declaration of a state of war in May, he had held a meeting with the archbishop in which he had told the head of the Mexican church that "he found too great apathy on the part of the clergy and of the Church towards the war" and that "he felt the Church was not helping itself by this lack of a clearly defined attitude."[86] Because he was personally sympathetic to the cause of the Allies and because he was pleased with the slow but steady gains that the church was making under Ávila Camacho, Martínez would have come away from such a meeting willing to voice support for the government's decision to go to war and eager to do what he could to stay in the president's good graces. The archbishop had told Ambassador Messersmith in a meeting in May "that he was entirely satisfied with the attitude of the Government" toward the church, and he had indicated a desire to avoid antagonizing the administration, as "any pressures at this time could only retard the favorable development" of church-state relations then taking place.[87] Martínez made his effort to demonstrate to Ávila Camacho the soundness of the church's position on the war just a few days later, when he issued his May 30 statement. In August, Messersmith would report his impression that Ávila Camacho still did not judge the response of the archbishop and the church to the war to be "as yet adequate," but by easing up on the enforcement of restrictions on church activity during his first year and a half in office, the president had gained a certain degree of leverage with the top ranks of the clergy, making it possible for him to call upon them for support in critical situations like the one that arose at the time that Mexico entered World War II.[88]

Other members of the Catholic hierarchy seized upon the declaration of a state of war as an opportune moment to make a subtle push for the expansion of the role of the church in a particular area of public life. The bishop of Chihuahua, like the archbishop, issued a statement acknowledging the right of the president to take the country to war and stating that it was the duty of the Mexican people to unite behind the chief executive, but he added an apparently generous offer that in fact had the potential to be quite controversial: "We [clergymen], who, by the disposition of Providence exercise the priesthood of Christ," he declared, "are ready to lend our services in the national army, at any time, and especially in the war, to aid the dying."[89] As an arm of the secular post-Revolutionary state, the Mexican Army did not include chaplains, and even the suggestion that priests play any kind of official role in the armed forces would elicit howls of protest from the left. The bishop of Chihuahua apparently sensed that Mexico's entry into the war provided an opportunity to raise this issue in such a way that it would seem to be a patriotic offer of wartime service on the part of the church rather than a frontal assault on the regime's ideology. However, the prudent desire of the archbishop to proceed slowly and cautiously in the negotiation of a new relationship between the church and the state kept this issue from becoming a major source of discussion in the months immediately after Mexico formally joined the fight against the Axis.

The Mexican declaration of a state of war did more than reduce the vulnerability of the administration to possible opposition from the right, however. By entering the conflict, the government also gained important leverage in its relationship with organized labor. Because leftist labor leaders like Lombardo Toledano of the CTAL and Velázquez of the CTM had been such avid proponents of participation in the fight against fascism, they and their organizations naturally pledged their full support to Ávila Camacho when he called for Mexico to enter the war. In their eagerness to back the Allied war effort, however, these groups surrendered some of the tools that they had at their disposal to protect the interests of their members and to exercise influence over the administration. In a "Pact of Labor Unity" signed just days after Mexico entered World War II, the leaders of six different labor confederations pledged not just to set aside "all inter-union struggles" and to eliminate "all activity that provokes the weakening or splintering of labor organizations" but also to suspend strikes and work stoppages and to refer any worker-employer conflict that could not be resolved through negotiations to the president for arbitration. The union representatives, who had been brought together by Labor Minister García Tellez, also bound themselves to a policy of "frank and decided cooperation with the Government of the Republic in the defense of our territory and institutions."[90]

Far from expressing concern about the loss of workers' ability to strike in defense of their interests, an editorial in the CTM newspaper, *El Popular*, hailed the labor leaders' pledge as "a decision that reveals the very high degree of patriotic consciousness that inspires the working class and its directors." While the author noted in passing that the promise to forego strikes for the duration would have to be "met with an equally patriotic attitude from the employer class," he interpreted the move not as an abandonment of the labor movement's most effective weapon but rather as a clear sign that "the workers are already in the vanguard of the defense of the Fatherland, in the first ranks of the great national union forged to reject the aggression of the totalitarians."[91]

The Pact of Labor Unity also provided for the creation of a Consejo Nacional Obrero (CNO), a national labor council that would include members of each of the agreement's six signatories: the CTM, the once favored but by then marginalized Confederación Regional Obrera Mexicana (CROM), the new Confederación Proletaria Nacional (CPN), the independent Unión Mexicana de Electricistas, and two smaller groups—the anarcho-syndicalist (but relatively inactive) Confederación General de Trabajadores (CGT) and the new Confederación de Obreros y Campesinos de México (COCM). The stated purpose of the council was "to avoid worker-employer and inter-union fights, to accelerate pro-duction, and to strengthen national unity during the period of emer-gency created by the war."[92] But because the different parties to the pact had equal representation on the council, despite the fact that the CTM was vastly larger and more politically powerful than all the others, the creation of the CNO might also be seen as part of a broader administra-tive strategy to reduce the clout of the "official" labor confederation by building up more conservative rivals such as the CROM and the CPN.

To be sure, the Pact of Labor Unity did not succeed in preventing manifestations of labor unrest throughout the war years. Strikes did take place despite the terms of the pact. In fact, workers at the Mundet Bottling Works in Mexico City, who were members of the CPN, carried out a strike for higher wages on the day after the agreement was reached, and some smaller labor groups went on strike later in the summer of 1942.[93] More seriously, later in the war miners threatened to suspend their work extracting vital war materials from the subsoil, and work stop-pages by railroad employees disrupted the transport of those and other products. Nor did the structure of the CNO ultimately result in the displacement of the CTM as the country's leading labor organization. However, the pledges of cooperation made by union leaders at the time that Mexico entered World War II did tend to limit the options that were available to them and to reduce the amount of pressure that they could effectively bring to bear on the government and on employers. And faced with the reality that the administration was willing to recognize and work with other labor confederations and organizations, the CTM lead-ership might well have reached the conclusion that it would be unwise to clash with the president lest he turn increasingly to rival groups. In sum, the changes to the relationship between the government and the labor movement that took place as a result of Mexico's declaration of a state of war placed Ávila Camacho's government in a position that was substantially stronger than the one it had occupied before May 28, 1942.

By leading Mexico into World War II, Ávila Camacho strengthened his hand in his dealings with many of the organized forces that influ-enced the country's politics, but he also enhanced his prestige among the vast, unorganized Mexican public. To be sure, the declaration of a state of war was not a development that the average Mexican wel-comed enthusiastically, and ambivalence with respect to the war effort remained widespread. Immediately after the president's May 28 speech

Figure 10: The presidential decree declaring the existence of a "state of war" with the Axis is posted as part of a formal ceremony. (National Archives and Records Administration)

to the Congress calling for entry into the war, the U.S. assistant naval attaché reported that "the people's attitude is apparently one of lethargy, a disbelief of the fact that what is happening can happen." Noting that many seemed to feel that the declaration alone would be sufficient to vindicate the country's honor and that no further sacrifices would therefore be necessary, he concluded that "Mexico's status as a belligerent will [not] be overly popular unless the Government undertakes and maintains a vigorous program to stimulate such an enthusiasm."[94] An American diplomat reporting on reaction to the Mexican declaration concurred, saying that "apathy was fairly general on the part of the public" and that dispatches from all regions of the country showed that "this apathy was general throughout Mexico."[95] When news of the declaration of a state of war was announced by local authorities around the country in a ceremony known as a *bando solemne*, an observer of the ritual in Durango noted that "the attitude of the great majority of the people viewing the procession was quite apathetic, so much so that even some of the government officials participating commented upon the fact and remarked that the government will have to take severe measures to make the people realize that the country is at war and that they must support the government in the stand it has taken."[96]

However, those Mexicans who had watched Ávila Camacho's response to the crisis that brought the country into the war admired his calm tone and his statesmanlike stance, and they deeply appreciated his repeated reassurances that Mexico would not be dispatching troops to the fighting fronts. This was a message that the president took care to reiterate. In a radio address to the Mexican people on June 3, one day after his "state of war" declaration had gone into force, Ávila Camacho again told his countrymen that Mexico's military commitment to the war would be limited to the protection of Mexican soil and the defense of the Western Hemisphere. "We will take the military dispositions that might be necessary to assure the inviolability of our territory," he said, "and although we might not intervene [*aunque no intervengamos*] in actions of war outside the Continent . . . we will collaborate, if necessary, in the defense of America."[97]

Words like these had their intended effect. The U.S. consul in the border town of Piedras Negras, Coahuila, reported that initially public opinion "among all classes was generally against a declaration of war" but that the prevailing "sentiment of discontent was changed immediately by the Mexican President's address [to the Congress on May 28], especially by that part where he recognized Mexico's limitations and outlined the role that he thought Mexico should play in the struggle." He observed "that public opinion in Piedras Negras is now 100% in support of Ávila Camacho's policy."[98] The Mexico City newspaper *Novedades*, which, like the people of Piedras Negras, had at first been wary of calls for Mexican participation in the war, also praised the president for his measured response to the crisis. Expressing relief that "in the Presidency of the Republic there is a man whose fundamental personality trait is serenity," an editorialist wrote that Ávila Camacho had "neither flown off the handle in the face of aggression, nor has he obsessed himself with the cries of those who would demand a crazy expedition in search of the enemy." Fortunately, he said, "the President knows that our forces are limited," and "he has made it clear that the role of Mexico will be that of defending its coasts and its soil."[99]

It was Ávila Camacho who had made the decision to take his country into World War II, but ingeniously, by appearing to reject the calls of more radical voices for active involvement in the conflict, he received the gratitude of many of his countrymen who had opposed participation in the war. An analyst at the U.S. embassy marveled that the president "had achieved the almost unanimous support of the Mexican people even if he had led them into a war which they would generally have chosen to avoid." Ávila Camacho's effective speech to the Congress and his "calm and serene manner" had "elevated him to a leadership which he had not theretofore possessed." Almost miraculously, the potentially controversial—and possibly explosive—step of taking Mexico into a "not too popular war" had made the country "perhaps more nearly united politically now than at any time in its history."[100] Right-wing organizations opposed to the regime were pledging their support to the administration, the church called for cooperation with the government, organized labor promised not to call strikes for the duration of the war, potentially influential former officials and military officers offered their services to the government, and the public generally accepted Mexican belligerency once it was clear that the country's role would be a limited one. In the months that followed, the administration endeavored to strengthen and build upon this unity, emphasizing the seriousness of the international situation as a way of holding the nation together behind the government.

FOUR

"Orienting" the Public

JUNE 1942–JULY 1943

Recognizing that most Mexicans still viewed the Second World War as something far-off and abstract even after the country formally entered the conflict, the Ávila Camacho administration took various steps during the latter part of 1942 to convince the public that Mexican involvement in the war was real and that unity and discipline were necessary to face the emergency. For a time, propaganda efforts, the launching of civil defense initiatives and military training, and carefully staged displays of wartime political solidarity succeeded in convincing at least some Mexicans that their country was living through exceptional times. But with the fighting actually moving farther and farther away from Mexican shores as 1942 gave way to 1943, the government began to take bolder steps to convince a population with no firsthand experience of the war that Mexico really did have a stake in the conflict.

As a part of this effort, the government began to implement a program of compulsory military service at the end of 1942, instituting a draft for eighteen-year-old men. Also, officials began to suggest quietly that it might ultimately be necessary for Mexican soldiers to participate directly in the fight against the Axis. Although the government continued to handle this explosive issue very cautiously, those who favored direct involvement in the war were taking small, gradual steps to prepare the public for the possibility that a Mexican expeditionary force would eventually be deployed overseas. If such a move could be made without generating a destructive political backlash, it would demonstrate to the many Mexicans whose lives had not been touched directly by the fighting on other continents that their country really was at war, and that realization in turn would stimulate patriotic feelings and enhance the ability of the government to insist on its program of national unity.

★ ★ ★

In the first few months after the declaration of a state of war, the administration attempted to ensure that the people of Mexico understood the country's position in the worldwide conflict, and officials sought to gauge popular attitudes regarding Mexico's role in the war. In the cabinet meeting at which the determination was made to declare a state of war against the Axis, Ávila Camacho's ministers had recognized that long-standing anti-U.S. sentiment would make it difficult to build up widespread enthusiasm for the Allied war effort, as would the admiration that existed in some circles for the efficiency and apparent strength of the Axis powers. Agriculture Minister Gómez wrote to a friend after the May 22 meeting that "what concerned us most was the need to go about convincing our fellow citizens of the correctness of our decision resolutely to take that which seemed to us the only reasonable and decorous path." The cabinet worried that many "people of pure and intransigent patriotism, with the greatest good faith, are not capable of forgetting the offenses that [the United States] has carried out against us, and they are resolutely repulsed by a strengthening of ties with our neighbor to the North." The ministers acknowledged, too, that "others, seduced by the luster of the uniforms and by the great noise of the conflict, admire Teutonic gallantry and bow before it." Therefore, the administration resolved to try to explain to the public that the declaration of a state of war represented the Mexican tradition of defending national sovereignty without regard for the strength of the enemy.[1]

In one early effort to build support in the provinces for the government's international policy, a number of legislators set out during the summer of 1942 on a campaign of "orientation" that took them to population centers in the north and the west of the country. At each stop, the senators and deputies presided over rallies at which they explained why Mexico had entered the war and called for support of the war effort. Although these events drew large crowds and a few of them apparently generated some excitement, observers generally reported that the speakers at the rallies

(left to right) Figure 11: As part of official efforts to "orient" public opinion on Mexico's role in the war, this poster explained why Mexico had entered the conflict. (National Archives and Records Administration)

Figure 12: A Mexican propaganda poster designed to generate enthusiasm for the war effort. A youth carrying the Mexican flag responds to "the cry of war" (a reference to the lyrics of the national anthem) after the sinking of the *Potrero del Llano*, shown in the background. (National Archives and Records Administration)

Figure 13: The Mexican government sought to link participation in World War II with other defining episodes in the nation's history. Here, Ávila Camacho is shown alongside Miguel Hidalgo, Benito Juárez, and Francisco Madero—other Mexican leaders who had fought for "liberty" and "a better world." (National Archives and Records Administration)

failed to shake the apathy of the attendees, many of whom had turned out only because local authorities or their labor unions had pressured them to be present. In Durango, for instance, the U.S. vice consul wrote that between twenty-five thousand and twenty-eight thousand people—out of a total population of only thirty-five thousand—attended a mass meeting in late July, but he noted, too, that the governor had leaned heavily on local firms and unions to achieve such a high turnout and that "the utter lack of enthusiasm on the part of the crowd was most conspicuous."[2] Separately, *La Nación* published a copy of a directive from Durango's chamber of commerce that in effect ordered local businesses to close and to have their employees attend the rally, in accordance with instructions received from the governor. The PAN publication called such methods "the best way to sabotage patriotism," as Mexicans who otherwise would be willing to support the war effort would come to resent these directives from on high.[3]

In Guadalajara, too, "an apathetic reception was accorded the group of senators which has been touring the country for the purpose of informing the public on the motives for Mexico's entry into the war," and in the port city of Guaymas, Sonora, their arrival "was met with much indifference by the press and inhabitants of the district."[4] One of the deputies involved in the orientation effort, Antonio Betancourt Pérez, even admitted privately that during a swing through Zacatecas he had encountered "considerable indifference to the war" as well as continuing "resentment against the United States," Mexico's new ally.[5] While reports of positive responses to the legislators' oratorical efforts trickled in from a handful of places, in general it appears that their tour did not lead to the development of deep enthusiasm for Mexican participation in the war.[6]

But even if the orientation effort failed to elicit much additional support for the government's decision to declare a state of war, the campaign was useful to the administration as a means of measuring the depth and intensity of resistance to the idea of active military participation in the conflict. In their speeches to audiences in various cities, Senator León García, a peasant-sector representative from San Luis Potosí, and Senator Eugenio Prado of Chihuahua suggested that Mexico should be preparing to send soldiers abroad to fight the country's enemies. Ávila Camacho might well have indicated to the senators that he would not object to their circulating this idea. Indeed, it seems unlikely that the representatives would have advanced such a controversial proposal without some sort of backing from the executive branch, particularly since García and Prado were considered to be close allies of the president.[7] A U.S. diplomatic report suggested that the legislators were making their calls for an expeditionary force "probably with the tacit consent of the president."[8]

For Ávila Camacho, it would have been useful to have the senators make a case for direct involvement in the war. Because of their prominence as public officials, their statements in support of an expeditionary force would be taken seriously. Certainly, at least some of the Mexicans who heard the senators speak drew the conclusion that they were in effect laying the groundwork for a change in government policy when they referred to the possible deployment of the army overseas. After the congressional delegation passed through Guaymas, for example, people there "openly expressed the opinion that the trip of the Senators was to gradually influence the population to accept the fact that soldiers must be sent abroad."[9] However, if there were an unfavorable reaction to the idea, it would be easy for the president simply to reiterate his previous statements to the effect that Mexico would not send troops into combat. No awkward policy reversal would be necessary, inasmuch as the legislators were speaking as popular representatives and not as members of the Ávila Camacho administration.

Whether or not he had explicitly approved the senators' allusions to the possibility of deploying troops overseas, the president no doubt took note of the fact that the public's response to these suggestions was decidedly unenthusiastic and that a number of editorialists actually denounced them. After Senator García told an audience in Chihuahua that "we Mexicans ought to be ready to take up arms and to go to fight in Asia or in any country of that or other continents," *La Nación* stated that he had committed a "censurable error" by contradicting "the program clearly fixed by the President of the Republic, who repeatedly, personally or through the Chief of Staff, has solemnly declared that the Mexican Army will be dedicated *to the defense of our territory* and that Mexican troops will not be sent to fight outside of the fatherland."[10] In Guadalajara, the U.S. consul reported that "the statement of one of the senators that Mexico may have to send troops abroad was roundly condemned," and an American official in Manzanillo wrote that Senator Gilberto Flores Muñoz's suggestion at a rally there that "Mexican lives may have to be sacrificed on foreign soil" likewise drew much criticism, demonstrating "that the public is not yet ready for anything but a defensive war."[11]

In an interview granted during the course of their tour to the editor of *Excélsior*, Senators García and Prado spoke of an expeditionary force of four hundred thousand men and of the need to "create a national atmosphere of such a nature as to permit the First Magistrate, at the request of the people, to order the transfer of our armed forces to the far-away trenches which are withstanding the attack of Nazi-Fascism." But *Excélsior* answered with an editorial charging that García and Prado spoke "with a lack of good sense and of reality [that is] truly regrettable." Noting that the country's armed forces were still too small and too poorly trained to be effective at the fronts and that the United States would never permit an Axis invasion of Mexico, the newspaper dismissed the senators' claim that Mexico was in danger of being overrun by its enemies, and the editorial argued that the country was adequately fulfilling its duty by increasing its production of strategically important materials.[12] Given the wary response of the public to the senators' calls for an expeditionary force and the denunciation of their speeches that came from both opposition groups (the PAN, through *La Nación*) and the mainstream press (*Excélsior*), it would have been clear to the president and his allies that the subject of military participation in the war was one that would continue to require careful handling.

Although he had promised his compatriots that their soldiers would remain at home, Ávila Camacho was aware of growing interest in military circles in the possibility of an active Mexican role in the war, and he himself was quietly sympathetic to the idea of a deeper commitment to the Allied cause. When Ambassador Messersmith met with Ávila Camacho on July 8, 1942, the president told the U.S. representative that a number of Mexican generals "who were very eager to do something" in the war had approached him to suggest that regiments should be raised in Mexico and other Latin American countries to be made available to go wherever they were needed to support the war effort. Ávila Camacho said that "he had told these Generals that if such a step were taken in a number of the other American Republics simultaneously he thought it would be a good thing," probably because he felt that it would be easier for his administration to reverse course on the overseas deployment of troops issue if such a step were made as part of a multilateral, regionwide effort. For the time being, though, the president said that he had "asked them to proceed discreetly and altogether quietly until they knew that there would be similar action in a number of other Republics as well as in Mexico," and he explained to the U.S. ambassador that while "he could not openly give approval to this measure at this time," he "was certainly not discouraging it." In fact, Ávila Camacho told Messersmith, he "was privately viewing [the initiative] with sympathy."[13] To be sure, the president must have calculated that by sharing this anecdote with the American ambassador he might rise further in the eyes of officials in Washington who were inclined to view him as a reliable ally worthy of U.S. support. Nonetheless, the information that Ávila Camacho passed along to Messersmith is significant in that it indicates that both prominent military officers and the president himself were contemplating the possibility of direct participation in the war just a few short weeks after he had convinced the public to accept Mexican belligerency by promising that troops would not be sent overseas.

His interest in an active role in the war notwithstanding, the president recognized that moving to send Mexican military units abroad was not yet feasible, either politically or logistically. Indeed, the organizational challenges that would have to be surmounted before Mexico could become militarily involved in the war were, if anything, more formidable than the obstacles imposed by the reluctance of the public to take such a step. At this early stage of Mexico's involvement in the war, the country's army was still very small, poorly trained, and badly equipped. To be sure, the modernization of the Mexican armed forces was under way as the government acquired up-to-date equipment on favorable terms from the United States, and one of the direct benefits to Mexico of its entry into the war had been a renegotiation of its March 1942 Lend-Lease agreement with Washington that resulted in an upward revision of the amount of materiel that the country would be eligible to receive and a reduction in the amount that Mexico would ultimately have to pay in exchange for that aid.[14] However, the army would have to be reorganized, expanded, and trained in modern methods of warfare before any overseas deployment would be possible.

Moreover, the organization of a Mexican expeditionary force would require a level of coordination with the U.S. military leadership that would be difficult to achieve. As Roosevelt put it, very diplomatically, in his reply to Messersmith's report on Ávila Camacho's interest in the organization of Latin American regiments, "the possibility of the offer to us of this cooperation raises a number of extremely difficult problems."[15] Those problems, as seen from the point of view of American military planners, were spelled out in some detail a few months later, after Undersecretary of State Sumner Welles informed his colleagues in the U.S. War Department in November 1942 that Ávila Camacho was interested in sending a Mexican division into combat sometime early in the following year. The exact form in which this proposal emanated from Mexico City is unclear, as Mexican presidential and diplomatic records do not include any reference to such a proposition being made at this time, and the Mexican administration was then publicly denying any intention to send troops overseas. Nonetheless, the "desire [of the Mexican president] to prepare a division of troops for employment overseas by the Spring of 1943" was apparently conveyed informally to State Department officials in Washington around this time, given that Welles referred to such a desire in a meeting of the State-War liaison committee on November 16, 1942.[16] In their response to the proposal, U.S. military authorities acknowledged that allowing Mexican forces to take part in the war might have some political advantages, but they concluded that for the time being, at least, "the active participation abroad of even token forces representing Latin American Countries is entirely out of the question," in part because of the "serious complications having to do with their equipment, armament, and supply" that would arise, but also because "the further matter of providing the necessary shipping and naval escort to transport this unit to an active theater of combat" would be difficult to address. Moreover, in light of the difficulties already involved in coordinating the efforts of a combined Allied force made up of units of different nationalities, the War Department did not wish to introduce "an added racial element into what already appears to be a sufficiently complex situation."[17]

During the November 16 liaison committee meeting, Welles had stated his intention to share any War Department reservations about Mexican participation in combat with Ávila Camacho's government, so the president was almost certainly made aware that the deployment of an expeditionary force would not be possible in the immediate future.[18] However, Ávila Camacho would not necessarily have viewed this response as a setback. The president would have been aware of the logistical obstacles that stood in the way of effective Mexican participation at the fighting fronts, and it is entirely possible that he anticipated that his offer of troops, in whatever form it was actually made, would be rejected. But if his real purpose in expressing a "desire" to send troops abroad at this point had been to signal to U.S. officials the depth of his government's commitment to the cause and perhaps also to prompt American policy makers to begin considering the circumstances under which Mexican participation in the war might be feasible later on, he had succeeded. Expressions of enthusiasm for and a willingness to participate in the war effort made it more likely that military equipment and other forms of aid would continue to flow to Mexico throughout the war years, despite its diminishing strategic importance after the Japanese defeat at Midway made an Axis attack on the Pacific coast of the Americas unlikely. Such offers of material assistance also made it more likely that the country would eventually, when its people were ready, win some kind of more direct role in the conflict, which would in turn stimulate patriotism, placate the military, and enhance Mexico's geopolitical clout in the postwar world.

Figure 14: Military drills for civilians were introduced in 1942, largely to raise consciousness that the country was at war. (Fototeca Nacional, Instituto Nacional de Antropología e Historia; © 54097 CONACULTA.INAH.SINAFO.FN.MÉXICO)

Back on the domestic front within Mexico, despite the impossibility of sending a Mexican force overseas immediately, the Ávila Camacho administration pushed ahead with policies and initiatives designed to emphasize the seriousness of the country's involvement in the conflict and to prepare the Mexican people gradually for a more direct role in the war. For a start, the government instituted weekly military training exercises for civilians around the country. In many places, at least at first, it appears that the programs were well attended by a willing citizenry, even though a shortage of weapons deprived most of the drills of any real military value. An American representative in Guaymas informed his superiors in September 1942 that the training sessions "have awakened a fervor of enthusiasm among the young men" of the town, and U.S. consular officials elsewhere in Mexico reported that the exercises were successfully raising consciousness of the war in various other cities, including Nuevo Laredo, Nogales, Tampico, and Tijuana.[19] With these observations in mind, no doubt, the embassy sent word to Washington that the "introduction of civilian military training has perhaps done more to arouse patriotic sentiments toward the Mexican war effort than any other single measure or event."[20]

After the first few weeks of the program, however, with the novelty of the drills wearing off, signs began to appear that the exercises were generating more resentment than enthusiasm. In Guadalajara, where twenty thousand civilian trainees had marched in an Independence Day parade, attendance at weekly exercises dropped off precipitously immediately after the September 16 holiday in the wake of the publication by the local newspaper *El Occidental* of a report that Mexican troops would soon be sent into combat. Many participants in the drills reportedly said "that if it was their government's intention to use them as cannon-fodder abroad, they were through training," and military authorities in the region scrambled to deny the controversial newspaper story and to boost suddenly slumping attendance figures at their training sessions.[21] Meanwhile, residents of rural areas and remote regions began to complain that productive tasks in the countryside were being neglected because local men had to spend long hours traveling to and from the nearest town for military exercises.[22] And elsewhere, there were complaints about abuses committed by the military officers in charge of the drills. Two men from Gómez Palacio, Durango, informed Ávila Camacho in a letter that their instructor, a Lieutenant Colonel Federico Bonilla López, was charging them twenty-five centavos for each session they attended—and that he was imposing fines of one peso for any session they missed.[23]

The same U.S. officials who, just a few weeks earlier, had described the positive response of the Mexican people to the initiation of the military training program noticed a change in the public's attitude. In Tampico, where the consul had noted enthusiasm for the drills in September, it was reported in October that "a spirit of resentment towards compulsory training is becoming manifest." And in Veracruz, a U.S. diplomat wrote that many attendees were clearly being compelled to take part in the exercises, as they said that they had "received notice that, if they do not turn out, things are likely to be unpleasant for them."[24] By the end of the year, in an effort to prevent any deepening of the bitter feeling that had been generated by the military training program, President Ávila Camacho had announced that participation in the weekly drills would be voluntary, but reports of forced attendance and abusive behavior by the officers in charge of the sessions in outlying areas continued to reach the capital in the months and years that followed.[25]

Shortly after military training programs were launched in the fall of 1942, the government made another effort to stress the exceptional nature

Figure 15: At the Acercamiento Nacional in September 1942, President Ávila Camacho addresses the crowd from the balcony of the National Palace, with Lázaro Cárdenas to his left and Plutarco Elías Calles to his right. (Fototeca Nacional, Instituto Nacional de Antropología e Historia; © 655302 CONACULTA.INAH.SINAFO. FN.MÉXICO)

of the times and the vital need for unity by staging the Acercamiento Nacional, or "National Coming-Together," in conjunction with the Independence Day festivities that took place in mid-September. The event centered around the September 15 rally in the Zócalo referred to at the beginning of this study. Similar ceremonies had been organized on a much smaller scale in previous years, but with the country formally at war in 1942, the administration seized the opportunity to mount a dramatic display of political unity by having Mexico's six living ex-presidents make an unprecedented public appearance with Ávila Camacho.[26] The sight of Lázaro Cárdenas, Abelardo L. Rodríguez, Pascual Ortiz Rubio, Emilio Portes Gil, Plutarco Elías Calles, and Adolfo de la Huerta on the same stage would have been a deeply impressive one to Mexicans who knew of the deep divisions that had existed between many of these men during the years preceding World War II. The event was important not just as a symbolic display of wartime solidarity; it also served to confirm the subordination of six potentially powerful political figures to the leadership of the sitting president. Indeed, since Mexico's entry into the war, the most influential former presidents had accepted positions that limited their political independence and required them to support the Ávila Camacho administration. Rodríguez appeared at the rally in uniform as the commander of the newly created Región Militar del Golfo, Calles had recently returned to active military duty, and most importantly, Cárdenas had just days earlier reaffirmed his loyalty to his successor—and his intention to stay out of politics—by joining the cabinet as defense minister.

At the Acercamiento, reporters watched in vain for signs of a reconciliation between Cárdenas and Calles, who had been enemies since the former had forced the latter into exile in 1936. The two rivals did not acknowledge each other during the course of the public event, but Cárdenas recorded in his diary that the assembled ex-presidents had "greeted one another with cordiality" in the National Palace before their joint appearance, despite past "political events that put distance between us." He concluded that the National Coming-Together had "served to demonstrate to the nation that the government of the Republic has at its disposal six more wills [*seis voluntades más*], six soldiers united with the national whole that offer in full their services to the fatherland."[27] Even without a public greeting between the two men who had dominated Mexican politics since the Revolution, observers interpreted their presence together on a single platform as an important step toward the realization of the national unity that Ávila Camacho had promised.

Nor was the impact of the ceremony and its message of national unity limited to the capital. Just as Abelardo Rodríguez, the former president who had chaired the committee that organized the Acercamiento, told the crowd in the Zócalo that the danger and adversity brought on by the war were a small price to pay for the unity that the conflict had brought about within Mexico, similar sentiments were being expressed by officials elsewhere in the country.[28] At Independence Day celebrations in Monterrey, for example, the influential commander of the local military zone, General Eulogio Ortiz, told the assembled crowd that "war, a thousand times cursed, will be blessed if it unifies the Mexican family."[29] The success of the National Coming-Together, in Mexico City and beyond, was viewed as a personal triumph for the president, and it was possible only because Mexico was at war.

Aware of the increased prestige and political strength that they enjoyed as a result of Mexico's belligerent status, the same members of the administration who had favored Mexican entry into the war sought ways to expand the country's role in the conflict through the fall of 1942. On Independence Day, September 16, 1942, Foreign Minister Padilla told Ambassador Messersmith "that Mexico was only awaiting her opportunity to take her part in the front line with our troops." The remark came during an informal conversation just before the two of them made a joint radio broadcast to mark the holiday, and Padilla went on to say that "he hoped that the way in which they had handled the [war] material which we had given them" in the military parade that had taken place that morning "had shown us how desirable it was" for Mexico to take its place on the battlefield.[30]

A short time later, at the beginning of October 1942, a prominent journalist with close ties to Padilla, José C. Valadés, argued in the pages of the weekly magazine *Hoy* that Mexico had a duty to participate actively in the war. The foreign minister's former private secretary lamented that the country seemed to be unaware of its "obligation to make war on those upon whom war has been declared." He asked rhetorically, "Is it that we are going to wait until the hour of aggression from abroad arrives?" "No," he said, "it is indispensable to strike those who have stricken us morally and physically." Acknowledging that it would be impractical and unwise to send Mexican forces to Europe, where they would be overwhelmed by German mechanized units, he called instead for one hundred thousand troops to be sent to the Philippines, where the guerrilla tactics of the Mexican fighting man would be effective. Mexicans shared cultural ties with the Filipino people, Valadés noted, and the climate and the landscape of the archipelago would allow Mexican soldiers "to fight as they fought with Villa and Obregón."[31]

Activists on the left also continued to argue in favor of a deeper Mexican commitment to the fight against fascism. The CTM daily *El Popular* provided consistent support for a policy of more extensive Mexican participation in the global conflagration. In a September 4 editorial reflecting on "What Mexico Can Win in the War," the newspaper asserted that "if from the actual state of the war within our own borders we were to have to pass to direct war with the enemy, in our territory or outside of Mexico, the sacrifices would be undoubtedly much greater, much more painful, tragic, and terrible; but perhaps the fruits would also be more, much more, important and valuable." Therefore, the editorial concluded, Mexico should not shy away from an active role in the fight.[32]

In October, *El Popular* also praised the government's decision to allow Mexican citizens residing in the United States to be drafted for military duty under American selective service laws as an appropriate step toward a broader role in the war. Accepting the foreign ministry's explanation that Mexicans north of the border were subject to conscription as nationals of a cobelligerent in the fight against the Axis, the newspaper commented that "this is a war in which it cannot be allowed that sentimentalism, egoism, and panic obstruct the gigantic effort that ought to be made to save humanity and to give it a future of peace and liberty." Therefore, it said, "we ought to consider as something normal and logical—normal and logical within the conditions of war—that Mexicans begin to participate for themselves, not only with raw materials and manufactured goods, but with men, in the war against Hitler."[33] And even if, for the moment, the Mexican soldiers fighting against the Nazis were to be members of the U.S. armed forces rather than the Mexican Army, *El Popular* expressed the hope that arrangements could be made to have the Mexican flag brought to the battlefronts as a symbol of the country's direct participation in the war through its expatriate fighting men.[34] While conservative publications such as the PAN's *La Nación* blasted the government for abandoning the interests of its citizens in the face of U.S. military service requirements, *El Popular* and other observers on the left took encouragement from all signs that the country was starting to play a bigger part in the war.[35]

The enthusiasm of the left for the administration's war policies grew in November 1942, when the Mexican government restored diplomatic relations with the Soviet Union, citing the new wartime partnership that existed between the two countries in the fight against the Axis. Foreign Minister Padilla announced on October 28, 1942, that Mexico would look favorably on the reestablishment of direct ties with Moscow "as a tribute of admiration for the immense service rendered to the cause of the Democracies and for the heroic resistance of the Soviet people before the terrible aggression of the Nazi dictatorship."[36] Talks between the Mexican and Soviet ambassadors in Washington followed, and on November 19, they reached a formal agreement on an exchange of envoys between the two countries.[37] The resumption of contact with the Soviet government came almost thirteen years after the Mexican government had broken off relations with Moscow to protest communist agitation in the country.[38] Mexican communists and leftist labor leaders such as Lombardo Toledano had long been calling for the restoration of links with the USSR, but even Cárdenas's left-leaning administration had not taken that step. Instead, it was the more moderate government of Manuel Ávila Camacho that took advantage of a dramatically changed geopolitical situation by resuming ties with Stalin's regime, thus gaining credibility with and winning more committed backing from leftist elements within Mexico that might otherwise have opposed the conservative drift of his government's policies in other areas.

The Partido Comunista Mexicano reportedly responded to this change in the government's policy toward Moscow by issuing a circular stating that the party no longer feared that Ávila Camacho would roll back the reforms carried out by Cárdenas. The document stated that although the PCM had been worried about the ideological orientation of the administration, recent events, including the appointment of Cárdenas to the defense ministry and, above all, the restoration of relations with Moscow, had shown that the interests of the people were secure and that Ávila Camacho was the right man to lead Mexico.[39] Just as he had secured backing from those on the left who might otherwise have opposed or distrusted him in May by leading Mexico into the war, the president won additional leftist support in November by taking this symbolic step toward a closer relationship with the Soviet Union.

As for the position of the Mexican armed forces on the prospect of direct involvement in the war, although the officer corps gave no public indication of a desire to take part in the fighting at the battlefronts during the latter part of 1942, U.S. officials who came in contact with Mexican military men around this time found that many did hope for such an opportunity. Shortly after Mexico entered the war, the military zone commander for the state of Guerrero, General Juan Domínguez Cota, told an American consular officer in Acapulco that if his country "were given the weapons, she would not be content to defend her own shores, but would fight by our side throughout the world."[40] Similarly, the local commander in the border city of Ciudad Juárez, Chihuahua, "on a number of occasions intimated to [the U.S. consul general] that if the situation becomes critical he hoped to see Mexican troops pressed into service any where in the world against the common enemy," and he stated "that Mexico would be proud to fight side by side with her allies in defeating the Axis powers."[41] After returning from an official visit to Mexico in September 1942, Admiral Alfred Johnson of the Joint Mexican–United States Defense Commission noted that Mexican military men "were apparently taking it as a matter of course that the Mexican Army would participate actively in the war sooner or later."[42] And later in the year, U.S. naval reserve officer John Reinhardt, who spent part of the fall of 1942 in Mexico gathering footage for an OSS propaganda film on the country's war effort, wrote that one of the army's more progressive, pro-American officers, Cristóbal Guzmán Cárdenas, had told him that plans were being drawn up in the defense ministry for direct participation in the war. Reinhardt reported that Guzmán Cárdenas "and several high ranking officers, among them General [Eulogio] Ortiz, Commander of the Monterrey Military Zone, are highly enthusiastic about the idea," and he came away with the understanding that Ortiz would be named commander of any expeditionary force that might be organized.[43]

The prospect of direct participation in the war did more than generate enthusiasm in military circles; it was also beginning to prompt significant changes in the structure and outlook of the Mexican armed forces. The acquisition of modern, U.S.-made equipment through the Lend-Lease program made it possible for the Mexican Army to form its first mechanized unit. At the beginning of September 1942, with new military hardware piling up at Military Base Number One outside of Mexico City, Guzmán Cárdenas left his post as military attaché in Washington to become the commandant of the new motorized forces at the base. At the beginning of December, his growing unit was designated as the army's Motorized Brigade.[44] The new airplanes and armored vehicles that Mexico had received during the first months after its entry into the war were proudly displayed in the traditional Independence Day parade that took place on September 16, 1942. A U.S. diplomat who saw the parade observed that "it is the evident intention of the Ávila Camacho administration to build up an armed force which will have combat strength under modern battle conditions and one which will be worthy of the dignity and capacities of the country."[45]

Ambassador Messersmith also noted that U.S. support for the buildup of the Mexican Army was helping to create a growing sense of goodwill toward the United States among Mexican military officers. When the U.S. envoy congratulated General Sánchez on the fine showing the army had made in the parade, the head of the Estado Mayor Presidencial "put

Figure 16: Modern military equipment passing the National Palace during an Independence Day parade. (Fondo Fernando Torreblanca, Fideicomiso Archivos Plutarco Elías Calles y Fernando Torreblanca)

his hand on my shoulder and said: 'My friend, we could not have done this if it had not been for the help of you all.'" Messersmith observed that "as our Mexican friends are not very voluble in their expressions, this coming from General Sánchez means a great deal," and he suggested that the impressive display of U.S.-supplied equipment had made "a tremendous impression not only on the Mexican people, but on some of the Army officers who have been skeptical and critical" of the United States in the past.[46]

Meanwhile, the defense minister and his advisers moved to reorganize the military so that the armed forces would be better prepared for the demands of contemporary warfare. On November 9, 1942, President Ávila Camacho approved Cárdenas's plan for the restructuring of the armed forces.[47] A circular sent to military officers explained that the reorganization was based on the "imperious necessity of freeing the army from urban and rural police functions, in order that it might be able to dedicate itself to its fundamental mission: to be instructed and to be prepared for war." To that end, thirty Regional Guard units were to enter service on January 1, 1943, to maintain order in the countryside, allowing the bulk of the army to focus on training in the modern methods of warfare. At the same time, the army would grow with the addition of two infantry divisions to be made up of conscripts, and new units were to be created to make use of the specialized equipment that the country was receiving.[48] Cárdenas also took steps to consolidate military planning and command functions in a general staff that would be based in the defense ministry. Before the war, Mexico did not have a modern general staff that could effectively coordinate the activities of the country's armed forces. Efforts had been made in the early part of 1942 to build up the Estado Mayor Presidencial to fill that role, but with the country now officially at war, Ávila Camacho issued a decree transferring some functions to the new defense ministry general staff.[49]

The armed forces also began staging war games as a way to develop the skills of the army's officers and men. In addition to their importance as training sessions, these events served as a demonstration to the public of the improvements that were being made to the army and as yet another reminder that the country was at war. When the defense ministry staged one such exercise just outside Mexico City in conjunction with the Anniversary of the Revolution holiday in November 1942, it invited the public to observe the simulation, which was also attended by the visiting president of Ecuador and a high-ranking U.S. general.[50] In addition, Cárdenas announced plans to hold a series of conferences at the national war college in which military commanders would receive training in modern strategy and tactics. The stated purpose of the first "Cycle of Information for Generals," which opened on January 4, 1943, was "to bring the personnel who attend up to date on the latest changes to tactics that have taken place as a consequence of the experience of the current war" and also to brief them on the changes that had been made to the general staff and command structure of the army "in order to satisfy the demands of modern war, which necessitate great speed in the assessment of situations and in the issuing of orders and an adequate utilization of the troops, in accordance with our means and the interests of the Nation."[51] Thus, Mexican generals would be informed of the need for them to focus on military rather than political matters and of the increased coordination and control to which they would be subject as a result of the war-inspired reorganization that was under way. Though the changes that were taking place within the armed forces tended to reduce their political clout, most military officers welcomed the opportunity the war provided to bring about the modernization of their institution, and as they enthusiastically observed the arrival of new equipment and the growth of the army, many hoped for a chance to prove their military skills on the battlefronts of the Second World War.

But while some generals and officials privately supported the organization of an expeditionary force, and a few commentators outside the administration were beginning to advocate such a step, hostile public reaction to occasional press reports on the possibility of military involvement in the war hinted at the difficulties that the government would still face if it attempted to change its policy of refraining from direct participation. The fallout from the article in *El Occidental* that appeared in Guadalajara in September 1942 and the criticism that the government received in October after it was announced that Mexicans in the United States could be drafted have already been noted. Another furor ensued in November, when *La Nación* translated and published a *New York Times* story claiming that Mexican mechanized divisions were being prepared for service overseas. According to the "authoritative sources" cited by the *Times* correspondent, news of the country's imminent military participation in the war was "being withheld from the Mexican people because it is the intention of the government to prepare the population gradually for this new development."[52] In its commentary on the report, the PAN magazine blasted the administration for its failure to take seriously the challenges posed by the war, seizing upon recent comments made by the foreign minister in an interview to charge that Padilla and his associates had taken the country into the conflict simply because Mexican participation seemed to them "a romantic idea." Now, the opposition publication contended, Mexicans faced the possibility of being called upon to fight and die for the cause of democracy, even though they were deprived of many democratic rights at home.[53]

Though it wielded little influence, the even more conservative newspaper *Omega* also commented on the story in the *Times*, saying that it was a grave matter that "after so many years of fratricidal struggles that have cost Mexico torrents of blood, another bloodbath might be imposed upon us and for a cause that ought not to affect us." In alarmist fashion, the *Omega* editorial noted the creation of new military units that were "unnecessary for internal needs" and "the justified alarm" caused by rumors of forced military recruitment in the countryside, and it called upon Ávila Camacho to clarify the situation to avoid a deepening of distrustful attitudes toward the government.[54] Less partisan media outlets agreed that the *Times* article had caused much worry and consternation. In December, the weekly news magazine *Tiempo* noted that in remote areas rumors that an expeditionary force would be sent to the fronts "had made an extraordinary surge during recent weeks" and that the "affirmations of the *New York Times*, according to which Mexico would send soldiers abroad as soon as the people became accustomed to the idea, had taken root even in the most distant corners of the country."[55] An analyst in the naval attaché's office at the U.S. embassy noted that "the great majority of the Mexican public, especially the lower classes, have hardly felt the effect of war as yet" and "are not prepared to see their troops go overseas," and he lamented that articles like the *Times* piece therefore "can only cause unrest and create ill will."[56]

The chief of the Estado Mayor Presidencial, General Salvador Sánchez, denied the *New York Times* report, adding that government policy remained focused on the defense of Mexican territory.[57] However, sensationalistic newspaper articles continued to keep the prospect of direct participation in the war before the Mexican people. A banner headline in the widely read tabloid *La Prensa* on November 11, 1942, screamed, "They seek that Mexicans go to fight," after Aurelio Pamanes Escobedo, a career military officer then serving as a legislator, said during a congressional session that a Mexican army ought to have a presence alongside the Allied armies fighting for democracy. *Excélsior* reported that several other deputies supported their colleague's suggestion and would study the feasibility of creating a "Mexico Brigade" to serve on the front lines of the war.[58]

Moreover, before the controversy over the *Times* article had died down, another report surfaced claiming that Mexico's ambassador to Brazil, José María Dávila, had announced at a November 14 press conference in Rio de Janeiro that his government would send 250,000 men to the battlefronts "as an expression of the determination of my country to contribute in an effective form to the defeat of the Enemies of Humanity."[59] The story received front-page billing in *La Prensa*, which proceeded to denounce the diplomat for having spoken on such an important issue without authorization. The Mexico City daily cited military sources who called the statement attributed to Dávila "ridiculous." According to the editors of *La Prensa*, these military sources had said that "until now" no steps had been taken toward the creation of an expeditionary force, "without that meaning that there are not high military chiefs who believe that it is convenient that our country take a direct role in the present armed conflict."[60] While readers concerned about the possibility of being sent abroad to fight on distant battlefields might have been relieved to learn that Dávila's alleged statement had no official backing, their worries would not have been dispelled, given the apparent interest of those unnamed military leaders in direct participation in the war.

Dávila, a former senator with political ambitions in his native Sinaloa, wrote to President Ávila Camacho's private secretary, blaming the negative press coverage he was receiving on his enemies at home.[61] He also hastened to assure the foreign ministry that he had been misquoted. He had been speaking of the expansion of the Mexican Army, he said, but he had made no reference to an expeditionary force.[62] Nonetheless, *La Nación* cited Dávila's reported words as another example of the "declarations and rumors that maintain justified alarm in public opinion," even after the "lukewarm and hardly definitive clarifications" that had been issued by the government in response to the recent *Times* article.[63] Noting that reports on Dávila's alleged statement had "caused an impression of painful surprise," *Omega* also reiterated its call for full disclosure by the government of its plans for Mexican involvement in the war. The newspaper observed that "when General Ávila Camacho himself, President of the Republic, has stated with full solemnity that Mexico will not send even a single man to fight outside of our territory, the declarations of Dávila, affirming that two hundred fifty thousand soldiers will be sent, had to cause the effect of an explosion."[64]

As early as mid-October, an assistant military attaché at the U.S. embassy had reported that the Mexican public in general seemed to believe "that a move to send Mexican troops into combat is being prepared," and he had observed that reaction to this possibility was "decidedly unfavorable," though the level of resentment generated by the suggestion of direct participation in the war varied "depending on how the subject is treated and on the locality (remote regions being the least interested as a rule)."[65] A month later, with these new reports on plans for an expeditionary force creating anxiety and controversy, Padilla made a statement reiterating that the government did not have any plans to use the armed forces for any purpose other than national defense. In a November 17 meeting with members of the press corps, the foreign minister explained that "until now, the exigencies of the war have not demanded the cooperation of our armed forces outside of the national territory" and that therefore "the effort of our collaboration, from the point of view of armed contingents, consists at the present time of the safeguarding of our territory, the vigilance of our coasts, and the ever more effective preparation of our Army."[66]

While it is clear that Padilla's statement was intended in part to reassure citizens who feared the imminent deployment of Mexican troops overseas, the use of the phrases "until now" and "at the present time" made this declaration considerably less unequivocal than Ávila Camacho's earlier pledges that no soldiers would be sent abroad. Lest there be any doubt that the administration wished for the public to be prepared in the future for the possibility of direct participation in the war, Padilla went on to say in his remarks to the reporters that "if the threat against human liberties and the destiny of the democracies were to demand the support from Mexico of armed contingents," then "the Government would present before the people the necessity of doing it," and he felt sure that the Mexican people would "respond affirmatively without the slightest vacillation."[67]

A report to the U.S. Office of Strategic Services noted that Padilla's declaration was "the government's first clear statement about the much discussed possibility of sending Mexican soldiers outside the nation's boundaries to fight." The intelligence agency's informant saw the foreign minister's remarks as an effort "to break the news as gently as possible to the populace that they might as well prepare themselves for such a move because if the emergency made it necessary, the government was prepared to put Mexican soldiers into the field shoulder to shoulder with their allies of the United Nations." Though the statement was only a very preliminary move intended to soften up the considerable resistance to participation in the war that then existed, the OSS report observed that "the administration was going as fast as it felt it dared to condition the people to this unprecedented step."[68] Observing these same events from the U.S. embassy, a diplomat there optimistically reported that war consciousness was gradually on the rise in Mexican society but that for the time being "the position taken by the Foreign Secretary in approving—for all practical purposes—Mexico's eventual armed participation in the war has nevertheless given the enemies of the administration and of the Secretary himself well-defined targets to shoot at." He reported that "the administration considers the situation delicate lest an organized attack against the Government arise."[69]

With the question of Mexican military involvement in the war thus left open, fears grew, especially in rural areas, that the government would send the country's young men to foreign fronts as "cannon fodder." In some places, these fears became acute in late November and early December of 1942, as local officials prepared to carry out a lottery that would result in the induction of ten thousand eighteen-year-olds into the Mexican Army. The draft was organized under the terms of an obligatory military service law enacted during the final months of the Cárdenas administration in 1940. After Mexico's entry into the war in 1942, the government moved to implement the law's provisions for a program of conscription that would expand the size of the country's armed forces.[70] The stated purpose of the draft was to provide for the defense of Mexican territory as well as to impart valuable skills and a sense of citizenship to young men from all over the country, but with rumors of an expeditionary force swirling, many believed the conscripts would ultimately be sent into battle overseas.

A lack of reliable information about the draft and a lack of faith in the promises of the government gave rise to great anxiety, especially in isolated areas. Shortly after the first draft lottery took place, a group of conscripts' mothers from a small town in Coahuila wrote to Ávila Camacho to "seek that their sons not [be ordered to] leave the country, and [to] ask if said service is going to be forever, or just temporary."[71] On November 26, 1942, just after the government had announced how the draft would operate, the newspaper of the Sinarquista movement noted that its leadership had received more than a few reports that parents were seeking to hide their sons from the authorities and that "'many are going into the hills' in a plan of frank rebellion, because they prefer, they say, 'to die of hunger or of a gunshot in their own fatherland, and not to go to leave their bones in a foreign land.'"[72]

The article went on to say that the UNS certainly did not wish to promote resistance to the draft—that, after all, "would be equivalent to an act of rebellion against a law, an attitude contrary to the principles that guide Sinarquismo"—but that serious questions were being raised as to the true purposes of the conscription program and that therefore the president should seek through his words and through the actions of his government "to calm the fears of the people." While Sinarquismo had "imposed on the people the duty of obedience," the newspaper said, the movement had an obligation of its own "to defend [the people] . . .

and to insist tenaciously before the Government of the Republic that it measure its steps in these difficult moments and—above all else—that it abstain from committing a single drop of Mexican blood outside of the country."[73] Elsewhere in the same edition, *El Sinarquista* published a more formal statement from the UNS chiefs informing Ávila Camacho that rumors of preparations for military participation in the war had caused "great uneasiness and discontent." "The people do not want to be taken to any foreign front," the open letter said, "and their determination ought to be respected, inasmuch as our obligation as Mexicans is limited to the defense of the national integrity." The message to the president also called upon him "to speak to the nation with all clarity" regarding his plans for Mexico's role in the war.[74]

Ávila Camacho did not respond directly to these demands for a reiteration of his pledge not to send soldiers abroad, but with the date set for the conscription lottery fast approaching, the defense ministry hastened to assure the nervous countryside that draftees would not be deployed overseas. The ministry had already received reports of isolated disturbances caused by fears about the true purposes of conscription. On November 29, during a military training session in a rural area in Aguascalientes, men and women armed with guns, knives, sticks, and stones had clashed with federal forces after hearing the announcement that young men born in 1924 should register for the upcoming draft. According to the military zone commander's report on the incident, the riotous citizens "wrongly interpreted this disposition," saying that they knew "that those boys were going to be enlisted in order to send them to the United States." The affray resulted in the death of at least one of the "agitators," and several soldiers were wounded. In his response to the report, the defense minister instructed the regional military headquarters to "make it known in the vicinity of said region and in all of that State that the establishment of Military Service has as its object the preparation of the conscripts in the service of arms for the defense of the Fatherland and not sending them abroad."[75] On December 2, in an effort to get this message out more broadly, the military authorities provided Mexican newspapers with a communiqué taking note of the "false and tendentious" rumors that draftees were to be deployed overseas. The circular telegram instructed all regional and zone commanders throughout Mexico to "make it known to the public that the conscripts, as the Law itself stipulates, will be destined exclusively to serve within the national territory."[76]

Significantly, this comforting promise, which received wide publicity in the Mexican press, came over the signature of Lázaro Cárdenas, who, as noted previously, had been serving in the cabinet as defense minister since September. While a number of the generals nominally under his command clearly did hope to lead Mexican troops into action before the end of the war, the ex-president had opposed Mexican entry into the conflict and was not a proponent of military participation in the struggle. Therefore, while the hawkish foreign minister had been notably unwilling to foreswear the option of direct involvement in the war when he had addressed the issue in mid-November, Cárdenas no doubt found it relatively easy to state categorically that conscripts would not be sent abroad. Moreover, it is likely that Cárdenas's reassurance was particularly effective because of the prestige and popularity that he still enjoyed in much of the countryside as a result of his role during his presidency as a champion of agrarian reform.

Certainly his statement and a subsequent defense ministry declaration that "parents ought not to harbor any fear that their sons will be sent to distant lands" were widely lauded in the Mexican press.[77] The relatively conservative Mexico City daily *Novedades* praised Cárdenas's message as a reconfirmation of what it saw as the premise underlying Mexico's participation in the war. According to the newspaper, the purpose of Mexico's entry into the conflict had simply been to maintain the country's dignity in the wake of the German submarine attacks of May 1942. The declaration of a state of war had not carried with it "any promise of bellicose aggression on the part of our army," but rather it had been "the rising up of a people to defend itself from a possible aggression from those who had already attacked before." Noting the widespread tension that existed in much of the country because of "the fear that parents have that their sons will promptly be shipped to distant lands," *Novedades* expressed the hope that the defense minister's circular would help to restore tranquility to the countryside.[78]

Other commentators seized upon Cárdenas's statement to criticize Padilla for his earlier remarks on the subject of direct participation in the war. The "editor's page" in the weekly magazine *Hoy* offered a pointed "Homage to Lázaro Cárdenas" after the publication of his telegram in early December. "With this circular," the editor wrote, "the people of Mexico have escaped from the anxiety generated by the excessive bellicosity of some officials who, allowing themselves to be carried away by

their personal enthusiasms, do not understand that their words can pro-
voke social alarm."[79] Although Valadés had argued for an expeditionary
force in the pages of *Hoy*, the magazine's official editorial position was
that the Mexican Army should not be sent overseas as it was needed for
defense at home. The publication had also launched various attacks on
the foreign minister, so the defense ministry's apparent dismissal of the
possibility of direct involvement in the war offered a perfect opportunity
for *Hoy* to reiterate its views through praise of Cárdenas.[80]

Even the UNS and the PAN, two groups that had arisen to oppose
Cárdenas and all he stood for, had to concede that the defense minister's statement was very welcome. *El Sinarquista* reported that many
followers of the movement continued to ask if these declarations might
not be part of a ruse to eliminate resistance to the draft. "These fears
are explicable," the newspaper said, "The people have been fooled many
times by their own authorities, for whom they have an instinctive dis-
trust." However, the Sinarquista daily went on, "in the present case we
are inclined to believe that the Secretariat of Defense will not flout the
categorical declaration that Mexican troops will not be sent abroad."[81]
For its part, *La Nación* did not miss a chance to launch another barb
in its long-running campaign against Padilla as it praised the circular
for "clarifying in a definitive manner questions left in half-light by the
Secretary of Relations."[82] The attacks on Padilla and the welcome given
to Cárdenas's statement highlighted the still limited willingness of much
of the Mexican public to countenance deeper involvement in the war.

The draft lottery took place in cities and towns across Mexico on
December 20. Undersecretary of National Defense Francisco L. Urquizo
announced that the process had been a "categorical success," considering
that conscription on such a scale had never before been carried out in
Mexico.[83] Urquizo admitted that "the lack of understanding of the matter on the part of good and simple people [who had been] badly informed
by perverse persons" had created scattered problems, but he said that
those difficulties had been resolved. Nonetheless, he wished to reiterate that the conscripts would be well treated and comfortably housed
and that "they will not leave Mexican territory to go to fight in foreign
lands as erroneously and malevolently has been said by persons of little
moral responsibility." The undersecretary stressed that the young men
inducted into the army would receive "physical, moral, and intellectual
training that will give as a result a spiritual unity amongst the national

population, in this way making national unity an undisputable reality."[84] With this statement, Urquizo sought to cast the controversial military service program in terms of the policy of *unidad nacional* so insistently promoted by the Ávila Camacho administration throughout the war years.

Largely unreported in connection with the draft lottery was the fact that the conscription process had been riddled with irregularities that had greatly angered Defense Minister Cárdenas. When the conscripts reported for duty, military authorities discovered that many of those who had been compelled to take part in the selection process were older or younger than eighteen, and some were clearly physically unfit for military service. It also emerged that local officials had in many cases accepted bribes to shield the relatively well-off from service and had occasionally simply resorted to the impressment of poorer youths.[85] These abuses eventually became sufficiently well known that the defense ministry publicly announced its determination to "avoid in the future the anomalies that have been observed in the 1924 Class [i.e., the group of conscripts born in 1924, inducted after the lottery of December 1942]" by insisting on strict compliance with "the legal precepts regarding age and state of health, as well as demanding from all the young men to whom it corresponds to enter active service the fulfillment of their duties, without regard to the social class to which they belong."[86]

Also unreported in the press during the final days of 1942 was the fact that the draft had prompted the emergence of isolated resistance movements in some parts of the country. The abuses already mentioned may well have contributed to these scattered outbreaks of violence, but it appears that the lingering belief that conscripts would be sent abroad to fight served as the primary justification for the rebels' resistance to the government and its program of conscription. On December 24, the interior ministry received a coded message from the secretary of the Puebla state government—future president Gustavo Díaz Ordaz—reporting that armed bands were moving between various towns in Morelos and southern Puebla. The rebels had detained four government tax collectors, and though an archbishop had encouraged them to lay down their weapons, they had pledged "to continue until triumph or death." The "hostile attitude" of these groups arose from their opposition to the implementation of the obligatory military service law, Díaz Ordaz said, and they alleged "that the President [had] committed himself to send two million Mexicans to war."[87] Reports also emerged of disturbances in the remote towns of Miguel Auza, Juan Aldama, Nieves, and Río Grande, in the state of Zacatecas, where villagers and residents of the countryside registered their opposition to conscription on December 27, 1942, by launching attacks on municipal buildings and killing some of the local authorities.[88]

In response to these incidents, the government launched a campaign intended to defuse the explosive situation in the countryside without alerting the country at large to the outbreaks of disorder that had occurred as a result of the conscription program. To this end, military airplanes dropped leaflets in areas where resistance had arisen, seeking to convince the country folk who had taken to the hills that the government had no intention of sending their sons into combat. The administration again capitalized on the links that it had been building with the church hierarchy by having the archbishop of Puebla sign one such leaflet. The prelate, Pedro Vera, assured the faithful that "from an authorized source we have learned that the Government will not send soldiers outside of the country, and the current registration does not have that end," and he implored those who had taken up arms to "abandon your attitude and return to order, to your homes." A second flier, this one unsigned, explained to simple country folk who might not fully understand the global situation that "the Germans, the Italians, and the Japanese have been killing Mexicans and therefore are our enemies," but it hastened to explain that "the Mexicans of 18 years of age are being called only in order to give them military instruction; no Mexican will go to fight outside of Mexico." Hence, "there is no reason to rebel against the Government."[89]

In another leaflet, a high-ranking general invited rebels to discuss their concerns as he made a tour through southern Puebla and Morelos. Donato Bravo Izquierdo, the commander of the country's most important military base, told opponents of the draft that they had been fooled "by those who always have wished every ill on Mexico" into thinking that conscripts would be sent overseas. That, he said, "is a crude lie." Military service would provide draftees with valuable instruction and education, the general insisted, and "once their preparation is finished they will return to their homes to be more useful to their people and their families." In closing, he told the people of the troubled region to have "absolute confidence that the democracies, for their triumph, which is the triumph of Mexico and yours, do not need the departure of Mexican soldiers."[90]

In addition to its efforts to communicate directly with armed opponents of the draft through leaflets, the government used the country's newspapers to repeat the message that Mexican soldiers would not be sent overseas. The administration took care, however, to conceal the fact that it was offering these reassurances in the face of active resistance to conscription. For example, when General Urquizo made his December 24 statement characterizing the draft lottery as a success and reiterating earlier pledges that draftees would not be deployed abroad, he intimated that the purpose of his declaration was simply to reassure those who had received misleading reports about the true purpose of conscription. He made no reference to an ongoing conflict over the policies. Mexico City newspapers published the words of the undersecretary of defense, but either because they lacked reliable information on the subject or because they did not wish to antagonize the government, they did not add any references to the disturbances in the countryside that had almost certainly played a part in prompting the statement.[91] Similarly, when the defense ministry announced just after Christmas that it was spreading leaflets throughout the country to reassure the population that Mexican soldiers would not be sent overseas, the banner headline in *La Prensa* read, "The Mexican conscripts will not go abroad," but the accompanying article did not mention the existence of armed groups that had rejected the obligatory military service policy.[92]

During the first few weeks of 1943, news of the clashes over conscription that were taking place in the countryside did not appear in the mainstream press. Nonetheless, the administration continued to find subtle ways to get its message into print. For example, while the pages of *El Universal* carried no references to unrest in Puebla, Morelos, and Zacatecas during the first half of January 1943, a number of unusual "public service announcements" did appear on various dates in small spaces between news stories or at the bottom of columns of text. In the past, these small blocks of bold-faced type had generally featured messages relating to public health, sanitation, and similar matters, but with fears of direct Mexican participation in the war driving a rebellion in the hills south of the capital, readers now received a reminder that "the President of the Republic declared that no Mexican will leave the national territory to wage war," and they were told that they "ought to have blind faith in the words of the President."[93] Another announcement explained that the rumor that an expeditionary force was being organized had "been circulated among the simple people by traitors."[94] In recognition of the fact that largely illiterate country folk were unlikely to be perusing *El Universal*, a third message exhorted those who were reading the paper to explain the truth "to all the people who do not read newspapers or listen to the radio, in order to prevent traitors from carrying out a crime of treason [*lesa patria*]."[95]

Elsewhere in the media, supporters of the government's war policies also reiterated the message that Mexico's contribution to the war would be economic rather than military in nature. For example, during the December 30, 1942, edition of his daily radio program on war news, the highly respected, staunchly pro-Allied commentator Félix Palavicini explained that what the United Nations needed most from Mexico was a steady supply of strategic metals and agricultural commodities. Therefore, the prominent journalist said, "our contingent of soldiers is not an effective aid, while our contribution of products has a high and advantageous significance." Although Mexicans were brave and had no fear of battle, he added, "in the current conflict, the best thing that we can offer is not a few million men" but rather a firm commitment to the production of vital war materials.[96]

Even the Sinarquistas, who had done so much during the final months of 1942 to nurture fears that Mexicans would be sent abroad in an expeditionary force, now sought to ease the tensions that had developed in rural areas largely as a result of their propaganda efforts. No doubt fearing that the UNS would be blamed for the resistance to the draft, the January 7, 1943, edition of the Sinarquista newspaper published an appeal to movement leaders on the local level, imploring them to "keep people from going into the hills" and to "maintain at all costs the peace of your regions." The message in *El Sinarquista* told readers that "going into the hills will not accomplish anything" and that the best way to ensure that soldiers would not be sent overseas would be to unite in a "powerful civic front" opposed to such a move. For now, though, Sinarquistas should "believe in the word" of the president and abandon any thoughts of insurrection.[97] With this appeal—and subsequent articles implausibly blaming the rebellions in the countryside on communists working through a group of ex-almazanistas—the Sinarquista newspaper became one of the few publications to acknowledge directly the existence of resistance to conscription.[98] It did so, however, because the Sinarquista organization felt compelled to voice support for the administration lest it face reprisals for the unrest in rural areas. To some extent, then, the outbreak of disorder on a limited scale in a few isolated areas actually strengthened the position of the president by forcing a group that had previously acted as a vocal critic of the administration's conscription policy to adopt a much more moderate tone.

In the specific areas in which signs of unrest had appeared in connection with the draft, the measures taken by the government, the press, and even the opposition to defuse the situation had only a limited effect. A clerk at the U.S. embassy who traveled to Morelos in early January 1943 found that "rather than diminishing, the movement is tending to increase," and the participants in the local uprising remained "convinced that by registering with the Mexican Army, as required by law, they will be sent to fight overseas."[99] The investigative branch of the Mexican interior ministry also found "countless armed bands between the States of Puebla, Morelos, and Mexico" that had arisen in opposition to the draft.[100] In the months that followed, a number of these groups achieved a more formal level of organization under local leaders such as Ruben Jaramillo, and they irritated the authorities by robbing (or seeking "voluntary" donations from) motorists on the Cuautla–Cuernavaca highway and by skirmishing with federal forces in the region. In the fall of 1943, the state government of Morelos was still seeking to put an end to disturbances in the countryside by strenuously denying that the government planned to send Mexican soldiers overseas. A September 30, 1943, leaflet addressed to communities in the southern part of the state and signed by the governor denounced those who had spread such rumors and called upon citizens not to heed "this seditious campaign that threatens our tranquility." The governor's message assured the people of the state that "the Federal Government is not forming armies of Mexicans to fight abroad" and that the government "only desires that Mexicans work intensely for the good of their homes in order to ensure the life of Mexico and in order to fight against the economic crisis that all wars bring on."[101]

But while the resistance to the government's conscription policy lived on for many months in the old heartland of *zapatismo*, most of the country remained quiet, and as 1943 began, the administration carefully pushed ahead with its efforts to prepare the Mexican people for a more active role in the war. In his New Year's Eve message to the nation, Ávila Camacho himself told his countrymen that in the face of the sacrifices being made by Mexico's allies, "we cannot remain indecisive or indifferent." In the global conflict "our intervention will have to consist not solely of an attitude of expectant and hopeful sympathy." In a statement strikingly like the one delivered so controversially by Padilla in mid-November, Ávila Camacho expressed his certainty that "if the eventuality of a direct action were to present itself, no Mexican would hesitate." "Between dishonor and combat," he said, "each one of us, since childhood, has made his choice." At the same time, keenly aware that the prospect of direct participation in the war was sparking resistance in some areas, he quickly added that "our front is for now in the factories and in the fields" and emphasized that "in the present state of things, our most important effort lies in production."[102]

Early in the new year, the president made another, more direct suggestion that Mexico would be willing to send its armed forces into combat, but significantly, he made his statement to a U.S. journalist rather than to a Mexican audience. While traveling in Chiapas in February 1943, Ávila Camacho told United Press correspondent Edward Morgan that Mexico would continue to focus on the production of strategic raw materials but that his government would be willing to contribute soldiers to the war effort if necessary. "If, along the sure road to victory, the question of materials becomes secondary to the need for fighting men," he said, "Mexico will arise to the emergency as her warriors have always done in the past."[103] The wire service helpfully prepared different versions of the article for distribution in the United States and in Mexico, and Morgan explained to one of Ávila Camacho's aides that the Spanish text reflected "various changes of emphasis in dealing with the somewhat delicate issues."[104] While the English version of his piece highlighted the fact that Ávila Camacho had spoken of the possibility of Mexican military participation in the war, the Spanish version barely mentioned it. Those who read the report in the Mexican press learned only that "the president believes that the possibility that Mexico will have need to call its soldiers to fight at the battle fronts is very remote." Ávila Camacho must have been pleased with the response to this article. Senior U.S. lawmakers praised him for his commitment to the Allied cause, but his statements did not lead to an outcry in Mexico.[105] In fact, the president continued to tell Mexican journalists at this time that the country "will not send men to war nor have we received from them (the United Nations) the least hint that we should; our obligation up to now continues to be production."[106] So, even as Ávila Camacho signaled to his counterparts in Washington that he would be willing to go further in supporting the Allied war effort, he continued to proceed cautiously with his efforts to prepare Mexicans gradually for the possibility of direct participation in the war. It was left to lower-ranking officials to make the case at home that sending military units overseas might eventually be necessary.

As the months passed, war-related economic hardships, lingering anti-U.S. sentiment, and the persistent activity of right-wing groups continued to make it difficult for the government to convince the Mexican people that the country would benefit from a more active role in the global conflict. Because production was so largely oriented toward meeting the needs of U.S. war industries, Mexican consumers began to suffer from food shortages in 1943, and they saw their purchasing power erode in the face of wartime inflation.[107] Under these circumstances, it was easy for Mexicans to attribute the difficulties that they faced to their leaders' decision to enter World War II. By the spring of 1943, U.S. officials noted increasing undercurrents of dissatisfaction and anti-Americanism in different parts of Mexico. In Acapulco, the consul reported "considerable criticism and grumbling and a tendency to blame the United States for not supplying finished goods, for not supplying machinery with which Mexico could make its own finished goods, and on the other hand for its insistence that Mexico should continue to furnish raw materials." In Manzanillo, too, a U.S. official observed in April that "criticism of the United States was at its highest level since the beginning of the war due to the scarcity of goods and rising living costs."[108]

Right-wing, anti-American propagandists made the most of this opportunity. Toward the end of 1942, a flyer that circulated as an insert in a Sinarquista newspaper railed against the "Yankee Jews" and screamed that Ávila Camacho and his cabinet were "handing the whole nation over to the Yankee, leaving the fatherland under [U.S.] tutelage as 'a protectorate.'"[109] An equally shrill circular appeared in February 1943. The anonymous flier, which was sent through the mail to addresses in various parts of the country, claimed that Mexican "ports, landing fields, railroads, etc., have been placed in the hands of the Yankee," and it called upon the Mexican people to "look for a Francisco Villa who will know how to confront the Yankee in defense of your sovereignty and your honor."[110] This concern with the maintenance of Mexican sovereignty was reflected in a March 1943 letter to Ávila Camacho. A citizen writing from Guanajuato warned the president that "neither the Fatherland nor

History would justify the sending of Mexicans to the front in a war that will only leave us debts that will compromise [our] Independence." He went on, "You like Juárez ought to maintain national autonomy everywhere in the Country."[111] While labor leaders and pro-American elements within the government continued to call for a deeper commitment to the fight against the Axis, these rumblings meant that president could not yet openly advocate direct military participation in the conflict.

Another threat to Ávila Camacho's desire to move toward a policy of closer cooperation with Washington and deeper involvement in the war arose as some top Mexican officials and business leaders grew resentful of the refusal of U.S. economic planners to make machinery and other needed products available to Mexico. In a controversial April 1943 speech, Eduardo Villaseñor, the president of the Mexican central bank, pointed out that his country was making vital contributions to the war effort by giving the United States access to its resources on very favorable terms, and he argued that officials in Washington should therefore give Mexican needs higher priority when allocating the output of U.S. war industries. Import quotas based on prewar importation levels were insufficient, Villaseñor said, and he remarked upon some of the problems faced by Mexican industrialists and farmers as a result of the need for machinery, spare parts, tractors, trucks, and other items that could not then be produced in Mexico. The head of the Bank of Mexico spoke of "a factory that could supply the entire country with calcium arsenate—a very scarce article indispensable for fighting blights [as a pesticide]—if the United States would authorize the exportation of some compressors"; he also described the problems faced by a paper factory that had been waiting for spare parts for more than a year and a nail factory that could not begin production because it had not been able to obtain a specialized machine. He ironically suggested that the U.S. government streamline its export-control bureaucracy by creating a single "Office for the Negation of Any Petition," and he called the U.S. practice of blocking the transfer of essential machinery to Mexico an act "incompatible with the nature of allied countries."[112] The speech caused consternation at the U.S. embassy and at Los Pinos, but as Ambassador Messersmith observed, it represented "a current of opinion [within the government] here which believes that Mexico should follow pressure methods instead of the policy of full collaboration of the President and the Foreign Office."[113]

Recognizing that anti-American sentiment threatened to undercut his policy of strongly backing the Allied cause, Ávila Camacho sought a way to foster more positive feelings toward Mexico's northern neighbor. To that end, in December 1942 his ambassador in Washington raised the possibility of arranging a meeting between Ávila Camacho and President Roosevelt, and in a conversation with Ambassador Messersmith on January 13, 1943, the Mexican president himself suggested that Roosevelt visit his country. Such a gesture, he said, would "consolidate in a marked way the changed relationships between Mexico and the United States."[114] Roosevelt responded favorably to Ávila Camacho's invitation, and the U.S. president arrived in Monterrey for a brief visit on April 20. From there, the two leaders delivered radio addresses before traveling together to the naval base at Corpus Christi, Texas, so that Ávila Camacho could immediately return Roosevelt's visit.

On both sides of the border, the exchange of visits gave rise to rumors that the scope of U.S.-Mexican wartime cooperation would soon expand to include direct Mexican participation in the fighting along-side American units. Reporter Edward Morgan interpreted the presence in Monterrey of José María Dávila, the Mexican ambassador to Brazil who had allegedly endorsed the formation of an expeditionary force in November 1942, as a sign that Mexican leaders looked favorably on the possibility of military involvement in the war.[115] U.S. journalists also made much of General Francisco L. Urquizo's comment that "our government is always ready to send troops abroad," even though the under-secretary of defense had been quick to add that "we need money and equipment" before any overseas deployment would be possible.[116] In Mexico, only right-wing publications such as *Omega* openly drew the conclusion that Roosevelt's visit would lead to a Mexican presence on the battlefronts, but given the attention that the issue had received in the months leading up to the Monterrey meeting, many Mexicans must have wondered if the two leaders had discussed the subject when they met.[117]

In an effort to address such concerns, Foreign Minister Padilla was quick to deny that the matter had even been raised, and he sought to undermine the arguments of those who claimed that Washington was insensitive to the needs of the Mexican economy by announcing that the two presidents had discussed a possible agreement that would give Mexico greater access to surplus U.S. machinery.[118] Officials from both countries emphasized that the meeting had been arranged not as a

Figure 17: President Ávila Camacho and his wife welcoming U.S. president
Franklin D. Roosevelt to Monterrey in April 1943. (Fondo Fernando Torreblanca,
Fideicomiso Archivos Plutarco Elías Calles y Fernando Torreblanca)

prelude to Mexican participation in the war but rather as an opportunity
for the two presidents to get to know one another.[119]

The exchange of visits had the desired effect on Mexican views of the
United States. Apart from the less than effusive coverage of the event
offered by the conservative *Novedades* and the deliberately anti-American
angle adopted by far-right newspapers like *Omega*, in general the press
provided highly enthusiastic reports on the meeting between the two
presidents. Pride was expressed that Roosevelt had not simply stopped
along the border but rather had highlighted Mexico's importance by
traveling well into the interior of the country.[120] An American journalist concluded that the "'unexpectedness and graciousness' of Mr.
Roosevelt's visit have aroused the Mexican public to an active rather
than passive support of the government's war program."[121] Months later,
the U.S. military attaché observed that the visit "is still bearing fruit
in better co-operation and understanding between the two nations."[122]
In Monterrey, for days after the visit, American consular officials were
greeted by Mexicans from all walks of life who expressed admiration for
Roosevelt and for the United States. The consul there said that he had
"failed to find one critical or sour note in the press of Monterrey in commenting upon this historic meeting." Not only had President Roosevelt

won praise through his visit, he said, "but it appears that the meeting caused the press to make the most flattering and enthusiastic statements concerning President Ávila Camacho which have appeared since he has been in office." Considering that the northern city had been a bastion of support for General Almazán during the 1940 elections, the appearance of the two presidents together on the streets of Monterrey served not only to bolster support for Ávila Camacho's foreign policy on a national level but also to increase his prestige in a region that had been a center of opposition to the PRM and to his regime. In the aftermath of the Roosevelt–Ávila Camacho meeting there, the consul reported that "the common comment now heard is 'how fortunate it was that Ávila Camacho was elected.'"[123]

Around the same time that Roosevelt and Ávila Camacho were meeting in Monterrey, the Mexican government took what some saw as another small, subtle step toward direct participation in the war when a Mexican military delegation departed for North Africa, where it would spend sixty days observing Allied operations in that region. The mission was to have been headed by General Sánchez of the Estado Mayor Presidencial, whose appointment was seen as compensation for the authority that he had lost as a result of the reorganization of the armed forces.[124] U.S. military doctors found Sánchez medically unfit to make the long trip across the Atlantic, however, so his place was taken by General Luis Alamillo Flores, a former member of Cárdenas's staff who was then serving as the Mexican military attaché in Washington. Representing the Mexican Air Force on the mission to Africa was Lieutenant Colonel Antonio Cárdenas Rodríguez, an experienced pilot best known for completing a goodwill tour of the Americas in 1940. The deputy chief of the defense ministry's new general staff, Lieutenant Colonel Arturo Dávila Caballero, also traveled to the front. Known for his close ties with the defense minister, Dávila Caballero informally served as Cárdenas's personal representative on the mission. The relatively young Dávila Caballero told U.S. officers with whom he came in contact of the frustration experienced by his more professionally trained generation of Mexican military men as they waited for the ranks of generals from the Revolutionary era to thin so that they could finally be promoted. Since the early 1930s, Mexico's Escuela Superior de Guerra had been turning out staff officers, but its graduates remained stuck in junior and midlevel ranks, subordinate to senior officers who generally lacked any formal background in tactics, strategy, and military organization. The mission to Africa and Dávila Caballero's inclusion in it were likely intended to highlight the Mexican Army's growing commitment to military professionalism and to provide encouragement to those like him who envisioned a Mexican military establishment that would be efficient and focused on meeting the challenges of modern warfare.[125]

This group left Washington for North Africa on April 28, 1943, and arrived in Morocco in early May before continuing on to Tunis. Alamillo and Dávila Caballero were attached to the headquarters of the U.S. 5th Army, while Cárdenas Rodríguez arranged to participate in bombing missions over Sicily and Sardinia.[126] When Alamillo left the North African theater toward the end of May, he spoke to the press of the glorious role that Mexican troops might have played in the campaign there, providing another indication of the interest that existed in military circles in the formation of an expeditionary force.[127] Upon his return to Mexico in early June, the military attaché presented an enthusiastic report on what he had seen to President Ávila Camacho and Defense Minister Cárdenas, both of whom asked him whether the Allies had sufficient manpower and how much longer the war was likely to last, suggesting that the possibility of a Mexican contribution of troops was on their minds, as well.[128]

While some observers drew the conclusion that Roosevelt's visit to Monterrey and the military mission to North Africa foreshadowed a more substantial commitment of Mexican troops to the war effort, opposition to such a move remained strong, and the Mexican government still had not taken any formal steps toward the creation of an expeditionary force. Indeed, despite Ávila Camacho and Padilla's moves to prepare the public for direct involvement in the war, despite the continuing calls for military participation made by Lombardo Toledano and other leftist leaders, and despite the desire of many military officers to gain experience on the battlefield, not only was the public still apprehensive about the possibility of a deeper role in the war, so, too, was a key political figure, Secretary of National Defense Lázaro Cárdenas. When a reporter for the *New York Herald Tribune* asked him in early April 1943 if Mexico would send men to the battlefronts, Cárdenas dismissed the idea. He asked rhetorically with what weapons a Mexican expeditionary force would fight. "With arrows? With stones? Mexico lacks almost completely the equipment necessary for modern war," the defense minister said. Until the army is "properly equipped," he added, "its chiefs will not be able to send it to a fight in which it would not be appropriately armed."[129] While Cárdenas's response did not rule out Mexican participation in the war at some future date, and while the statement could be seen as an assertion that Mexico should receive more military aid from the United States, the emphasis that the defense minister placed on the long period of time—at least five years—that would be necessary to build up the country's military capacity suggests that he did not foresee and would not be in favor of a role for Mexican military units in the fight against the Axis overseas.[130]

As the anniversary of Mexico's declaration of a state of war approached, the Ávila Camacho administration sought to use the occasion to revitalize its campaign for national unity. The government declared May 28, 1943, to be a "Day of National Solemnity." Government offices were closed, and around the country, local and federal authorities organized patriotic events, often in memory of the sailors who had lost their lives in German attacks on Mexican shipping. An editorial in the official government newspaper reminded Mexicans of the need for "the democratic unity that is based upon an absolute and limitless support for the war effort of the Fatherland."[131] In a speech that was broadcast to the nation, Ávila Camacho commended all Mexicans for their contributions to the war effort. In contrast to his public statements a year earlier, however, the president now acknowledged the possibility that Mexico might eventually be called upon to participate directly in the war. "Until now, the test of fire has been avoided," he said, "but, if the circumstances should demand it, our men will confront it bravely, with the courage of a stoic people that does not know how to live in slavery."[132]

The president's speech and the day's ceremonies did not succeed in whipping up renewed enthusiasm for the war effort, however. The PAN's *La Nación* dryly noted that although the president had stated that the Day of National Solemnity "was not a holiday," "the limited official imagination did not find any other way to celebrate solemnity besides the usual parade, carried out all over the country."[133] And a diplomat at the U.S. embassy noted that observance of the occasion had been "unenthusiastic."[134] Nonetheless, the anniversary had provided an opportunity for the administration to remind the populace that the country was at war and that they might well be called upon to make additional sacrifices for the cause of democracy.

Within days, however, the misgivings felt by many Mexicans about the prospect of participation in the war and cooperation with the United States were again on display in the press. In an interview published in *Excélsior* on June 3, Senator Alfonso Flores M. charged that some 250,000 Mexicans were already fighting on the front lines all over the world as members of the U.S. armed forces, and he demanded that the Mexican government do more to protect the rights and ensure the welfare of its citizens who were serving under the American flag.[135] Mexican citizens residing in the United States had been subject to conscription since the preceding fall, an arrangement that was formalized in a January 22, 1943, agreement between the two governments.[136] However, Padilla responded to Flores's claims by asserting that fewer than six thousand Mexicans were actually enlisted in the U.S. military.[137] That figure corresponded with the information that the U.S. War Department had provided to the Mexican government, but opposition newspapers cited large numbers of Spanish surnames in lists of U.S. casualties as evidence that the foreign ministry's number was impossibly low.[138] *La Nación* suggested that even if Flores's claims were exaggerated, the true number of Mexicans in U.S. ranks was probably around ninety thousand.[139] The primary purpose of these charges, to be sure, was to diminish the prestige of Padilla, of whom both Flores and the PAN had long been outspoken critics. The political nature of the attacks was highlighted by the fact that Senator Nabor Ojeda, a political rival of the foreign minister from his home state of Guerrero, joined in, echoing his colleague's call for more protection of Mexican citizens serving overseas.[140] Nonetheless, the controversy that developed over this issue showed that the government remained sensitive and vulnerable to charges that it was seeking to send large numbers of Mexicans into combat.

Meanwhile, a new challenge arose to the administration's effort to build a more positive image of the United States as an ally and partner when news reached Mexico of a series of disturbances in Los Angeles. For several nights beginning on June 3, bands of U.S. soldiers and sailors ventured into Mexican neighborhoods there to confront groups of youths dressed in oversized "zoot suits," holding them responsible for a recent crime wave in the city. When they were unable to find young men wearing the incriminating attire, they often launched indiscriminate attacks on Mexican American residents. While the Zoot Suit Riots were taking place, a number of Mexico City newspapers carried brief wire service reports on the events in Los Angeles, but initially these small articles attracted little attention, as they barely hinted that there was any kind of racial dimension to the violence. *El Universal* at first ran a United Press story on clashes between servicemen and ridiculously dressed individuals known as "Tarzans," without alluding to the fact that the Tarzans were of Mexican extraction.[141] The government newspaper, *El Nacional*, picked up a different wire report characterizing the Tarzans as the "problem" in Los Angeles and claiming that soldiers and police were confronting the "idle and bad-living criminals" there.[142]

In the aftermath of the incident, however, commentators in the United States, including First Lady Eleanor Roosevelt, drew attention to the racial tensions and conflicts that lay behind the riots, whereupon critics of the Mexican foreign minister seized the opportunity to denounce Padilla for not doing more to protect Mexicans in California. Although the foreign ministry had been receiving reports on the events in Los Angeles for several days, it made no formal statement on the riots until after the Mexican press had begun to take note of the ethnic background of the so-called Tarzans.[143] On June 15, by which time it was becoming increasingly apparent that Mexicans had been the primary victims of the violence, Padilla sent a message to Secretary of State Cordell Hull expressing confidence that those responsible for the riots would be punished and that those who were injured or lost property in the riots would be compensated.[144] However, Padilla's detractors, including publications such as *Novedades*, *La Nación*, and *Omega*, and political rivals like Senator Flores, said he should have gone further, protesting more energetically or even flying to Los Angeles to look out for the interests of his countrymen.[145] The foreign minister replied that he had done all that he could appropriately do. While American-born individuals of Mexican descent had suffered attacks during the riot, there was little evidence that citizens of Mexico had been targeted or injured, he said, and traveling to the scene to claim a role in defusing the situation would have been inadvisable, inasmuch as it would have set a precedent for the interference of one state in the internal affairs of another that might someday be used against Mexico.[146]

Nonetheless, many Mexicans continued to view Padilla's slow, understated response to events in Los Angeles as evidence of his subservience to Washington, and they saw the riots themselves as proof of the hollowness of American claims that the United States was a "good neighbor" fighting against the totalitarian doctrine of racial hierarchy. On June 25, an angry demonstration made up of several thousand students from the national university marched on the foreign ministry to protest the attacks on Mexicans in Los Angeles. The growing and increasingly violent crowd of demonstrators would have continued on to the U.S. embassy but for the intervention of the university's rector, Rodolfo Brito Foucher, who persuaded the students to return to their campus.[147] An observer reporting to the OSS wrote that "a cauldron of ill feeling, suspicion and downright anger has just begun to bubble in Mexico over these incidents."[148] The resentment toward Padilla and the United States that was generated by the Zoot Suit Riots thus momentarily slowed the momentum that the Ávila Camacho administration had been trying to build behind a policy of closer cooperation with Washington and deeper involvement in the war.

The news from California did not long remain in the headlines, however, as Mexico looked ahead to the midterm congressional elections that were scheduled for July 4, 1943. In their preparations for the vote, President Ávila Camacho and his Partido de la Revolución Mexicana (PRM) used the fact that the country was at war to gain an unusually high level of control over the electoral process. Since its establishment as the Partido Nacional Revolucionario (PNR) in 1929, the PRM had used a combination of large-scale organizing efforts, machine politics, and fraud to determine the outcome of elections. Though popular challengers to official candidates did arise during the 1930s and 1940s, these tactics were generally effective in ensuring that political power remained in the hands of members of the "Revolutionary family." In 1943 the dominant party took advantage of the international situation to tighten and centralize control over the naming of its own candidates, who would then be guaranteed election through the same mechanisms that had been employed since the party's foundation. As early as August 1942, the PRM had begun informing its members that because of the "situation created by [the] state of war between Mexico and [the] Axis powers," "premature agitation or advance electoral politics" was to be avoided and campaigning should begin "only on the dates fixed by the respective election calls and not before."[149] By the beginning of 1943, the party had announced that it would nominate a single candidate for each congressional seat through an internal process. The PRM decided on this procedure, it claimed, in order to reduce the intensity of political agitation during a wartime election.[150] These measures succeeded in limiting the length of the 1943 political season. A U.S. diplomatic report in April noted that while election years often were marked by disorder and signs of instability in Mexico, that year "the effervescence has been mild[,] with campaigns just getting under way."[151]

The PRM did not announce its official slate of candidates until early June 1943, less than a month before election day, and when it did, many of the nominees came not from the party's traditionally more radical labor and peasant wings, represented by the CTM and the Confederación Nacional Campesina (CNC), respectively, but rather from the new "popular sector," a catchall grouping of moderate, largely middle-class elements loyal to Ávila Camacho's brand of political centrism.[152] A small number of PRM members who had been passed over for candidacies refused to accept their exclusion from the ballot and ran as "independents," but for the most part party discipline prevailed, with CTM and CNC representatives yielding their claims to congressional seats in the name of wartime unity.[153] In some districts, the "Revolutionary" candidates for congressional seats faced other challengers, either from the PAN, which had decided to contest an election for the first time, or from leftist organizations such as the PCM and Narciso Bassols's Liga de Acción Política. The participation of these elements in the election, as well as the emergence of a few voices for reform within the PRM, gave rise to faint hopes that a truly democratic election might take place on July 4.[154]

The elections themselves were marked by apathy and fraud, however. The PAN documented and denounced cases in which ballot boxes were stolen by gunmen and in which peasants from surrounding states were bused in to vote in Mexico City districts with contested seats. Opposition candidates presented evidence of widespread irregularities to the Chamber of Deputies when it met the next month to certify the results of the elections—one even dramatically committed suicide in the well of the chamber after lodging his protest.[155] Nonetheless, only PRM candidates and a small handful of nonthreatening "independents" received credentials as deputies in the new Congress.[156] *La Nación* and other opposition outlets were naturally vocal in their denunciation of the way in which the election had been carried out, but even mainstream newspapers criticized the PRM for its undemocratic practices. "The P.R.M., like all the groups that before it have arrogated to themselves the political representation of the Revolution, has failed as a means of fomenting the civic progress of the country," *El Universal* wrote in an editorial shortly after the election. "Thanks to the official parties, faith in the effectiveness of the suffrage, far from growing, has diminished over time," it said. "The P.R.M. almost managed to finish the job, annihilating the democratic hopes that surrounded the elections of July 4."[157]

Despite these signs of disappointment and disillusionment, the official party had in fact succeeded in strengthening its grip on the political system, and it had accomplished this in large measure by insisting that Mexico's participation in the war made it necessary for the ambitious individuals in its ranks to focus on the "national program of unification and preparation of military and civil defense outlined by President Ávila Camacho" rather than their own political campaigns. By centralizing control over the selection of PRM candidates, the party leadership minimized the level of open, visible political activity and conflict, thus ensuring that election day would be calm and basically peaceful, even if the polling that was taking place was still not free and fair. "The election was a farce but an orderly one," an observer reported to the OSS. Indeed, he said, "at no time since the 1910 Revolution was an election accompanied by less gun-play."[158]

Though the nature of the July 1943 legislative elections highlighted the irony of Mexico's repeated affirmations of loyalty to the cause of "democracy," President Ávila Camacho must have been highly satisfied with their results. Violence and disorder had been avoided, and a new group of deputies who owed their seats to him would soon be taking office. His party's grip on political power was stronger than ever, and despite a widespread recognition that the elections were deeply flawed, questions about the legitimacy of the results had been cast aside relatively easily. In any event, the president had already found that Mexico's involvement in World War II could provide a convenient justification for the dismissal of challenges to the official outcome of an election. When Ignacio García Téllez, a close associate of Cárdenas who had also served in Ávila Camacho's cabinet, protested privately to the president that fraud had deprived him of victory in Guanajuato's gubernatorial poll earlier in 1943, Ávila Camacho cited the war as a reason that he would be unable to tolerate any postelection conflicts over the succession in the state. The president told his former labor minister that if he accepted his defeat, he would "give all kinds of guarantees and considerations to the deputies of your group that have triumphed [in congressional elections] and for you the doors of my friendship and of the administration will be open." However, if García Téllez's followers attempted to prevent his rival from taking office in Guanajuato, the president said, "federal forces will have to repel them." Such a drastic step would be necessary, Ávila Camacho explained, because "we are in a difficult international situation, and unrest in Guanajuato would have grave repercussions." Therefore, the defeated García Téllez was informed, no resistance to the imposition of his opponent would be permitted.[159]

With the distractions and the potential disruptions of election season out of the way, the president would be able to forge ahead with his efforts to deepen Mexican involvement in the war. Indeed, just as Mexicans went to the polls, Foreign Minister Padilla was opening discussions with Ambassador Messersmith about the possibility of a limited Mexican military commitment to the Allied cause.[160] It would take another year, however, to complete the work of preparing the Mexican public for that step.

FIVE

Toward Direct Participation

JULY 1943–JULY 1944

With the midterm elections safely concluded, the Ávila Camacho administration continued to make subtle moves to prepare the population for the possibility of direct participation in World War II, but also, for the first time, it began to take concrete steps behind the scenes toward the formation of an expeditionary force. Preparations for the deployment of a Mexican military unit began with informal discussions on the subject between Foreign Minister Padilla and Ambassador Messersmith in July 1943. In the months that followed, carefully staged presidential statements on Mexico's role in the war laid the groundwork for the announcement that Mexican troops would go to the battlefronts. For logistical and political reasons, however, the administration concluded that Mexico's military contribution to the war effort would be limited, at least initially, to a relatively small air squadron. Integrating larger ground units into the Allied forces would create headaches for war planners in Washington and for commanders on the front lines. Moreover, Mexican leaders judged that the public at home was less likely to resist participation in the war if only a small group of professional military pilots and support personnel were sent into action.

When the newly organized Squadron 201 of the Mexican Air Force left Mexico City for training in the United States in July 1944, there was no outcry over the news that the unit would ultimately be destined for service overseas in the fight against the Axis. Although the belief that Mexico might send its soldiers abroad had been enough to trigger rebellions in the countryside during the first year after the country had declared war, the government's cautious handling of the issue over many months allowed it to avoid any serious resistance when it finally did acknowledge that an expeditionary force would carry Mexico's flag into battle. Indeed, not only did the Mexican decision to participate actively in the war contribute to the administration's efforts to professionalize the armed forces and to raise the country's standing in the international community, it also generated a burst of patriotic feeling that enhanced the president's authority and prestige. And by the middle of 1944, any additional leverage that the government could gain through a deepened public commitment to the war effort would have been welcome to the country's leaders, given the ominous signs of discontent and instability that were beginning to appear at that time.

★ ★ ★

When Padilla raised the possibility of Mexican military participation in the war in a conversation with Ambassador Messersmith early in July 1943, he made it clear that his government's interest in the matter arose largely from a desire to deepen the Mexican people's consciousness of what was at stake in the global conflict. He noted that with Mexico becoming geographically "further away from the war" and with the prospect of an attack on Mexican shores becoming "more remote," "it was difficult for the great masses of the people to appreciate all of the implications of the war for Mexico."[1] Participating in the conflict directly would make the importance of the conflict clearer to the Mexican public, the foreign minister implied. Though Padilla did not say so, it is very likely that he and his colleagues calculated that a deeper emotional investment in the outcome of the war would cause the citizenry to rally around President Ávila Camacho and to curtail its criticism of the government. In light of the unwelcome attention that the regime was then receiving for its inability to control inflation, its failure to punish the grafters in its ranks, and its underhanded tactics during the recent congressional elections, the president and his ministers were no doubt eager to find ways to rekindle the spirit of "national unity" that had been on display for brief periods during the first few months after Mexico entered the war.

Padilla also told Messersmith that many of the country's military leaders were anxious to take part in the fight against the Axis. In their view, he said, "it was not in accord with Mexico's dignity and her place among the United Nations that her army did not bear a part of the sacrifices of the war." According to Padilla, these officers "were very outspoken and definite in their opinion," and many of them were "chagrined" that General Cárdenas had denied that the army was prepared for combat. In widely publicized comments to a reporter in April 1943, the defense minister had dismissed the possibility of Mexican participation in the war, asking whether the country's troops would fight with stones or with arrows, but other military figures "resented his statement," Padilla said.[2] Finding a role for Mexican troops on the front lines would thus please the country's officer corps, and it would be a sensible step forward in Ávila Camacho's quiet campaign to make the Mexican Army a more professional, less political body. If the Mexican armed forces were engaged in intensive training and preparations for combat, there would be little time for generals to engage in political maneuvering. With ambitious public figures already beginning to look ahead to the 1946 presidential election, the time appeared to be right to move forward with efforts to focus the attention of the officer corps on military matters.

Finally, the foreign minister told the U.S. ambassador that, for his own part, he worried that there would be a reaction against Mexico in the United States and other allied nations if the people of those countries came to feel that "the American Republics had not done their share in the way of actual sacrifice" during the war.[3] This statement suggests that Padilla and his associates in the administration were concerned about Mexico's place in the postwar world. Direct participation in the conflict would presumably assure Mexico of a privileged position among the victors at any peace talks or international conferences that might follow the cessation of hostilities, while a failure to provide at least a token military contribution to the fight against fascism could diminish Mexican influence in Washington and in other centers of power after the war. In this regard, Padilla might also have been influenced by reports that Brazil was preparing to send an expeditionary force overseas.[4] If the Ávila Camacho administration did not make a similar gesture, such a move by Rio de Janeiro could threaten Mexico's claim to regional leadership and preeminence after the end of the global conflict.

This July 1943 conversation between Padilla and Messersmith was not the first in which a Mexican official had brought up the issue of possible participation in the war. As noted previously, Ávila Camacho himself had told the U.S. ambassador a full year earlier of the desire of some Mexican military men to form an expeditionary force, and while Padilla had denied that Ávila Camacho and Roosevelt had discussed the issue when they met in April 1943, the foreign minister apparently took advantage of the meeting in Monterrey to mention the matter informally to Undersecretary of State Sumner Welles.[5] However, the Padilla-Messersmith discussions of July 1943 were the first in which the subject was raised with a view toward carrying it forward. After stating that "he personally, and he was sure the President, felt . . . that it would be a very good thing all around if there could be some participation by Mexican elements in the actual conflict," Padilla sought to "explore the situation" with the ambassador. Messersmith reminded the foreign minister of the logistical difficulties that stood in the way of large-scale Mexican participation in combat, but he agreed that it would be desirable for Mexico to take part in the fighting overseas. He therefore suggested that the most practical way for Mexican forces to participate in the war would be through an air unit, which could be prepared for action relatively quickly, since Mexico already had a corps of skilled pilots. Padilla agreed that "it would be a splendid thing" to have a Mexican squadron sent to a fighting front, and he expressed his belief that such a deployment could serve as "a fine entering wedge" that might lead to more extensive participation further down the road. Messersmith therefore asked Welles to get the reactions of top U.S. officials to the idea of Mexican participation in the war so that he could work with Padilla to determine the best way to proceed.[6]

State and War Department officials in Washington did not immediately rush to accept Mexico's informal offer to provide fighting men for the fronts. Welles took more than a month to respond to Messersmith's letter on his meeting with Padilla, and he replied only after the ambassador had sent him another dispatch, informing him that the foreign minister had asked again about the possibility of a combat role for Mexican troops.[7] When he finally did write back, in mid-August, the undersecretary said only that the question of Mexican participation in the war had been "taken up by our military people here," who had noncommittally informed him that "upon the receipt of a formal proposal from the Mexican Government, attentive consideration will be given to the military and strategic factors involved."[8] When Messersmith conveyed this message to Padilla on August 30, the foreign minister promised to discuss the issue with Ávila Camacho and to inform the ambassador of the result of their conversation.[9]

If the Mexican government was discouraged by the apparently luke-warm initial U.S. response to its overtures, high-ranking members of the administration nonetheless pressed ahead with efforts to convey their interest in participating in the war to American officials. When the U.S. military officers who served on the Joint Mexican–United States Defense Commission were in Mexico City for a meeting around the time of the Independence Day holiday in mid-September, Defense Minister Cárdenas took aside the commission's two ranking members, Major General Guy V. Henry and Vice Admiral Alfred W. Johnson, and he informed them privately that he hoped "that Mexican troops will be given an opportunity to do their fair share in combat," as he recognized that "after this war, no nation can hold its head up which has not participated to the best of its ability in the war." He acknowledged that he had once remarked that his men "were armed with sticks and stones and could not participate in modern war," but he added that "thanks to the generosity of the United States Government and the work of the Defense Commission, the Mexican Army is [now] reasonably well equipped with modern imple-ments of war[,] and we have worked hard to give it good training."[10]

Noting that Cárdenas had previously opposed direct Mexican par-ticipation in the war, Ambassador Messersmith later concluded that the defense minister made this statement to Henry and Johnson only because "his hand was somewhat forced by the President of Mexico and by the Foreign Minister and also by the attitude of some of the Mexican Generals who increasingly believe that there should be such participation in some form or other."[11] Nonetheless, his private remarks to the U.S. members of the Joint Defense Commission gave military officials in Washington a clear indication that the Mexican govern-ment was serious in expressing its desire to take part in combat. The same message was conveyed by President Ávila Camacho himself to the U.S. Army's chief of staff, George C. Marshall, who was also in Mexico City for Independence Day. Marshall and the Mexican president car-ried on extensive conversations during a dinner on the eve of the holi-day, and together they reviewed the military parade that took place on September 16. Padilla later told Messersmith that Mexican participation in the war was among the subjects that the two men had discussed.[12]

Significantly, however, the possibility of a Mexican role in combat operations was discussed only in private, high-level conversations and not during the regular meetings of the Joint Defense Commission that took place that September. During this early stage of their preparations for an overseas commitment, Ávila Camacho and his associates clearly wished to restrict the number of people within the government who were aware of their plans for an expeditionary force. Although the Mexican officers who served on the commission, as military men, probably would have been strong proponents of their country's participation in the war, they might have resisted the suggestion that Mexico's contribution be limited to an air force unit. Moreover, the president and his advisers almost certainly worried about how the public would react if word of their plans were to leak. In commenting on the fact that only very high-ranking officials raised the subject of involvement in the war to visiting U.S. dignitaries, Messersmith observed that "there is[,] I believe[,] a good part of the Mexican population which is still unprepared for such a move."[13]

To be sure, leftist leaders continued to advocate Mexican participation in combat. For example, during an August 29, 1943, rally organized by the CTM to express support for Ávila Camacho's efforts to control inflation, Vicente Lombardo Toledano had repeated his frequent calls for a Mexican expeditionary force. However, the U.S. military attaché observed that the labor leader's "advocation of armed participation in the war on the part of Mexico evoked unfavorable repercussions (for him) in all except his own paper, El Popular" and that "several papers implied that it would be a welcome moment when Toledano himself headed the armed participation which he suggests."[14] The Mexico City newspaper *Excélsior* reported that it could find only one member of Congress—Deputy Jesús Yurén, a labor-sector representative who had been present at the rally— who supported Lombardo's proposal for direct involvement in the war, while other legislators opined that it would not be necessary to send troops overseas or at least that such matters should be left to the president.[15]

At the same time, the leader of the UNS published an open letter to Ávila Camacho reporting that with the draft lottery for youths born in 1925 approaching, country folk across Mexico remained worried that their sons might be sent abroad to fight.[16] An article that appeared in *El Sinarquista* a few days later asserted that "everyone knows that the immense majority of Mexicans is not in favor of going to fight outside of the national territory" and that "therefore the words of Lombardo Toledano create a great lack of confidence among the parents of the boys of the class of 1925."[17] Signs such as these that resistance to participation in the war remained widespread prompted the president and his cabinet members to proceed cautiously in their handling of the potentially controversial issue, using personal contacts with upper-level U.S. officials to explore the possibility of a Mexican role in combat rather than going through the normal channels of diplomatic and military communication.

Despite the government's efforts to keep its plans for participation in the war secret, however, rumors began to reach some military officers that an expeditionary force might be organized, causing an upsurge in excitement in the middle and upper ranks of the armed forces. For example, General José Beltrán Moreno, then serving as the army's director of artillery and mechanized troops, wrote to the president on October 13 to inform him that he had heard hints from U.S. officers that a Mexican force might go to the fronts. Unable to contain his enthusiasm, Beltrán asked to be considered as a possible commander for such a unit, saying that "it would be a glorious conclusion for my life as a soldier, begun in the classrooms of the Military College, many years ago, and forged in all the campaigns of our Revolution, to lead soldiers of my fatherland, under the shadow of our banner, to distant battlefields, in defense of the principles that you and I foster as an inheritance from our fathers and a legacy for our children."[18] Shortly thereafter, another prominent military figure, General Abelardo L. Rodríguez, told an interviewer that "Mexico ought to send soldiers to the fronts" and that "the country ought to have at least a division in Europe." The former president, who was then beginning a term as governor of the state of Sonora, also offered himself as a possible commander for any Mexican expeditionary force, saying that he "would go not just with the satisfaction of a soldier, but with the satisfaction of a Mexican who knows how to fulfill his duty."[19]

Nor were such sentiments limited to the very top of the military hierarchy. An official in the U.S. military attaché's office who was in close contact with the Mexican Army observed in October 1943 that the "officers who are most ardent in their desire to see a Mexican unit in combat" were "principally Captains of the classes 1924–1928 of the Colegio Militar"—that is, relatively young, professionally trained military men whose prospects for promotion were dimmed by the fact that the higher ranks were filled with aging veterans of the Revolution who were generally less technically proficient. For these ambitious junior officers, participation in the war would offer a chance to prove their military skills and perhaps to revive their stalled careers, and therefore they were strong advocates of the organization of an expeditionary force.[20] While indications such as these that the military leadership was eager to take part in combat must have been encouraging to the administration officials who were attempting to arrange for direct Mexican participation in the war, the president and his advisers almost certainly worried about how the general public would respond to the organization of a Mexican expeditionary force.

Perhaps more than fortuitously, the government had an opportunity around this time to gauge the extent to which the views of the public had evolved with respect to the question of Mexican participation in combat. On October 14, 1943, the lead story in *Excélsior* reported that "Mexico is disposed to send abroad an expeditionary military force." Citing unnamed "reliable sources," the article stated that the move toward participation in the war had not originated in political circles; rather, the initiative came from "the patriotic and visionary impulse of a group of generals, staff officers, and pilots who have informed their superiors of their desire to be considered among the first ranks in any military unit that Mexico decides to send overseas." Nonetheless, the *Excélsior* report continued, "the proposal for the formation of this expeditionary force is not looked upon badly by the Government because Mexico could not remain behind other Latin American nations that are already making the same preparations." With rumors circulating that Brazil and Cuba were planning to send troops into action, there was reportedly a fear within the administration that Mexico's "position would be diminished and even dishonorable" if it did not join its neighbors in combat. Moreover, the article continued, "a truly combatant and determined Mexico would have as well the advantage of being able to have an effective voice in the peace negotiations and in the resolution of the problems inherent to the postwar period." Indeed, the report concluded by offering the view that "a symbolic gesture of active participation in the war on the part of Mexico and other Latin American countries would promise to them a status in the future of the world which they would be able to obtain in no other way."[21]

However, even as it predicted that a ten-thousand-man expeditionary force would be ready for service overseas within six months, *Excélsior*'s report offered some reassurance to those Mexicans who might have worried that they or their husbands and sons would be used as "cannon fodder" in fierce fighting on the front lines. First of all, the article noted that the officers who advocated participation in the war envisioned the deployment of "some two divisions *of volunteers*," indicating that conscripts and other Mexicans would not be sent into action against their will. Furthermore, the report suggested that "as our soldiers would be at first novices for combat on the front lines, it is believed that in any case they would be assigned for now to garrison duty in occupied territories."[22] Thus, they would win for Mexico a place at the peace table without facing significant enemy fire or exposure to the perils of the battlefield.

In the days that followed, *Excélsior* moved from covering the story of the military's interest in participation in the war to launching a brief campaign in support of the idea. In case the effusive tone of the October 14 article did not make it sufficiently clear that the newspaper was in favor of sending troops abroad, an October 15 editorial explicitly endorsed such a move. The editorial acknowledged that for logistical reasons Mexican participation in the war would have to be limited in scope, and it insisted that any expeditionary force would have to be made up of volunteers, but it argued that the experience gained in combat by even a relatively small Mexican unit would be of great value to the young officers who would return from the fronts "with an outlook broadened by the perspective of a struggle on a grandiose scale." Moreover, the editorial went on, while Mexico had already earned its place at post-war conference tables through its economic contributions to the Allied cause, "a fraternity sealed by the struggle on the fields of battle" would give Mexico greater "moral force" at those meetings.[23]

The October 15 edition of the newspaper also reported that *Excélsior* had solicited the views of a wide range of political figures and, in contrast to the situation at the end of August, when it claimed to have been able to find only a single deputy who was willing to support the creation of an expeditionary force, "all our interviewees seem to agree that a step of this nature has to be the logical consequence of our position of decided and loyal support to the cause that we defend." While government officials such as Undersecretary of Defense Francisco L. Urquizo and Foreign Minister Padilla were careful to disavow any knowledge of plans for an expeditionary force, the newspaper emphasized that their statements did not constitute outright denials of its report. Furthermore, after expressing "surprise" at *Excélsior*'s story, Padilla was quick to add that "if the opportunity presents itself and Mexico has the necessary equipment, I am sure, because I know the military spirit of the army, that our country will fulfill its commitments as a belligerent."[24]

A PRM spokesman and Deputy Federico Medrano Valdivia, the party's whip in the lower chamber of Congress, both said only that it would be up to President Ávila Camacho to define Mexico's role in the war, but numerous other legislators were less circumspect in their endorsement of direct involvement in the conflict. Given the backing that the CTM had long given to the idea of participation in the war, it was unsurprising that senators and deputies with ties to the left-leaning labor sector were among the more outspoken proponents of an expeditionary force. Deputy Ruffo Figueroa of the Federal District, a powerful public-sector union leader, said that "we are at war, and nothing is more logical than that we provide what the war demands," and Senator Alejandro Peña of Sinaloa, a member of the CTM, stated that "Mexico ought to cooperate in this war, offering its generous blood."[25] Another cetemista senator, General Celestino Gasca of Guanajuato, reiterated his long-standing support for the creation of an expeditionary force, as did Senator León García of San Luis Potosí, a peasant-sector representative and a close ally of the president who had advocated direct participation in the war during the 1942 "orientation" campaign in the north of the country.[26]

Significantly, however, *Excélsior* was also able to collect favorable comments on the possibility of participation in the war from more conservative figures such as Senator Gilberto Flores Muñoz, known as a disciple of San Luis Potosí strongman Gonzalo Santos, and Senator Noé Lecona of Puebla, who had close ties with the rightist communications minister, Maximino Ávila Camacho.[27] Naturally, Fidel Velázquez of the CTM, Vicente Lombardo Toledano of the CTAL, and the secretary-general of the PCM also expressed satisfaction that a Mexican force might soon be in the field fighting against fascism, but it was the "plausible serenity" with which the rest of the country had accepted the news and the fact that "no official source" had gone so far as to "deny the information published yesterday" that caused *Excélsior* to conclude that the deployment of Mexican troops abroad was indeed imminent.[28]

Excélsior's suggestion that a national consensus had developed in favor of direct participation in the war was exaggerated, however. While the CTM's *El Popular* welcomed the newspaper's support for the organization of an expeditionary force, most mainstream press outlets reiterated their opposition to military involvement in the global conflict.[29] The relatively conservative Mexico City daily *Novedades* answered the reports in *Excélsior* with an editorial emphasizing that this proposal for military action abroad did not come from the president, who was "the only one who has the authority and the responsibility for these decisions." Furthermore, the editorial went on, given the many domestic social and economic problems that required the government's attention, "it would be unfortunate if far-off adventures were to be placed above urgent internal necessities."[30] The tabloid *La Prensa* agreed and added that the Mexican armed forces were not adequately equipped for service on the front lines.[31] Salvador Novo, a well-known commentator for *Novedades*, reflected both privately and in his column on "the impolitic nature of a propaganda that establishes the contribution of blood as an indispensable condition for the rights of victory" and on "the stupidity of an inferiority complex that does not perceive that in the nuances, in the differences of the very contributions of the United Nations lies the free and democratic nature of their union."[32]

More right-leaning organizations and publications also continued to oppose direct participation in the war. The PAN's *La Nación* asked by what right this group of "young generals and officers" had arrogated to itself the right to propose such a drastic expansion of Mexico's role in the war, and it denounced those who called for participation in the war without giving careful consideration to the army's technical capacity to be effective in combat.[33] For their part, Sinarquista publications blamed the reports that troops would soon be heading to the fronts on communists, charging that the "reds" intended to destabilize the government by raising the unwelcome prospect of Mexican participation in the war or that the communists would take advantage of the army's absence from Mexican soil to launch a revolution.[34] Such dire warnings did cause at least some consternation; after reading *El Sinarquista*'s commentary on the alleged communist conspiracy that was behind calls for an expeditionary force, a concerned woman from Saltillo, Coahuila, informed President Ávila Camacho in a letter that "we desire above all else to know what is the reason for which our men might go abroad; for you have assured us that they would not leave for foreign lands, and now it turns out that this is a lie, and we want you to tell us the reason, for we do not have any other person besides you who might give us the answer."[35]

But if *Excélsior*'s advocacy of direct involvement in the war failed to win over opponents of participation in the conflict, the newspaper's reports and the various reactions to them did allow observers to take note of the decreasing intensity of public feeling on the issue. Despite the predictable chorus of voices that had rejected the newspaper's call for an expeditionary force, a number of analysts noted that resistance to the proposal was far weaker than might have been expected. A U.S. diplomat reported to Washington that "so far as reaction can thus far be gauged to Excélsior's article, the principal enthusiasm for a Mexican expeditionary force" remained "with leftist leaders like Lombardo Toledano and with a sector of officers in the Army," but he also commented on the "noteworthy" fact that "the consideration of the possibility by public opinion has developed no bitter opposition—opposition which could have been expected to develop several months ago." If the general response to the article was "not affirmatively enthusiastic," he wrote, "the opposition was less bitter than might have occurred."[36] The U.S. embassy's military attaché agreed, calling public reaction to the proposal "apathetic" and noting that "strong opposition did not develop, as certainly would have been the case six months ago."[37] The lack of a more robust response to reports of possible moves toward Mexican participation in combat thus provided encouragement for those within the government who were preparing for such a step.

Indeed, it is highly probable that advocates of direct involvement in the war within the administration were responsible for the appearance of the articles and editorials that were published in *Excélsior* in October 1943 and that the true intention of these reports was to prepare the public for the forthcoming expansion of Mexico's role in the war. As noted previously, *Excélsior* had rejected the argument that a contribution of blood was necessary to secure Mexico's place at the peace table as recently as August 31, in response to Lombardo Toledano's speech advocating an expeditionary force. The abrupt change in the newspaper's position on the issue suggested that its publishers had received some sort of quiet official encouragement to adopt a new stance.[38] *El Popular* took note of the sudden shift in *Excélsior*'s views on the subject but preferred not to raise too many questions about how it had come to gain an ally in its campaign for a Mexican military role in the war.[39] *Novedades*'s editorial on the subject, however, asked if the alleged military officers' proposal might be "simply a preparation of the environment," so that plans for participation in the war that were already on the drawing board "will sound less strange" when they are made public.[40] The press officer at the U.S. embassy received word from one of *Excélsior*'s chief political writers that the October 14 article had in fact been "inspired by the

Foreign Office," and another American diplomat concluded that, even if the provenance of the report was not entirely clear, "Excélsior's article was, in any event, a trial balloon" meant to test the public's response to the idea of direct participation in the war. Having received indications that opposition to the creation of an expeditionary force would not be insuperable, the administration quietly moved forward with its plans.

Just a little more than a month after *Excélsior*'s reports announced to the Mexican people the possibility that a military unit from their country might be bound for the battlefronts, Ávila Camacho himself took a significant step to prepare the public for such an eventuality. On November 16, the president made a speech to about a hundred of the country's highest-ranking military men at the closing session of the defense ministry's second "Cycle of Information for Generals." For more than two weeks, the officers in attendance had received instruction in the methods of modern warfare, and, in accordance with Ávila Camacho's desire to create a more professional, less politically active army, they had heard what Messersmith described as "any number of lectures, including one by General Cárdenas himself, emphasiz[ing] the fact that the Army is the servant of the civilian administration and must not mix in politics."[41] At the end of the conference, with former presidents Cárdenas, Calles, and Ortiz Rubio in attendance, Ávila Camacho sought another way to focus the attention of the armed forces on military matters by making his most explicit statement to date about the possibility of direct Mexican participation in the war. The president told the assembled military commanders that although the country had theretofore been far removed from the battlefields of the war, "the Mexican Army is disposed to act where the circumstances demand: here in our territory, if the war thus requires it, and also outside of our territory if for justified reasons our allies seek it from us." Ávila Camacho also stipulated that any Mexican contribution should "not be lost in the confusion of an anonymous mass" and that therefore any expeditionary force would have to be assigned a distinct sector of operations of its own.[42]

The conditions that the president placed on any Mexican involvement in combat took Ambassador Messersmith by surprise, as he had made it clear in his discussions with Padilla that the U.S. government would welcome a Mexican proposal on participation in the war but that Washington had no intention of making a formal request for a Mexican force. The ambassador therefore concluded that the content of Ávila Camacho's speech had been influenced "by considerations which General Cárdenas brought to bear and also by the fact that he knew that a certain part of the Mexican population was not yet prepared for what he was saying." In a report to the State Department, Messersmith cited "first-hand and responsible information that General Cárdenas was not at all pleased that President Ávila Camacho deemed it advisable and convenient to make any statement with regard to this matter of participation at the combat fronts." However, the defense minister was "forced to agree to such a statement being made by the fact that he knew that the great majority of the Generals were in favor of such action."[43]

Indeed, the ambassador concluded, the president probably felt obliged to make some reference to the subject, given the intensity of the generals' interest in an active role in the war: because "there was an obvious desire on the part of the majority of the Generals that some action should be taken by the Mexican Army with regard to participation at the combat fronts," Ávila Camacho might have felt compelled to address the issue "before he was quite ready," and "in view of Cárdenas and the somewhat unprepared state of public opinion, he could not go all out as he desired."[44] A U.S. assistant military attaché agreed that the restrictions that the president said he would impose on the country's military involvement in the war "may very possibly have been inserted in the speech by way of appeasement of the Mexican public," and his report suggested that the address was "in line with President Ávila Camacho's step-by-step development of anti-Axis, pro-Allied feeling" among the Mexican people. "Whether or not they agree with him thoroughly," the U.S. Army officer observed, "all present indications are that Mexico will follow his lead, always provided that his actions are carefully planned to suit the Mexican temperament and are not entered into precipitously."[45]

Perhaps in part because of the conditions that Ávila Camacho had attached to the possibility of Mexican participation in the war, and certainly because in this case the proposal was coming directly from the president himself, the November 16 speech prompted little open criticism. Although *La Prensa* had opposed the creation of an expeditionary force when such a step had been proposed by *Excélsior* the month before, the Mexico City tabloid now hailed the president's words, "which undoubtedly will be received by all Mexicans with great enthusiasm, since they entirely reflect Mexican sentiment, the true patriotism and the ardor of the people." Predictably, *El Popular* and *Últimas Noticias*

(*Excélsior*'s afternoon edition) also celebrated Ávila Camacho's speech, reiterating their previously articulated arguments that participation in combat would be necessary to assure Mexico of a place at the peace table. Interestingly, the government newspaper, *El Nacional*, focused its editorial comments on the modernization of the army rather than the possibility of an expedition to the battlefronts, suggesting that the administration did not wish to draw too much attention all at once to the issue of participation in the war. However, in the closing paragraph of its commentary, the official daily did echo Ávila Camacho's address by noting the willingness of the "new Mexican Army . . . to fulfill the duties which circumstances may demand" by fighting on foreign battlefields, if necessary. *Novedades* alone among the major mainstream press outlets remained opposed to direct involvement in the war, holding out hope that "the Government of the Republic will not demand this sacrifice of our people unless the conditions are urgent, unavoidable and vital, really meriting a sudden and radical modification of the nature of our participation in the war."[46] Meanwhile, the president of the Senate, various deputies, and Communist Party officials publicly offered their support for the idea of an expeditionary force, and individual officials and citizens wrote to Ávila Camacho to congratulate him on his speech.[47] One Juan Silveti sent a telegram to the president informing him that during a trip from the capital to Guadalajara, "in all the towns through which I have passed I have noted the patriotic effect that the speech you made at the generals' banquet has had."[48]

If the reaction of the public to the president's speech was generally neutral if not positive, the reaction in military circles was overwhelmingly favorable. Immediately after the conclusion of the conference, the thirty-one military zone commanders who had been present signed a message congratulating the president on the "pure patriotism laid out in the doctrine contained in your brilliant speech."[49] These generals and others who had attended the meetings happily returned to their posts to await orders to prepare for service abroad. The U.S. consul in Nuevo Laredo reported on November 24 that the commander of the garrison there, General Pinal Villanueva, had arrived back in that border city "well pleased with the conferences" and hopeful that he might "get some overseas service himself."[50] The head of the air force, General Gustavo Salinas Camiña, was so encouraged by the apparent possibility of direct Mexican participation in the war that he effectively began to lobby for the deployment of his branch of the country's armed services. In late November, he told a reporter that the air force was "ready to go wherever the President sends us," and he argued that the most practical way for Mexico to take part in the fighting would be through an aviation unit. "A contingent of 500 planes would be as efficient as 150,000 soldiers," he said, "and their action would be less expensive and less complicated."[51] Salinas again expressed his desire for air force participation in the war in a December 15 speech at the U.S. naval air station in Corpus Christi.[52] Statements such as these gave rise to stories in the press that an air unit would soon be sent into battle, prompting the head of the defense ministry general staff to deny that any overseas deployment was imminent.[53] In refuting these reports, however, General Tomás Sánchez Hernández perhaps revealed his own enthusiasm for an even more extensive level of Mexican participation in the war when he said, "When the moment arrives, Mexico will not send a fraction of troops of a certain type, [but rather] she will send a land and air army that will work together."[54]

Early in December, Ávila Camacho followed up on his speech to the generals' conference with further guarded comments on Mexico's willingness to provide fighting men to support the Allied cause. On December 2, while touring a dam construction site in Puebla, the president answered a reporter's query on the possibility that a Mexican expeditionary force would be sent into battle by saying that his administration still had not received any request for troops from its allies but that the government was preparing for such a contingency because it might later "face this eventuality."[55] On December 6, Ávila Camacho kept the issue in the news, but again downplayed the likelihood that Mexican soldiers would soon be deployed overseas, when he told a group of senators that there appeared to be no shortage of Allied manpower on the front lines. He assured the visiting legislators, too, that if Mexico did participate directly in the war, its role would be "in accordance with our ideology and national sentiment, respecting the sovereignty of other peoples."[56] His statement that the Mexican Army, if asked to go to the fronts, would want to help "free conquered countries, such as the Philippines, for example," was taken by some to mean that the president was planning for the deployment of a Mexican unit in the Pacific theater, but the U.S. military attaché interpreted Ávila Camacho's remarks as an effort to keep the possibility of participation in the war before the public and as "a suggestion to Allied leaders that Mexico's assistance should be asked for."[57]

What most impressed Mexican newspapermen was the cautious tone that the president maintained when discussing the issue. A local reporter who brought Ávila Camacho's December 6 comments to the attention of the U.S. embassy noted the belief "in newspaper and other circles that the President himself is in favor of taking immediate steps to send Mexican troops to active fronts" but that he had so far limited himself to making cautious statements because of "the influence of former President General Cárdenas, who is generally believed to be personally opposed to such action," and to have acquiesced in public discussion of the subject only "because of strong feeling on the part of Mexican generals that Mexico should take an active part in the fighting."[58]

But if the nationalistic defense minister remained unconvinced that it was in the country's best interest to send troops into combat, he was not alone. While Cárdenas was at least willing to conceal any negative feelings he might have had about direct participation in the war from public view, the mercurial communications minister, Maximino Ávila Camacho, told reporters in early December that "recent Allied victories make our direct participation in this war more remote" and that he did "not believe that it is now necessary for us to take an active part" in the conflict. Long a bitter enemy of Vicente Lombardo Toledano and a target of attacks from the leftist labor sector, the president's brother could not resist the temptation to blame "professional agitators who are only looking for personal advantages, especially the demagogic leaders," for spreading disruptive reports that Mexican troops would be sent to the fronts.[59]

After reiterating the Sinarquista movement's belief that direct Mexican participation in the war would be unnecessary, a UNS spokesman had similarly seized upon the opportunity to take a swipe at Lombardo Toledano by repeating his organization's tongue-in-cheek suggestion that the labor leader and various leftist legislators who had advocated the creation of an expeditionary force should be sent abroad to fight as a "foreign legion."[60] In general, however, conservative organs such as *La Nación* and *El Sinarquista* devoted relatively little attention to the issue of military involvement in the war during the weeks and months immediately after Ávila Camacho's November 1943 speech. The lack of an outcry from the PAN and the UNS over the issue prompted a U.S. diplomat to observe at the beginning of 1944 that "there has been a noticeable change in favor of such action, especially on the part of *Acción*

Nacional and the *Sinarquistas*."[61] While the two groups certainly had not reversed course so completely that they now supported direct participation in the war, the apparently carefully considered statement of the president before the country's generals in November now made it difficult for them to claim openly that only irresponsible elements supported the idea of an expeditionary force.

Although there was little open resistance to the suggestions made in October and November of 1943 that Mexico should play a direct military role in the global conflict, Ávila Camacho waited several months before taking further visible steps toward the creation of an expeditionary force. The president perhaps wished to allow the idea of formal participation in the war to sink into the public consciousness. While he made relatively few direct references to the possibility of participation in the war during the period immediately following his speech at the generals' conference, Ávila Camacho did use both symbolic gestures and public statements to remind his compatriots of the difficult international situation and of the need to set aside internal differences while the country was at war. On November 19, for example, in conjunction with the celebration of the Anniversary of the Revolution holiday, he presided over a ceremony in front of the National Palace in which torches carried from around the country were brought together to light a symbolic flame to represent the unity of the nation. In an event clearly intended to impress Mexican citizens who might have forgotten the need for sacrifice and solidarity as World War II moved farther away from the country's shores—and as the rising cost of living became a more pressing daily concern—ten thousand schoolchildren sang the national anthem before the president lit the "Fire of National Unity."[62] Six weeks later, during his annual New Year's Eve message to the Mexican people, Ávila Camacho made a somewhat more explicit suggestion that citizens should be willing to accept some degree of hardship during wartime. "As a gentle hint to the people of Mexico that they should not complain, the President said that he did not wish to cite the examples of the conquered nations since he did not believe that the situation of Mexico should be compared with the sufferings of other countries," a U.S. diplomat reported in his summary of the December 31 speech. "Nevertheless, when he heard complaints about restrictions which the international struggle had imposed on Mexico he also thought of the fabulous losses which many friendly nations were suffering, and he could only consider that persons who made such criticisms do not understand the reality and do not clearly interpret the obligation of human solidarity."[63] The war thus gave the president an opportunity to put the economic hardships faced by Mexicans at this time into perspective.

Ávila Camacho's efforts to emphasize the need for discipline and collaboration with the government during wartime might also have been intended to help defuse persistent tensions between the left and the right, which continued to snipe at one another over the appropriate role of the church and of religion in various areas of national life. While the two ends of the ideological spectrum in Mexico had not abandoned their mutual hostility even during the heyday of "national unity" immediately after the Mexican declaration of war, there were signs that the conflict between the two camps was becoming more intense during the latter part of 1943. In an overview of the political situation at the beginning of 1944, a U.S. diplomat reported that the division between the left and the right on religious questions was "the political problem which has caused most unrest during recent months and apparently given the most concern to the President."[64] Conservative publications such as *La Nación* continued a long-running campaign demanding the repeal of Article Three of the Constitution, which dictated that education in Mexico be secular and socialist. In Congress, debate raged over the name of the Mexico City district in which the shrine of the Virgin of Guadalupe was located. Since the Revolution, the area had been known officially as "Villa Gustavo A. Madero," in honor of the murdered brother of President Francisco I. Madero (1911–1913), but many Catholics called for the restoration of the zone's traditional designation as the "Villa de Guadalupe Hidalgo." In October 1943, the legislature somewhat grudgingly allowed the old name to be applied to the immediate neighborhood of the basilica, but the Chamber of Deputies also took the opportunity to denounce "certain elements of the clergy and some groups of Catholics who have dedicated themselves to the task of flagrantly violating the [anticlerical and secularizing provisions of the] Political Constitution of the Republic, aiming not only to make the Mexican Revolution recede, but also to modify the Political Charter of the Nation in a regressive sense."[65]

Although Ávila Camacho had generally demonstrated a willingness to show greater tolerance toward the church and toward religious expression during his years in office, he apparently felt compelled at this time to demonstrate to the left that the regime's constitutional commitment to secularism was secure. A November 1943 presidential decree established a military rule forbidding church attendance by soldiers in uniform, and on November 10, 1943, Interior Minister Miguel Alemán circulated an order calling for the enforcement of constitutional prohibitions on the organization of outdoor public events by groups with religious affiliations.[66] Alemán's instruction came after church leaders held "Eucharistic Congresses" in Veracruz and Mazatlán. These large-scale celebrations included religious processions through the streets of those cities that were unlawful under the terms of the Constitution of 1917.[67] It was in this charged environment that, despite Alemán's order and much to the consternation of the Mexican left, tens of thousands of members of a Catholic labor union staged a pilgrimage to the shrine of the Virgin of Guadalupe on December 5, 1943.[68] With all of these issues and incidents contributing to mounting internal tensions, it is easy to understand why the president found it useful to make reference to the country's external enemies and to the need for unity in confronting them.

Meanwhile, in meetings with top U.S. officials during a visit to Washington in January and early February of 1944, Messersmith took up the question of Mexican participation in combat. After securing the approval of Secretary of State Hull, the ambassador reminded President Roosevelt of the growing desire in Mexican government and military circles that the country send an expeditionary force abroad. Messersmith reported that "the President of Mexico and the Foreign Minister were exceedingly anxious that Mexico should participate in some way at the combat fronts" and that, in his own opinion, "it was highly desirable that Mexico should participate in actual combat through at least an air squadron." Though in military terms Mexico's contribution would be small, Messersmith argued that direct Mexican involvement in the war should be encouraged for political reasons. Participation in the war would strengthen the country's claim to regional leadership in Latin America, and a stronger position for Mexico in the postwar world would be advantageous to the United States, the ambassador told the president, because Mexico had shown itself to be a loyal ally. Messersmith acknowledged that Allied military commanders might not be prepared to accept the challenge of integrating Mexican land forces into their units, but he argued that the deployment of a Mexican air force squadron should be feasible. Roosevelt agreed and told the ambassador that he could inform Ávila Camacho "that the participation of a Mexican air squadron or two or three, would be very acceptable and helpful." Upon receiving this news from Messersmith back in the Mexico City, Ávila Camacho "was much pleased," and he told the ambassador that after some additional consultations, he would be back in touch with his final decision on the matter.[69]

In the meantime, however, knowledge of preparations for the deployment of an expeditionary force remained restricted to a very small circle in Washington and Mexico City. Thus, even as the final necessary arrangements were being made to prepare the way for direct Mexican involvement in the global conflict, some Mexican military men were beginning to become frustrated at the lack of apparent progress toward active participation in the war. Early in February 1944, air force chief Salinas reiterated to the U.S. military attaché in Mexico, Brigadier General A. R. Harris, that "Mexico is very anxious to take the lead" in the formation of a regional expeditionary air force, and he expressed his hope that he himself might be considered as a possible commander for such a unit.[70]

The military attaché also noted that a long-time proponent of Mexican involvement in combat, General Cristóbal Guzmán Cárdenas, had asked him why the United States had made no request for Mexican troops in response to Ávila Camacho's November 1943 speech. Guzmán Cárdenas, who had just been named head of the defense ministry's general staff, said that "he and all the other Mexican officials who have been advocating closer collaboration with the Allies were greatly disappointed and somewhat hurt by the apparent coolness in which the President's offer of troops had been received by the Allies—especially the United States." Harris tried to explain that to the best of his knowledge the United States had not received a *formal* offer of military assistance from Mexico upon which it could act, but Guzmán Cárdenas expressed the view that the president's public statements on the subject made it sufficiently clear that his country was willing to contribute on the battlefield. The Mexican general told the U.S. military attaché that "about 90% of the Army is strongly advocating active participation in the war" but that these officers were "becoming impatient and a little dismayed" as a result of Washington's failure to acknowledge the president's "(to them) very important statement, which the leaders of the movement for active participation in the war have been advocating for months." To encourage Mexican officers' interest in the war, Harris recommended that the top ranks of the army be invited to visit the southwestern Pacific theater of operations, where Guzmán Cárdenas had suggested that Mexicans' knowledge of guerrilla fighting could be an asset.[71] That recommendation was placed on hold, however, while Messersmith and other U.S. officials awaited Ávila Camacho's decision on how best to proceed toward Mexican participation in the war.[72]

During the weeks immediately after Messersmith had informed Ávila Camacho that a Mexican squadron would be a welcome addition to the Allied forces, the president said nothing further on the subject to the U.S. ambassador. Early in March 1944, however, Ávila Camacho gave additional public indications of his desire to see Mexican troops take part in the struggle against the Axis, and he provided the Mexican people and the armed forces with an idea of the form that the country's participation in the war might take. A March 5 demonstration of the capabilities of the Mexican Air Force in the skies over the capital provided one hint; immediately after the exercises, the U.S. military attaché speculated that the true purpose of the event might have been "in the nature of preparing the public for an announcement that the Mexican aviation was ready for active participation in the war when requested by the Allies."[73] Three days later, on March 8, the president attended a banquet given by the air force in his honor. Speaking on behalf of the assembled officers, Major Javier González Gómez told Ávila Camacho that his fellow pilots would welcome the opportunity "to cooperate on the battlefields in the annihilation of the nazi-fascist hordes" and that if the president saw fit to send them into combat they would "know how to do honor to their flag, to their fatherland, to their people, and to their government."[74]

In a supposedly improvised but surely very carefully scripted response, the president reiterated that "until now no cooperation of that type has been required of us," and, presumably to dispel the popular belief that the United States wanted Mexican soldiers on the front lines as "cannon fodder," he stressed that the Allies were not pressing for Mexican military involvement in the war. Ávila Camacho added, however, that he understood "the anxiety of many members of our [military] Institute, of the diverse branches of service, who, as men, as Mexicans, and as brave warriors would want to participate in this conflict." The president therefore promised that in light of the desire of Mexican fighting men to do their part for the democratic cause he would "think about the possibility that Mexico . . . might participate, at least in a symbolic form, in carrying our flag to the theaters of war." He added, too, that "if this is decided, I believe that no one could carry it in a more efficient form than the Air Force."[75]

Ávila Camacho's remarks still fell short of an open declaration that Mexico would send its men to the front lines, but the president's pledge to explore the possibility of such participation was received enthusiastically by the air force officers at the banquet and by military men more generally. A number of soldiers and officers reacted to the speech by sending telegrams to the president's office asking to be considered as possible members of an expeditionary force, and defense ministry officials told the press that "thousands" of similar messages had arrived there, as well. Among the prominent generals who made public their desire to command a combat unit were former president Abelardo L. Rodríguez and Joaquín Amaro, who had been Calles's defense minister in the 1920s and was then serving as the commander of the Oaxaca military zone.[76] The conservative political affiliations of these two men accentuated the fact that enthusiasm for a Mexican role in the war came not just from the pro-Soviet left but also from military men with an interest in the modernization of the army. Some commentators noted and drew a distinction between the insistence of labor leaders like Lombardo Toledano that Mexico take its place on the front lines and the desire of the armed forces to play an active part in the war, judging the latter to be more honorable. An editorial in *El Universal Gráfico*, for example, observed that expressions of "loud, activist patriotism [*patrioterismo vocinglero*, something of which Lombardo and his colleagues had often been accused] that would push the soldiers into the fight" had "already been discarded in favor of the serene attitude of those," like the pilots of the air force, "who simply offer to fulfill their duty."[77]

For its part, *Excélsior*—reveling in the fact that its October 1943 reports on the army's interest in combat duty had now been vindicated— made what many Mexicans might well have considered a key point when it noted that because the president was responding to a clearly manifested desire on the part of the military to go into battle, any participation in the conflict would "not be the fruit of government coercion, but rather, on the contrary," it would be "the result of a collective will demonstrated persistently and bravely."[78] Ávila Camacho had managed to frame his statement that a Mexican unit might go into action in such a way that it seemed to be simply an accession to the wishes of armed forces rather than an imposition on an unwilling citizenry.

The announcement that any expeditionary force would be "symbolic" and that it would in all likelihood be led by professional military aviators probably calmed many of the lingering fears that the public might still have had about Mexican participation in the global conflict, but even as Ávila Camacho aimed to reassure the populace that huge numbers of Mexican teenagers would not be shipped off to the front lines, he also sought through his remarks to remind the nation once again that Mexico was at war. Such a reminder was necessary, an editorial in *El Universal Gráfico* observed after the president's speech, because the reality of Mexico's role in "a formidable conflict that will transform the course of history" was "being hidden by the smokescreen of the indiscipline of the railroad workers and oil workers"—some of whom were then engaged in wildcat strikes—and by "comments about the variety and intensity of the nightlife in Mexico," which was flourishing as the country's nouveaux riches sought ever grander diversions, frequenting nightclubs and attending horse races at the new Hipódromo de las Américas. "The real Mexico is not the one that organizes suicidal work stoppages or that escapes into the artificial paradises of elegant vice," the newspaper said. "The real Mexico is in the young group of aviators who demonstrated last Sunday their technical mastery over the modern apparatuses."[79] Just as Ávila Camacho had used previous celebrations of a supposed national unity and rhetorical references to the Allied war effort to rally public support and to inspire patriotism in the face of internal divisions and economic hardships, he now referred again to Mexico's responsibilities as a belligerent in an effort to divert attention from difficult domestic problems and to shore up the administration's political position.

In contrast to the situation in October 1943, when a number of newspapers had criticized *Excélsior* for advocating participation in the war, the reaction of the press to Ávila Camacho's speech in March 1944 was almost uniformly favorable. *Excélsior*, *El Universal*, and *El Popular*, among other publications, hailed the president's suggestion that Mexico might take a direct part in the war, and *La Prensa* launched its own campaign for military involvement in the conflict, inviting readers to write in to express their own willingness to fight for the Allied cause. While the editors of the Mexico City tabloid said they hoped that no Mexican blood would be spilled, they spoke of a need "to win for Mexico a place in the better world that is being forged," and their reporters found numerous senators and military officers who were willing to be quoted as saying the same thing.[80] Scattered disapproving perspectives could be found, to be sure: *El Sinarquista* expressed regret that the president "insists in offering that which is not sought from us," suggesting that the contribution of a tiny air squadron to the war effort would bring the country ridicule rather than glory.[81] Moreover, it was perhaps convenient for the administration that the Mexico City daily *Novedades*, which had previously criticized proposals for military involvement in the war, was not then appearing on newsstands because of a strike by a faction of its employees.[82] Nonetheless, a remarkably complete cross section of the mainstream national press responded to Ávila Camacho's March 8 speech by commending the president and the air force pilots for their patriotism and by embracing the idea of limited, symbolic Mexican participation in combat.

No doubt encouraged by the positive response to his statement on the possible deployment of an air force unit overseas, Ávila Camacho sent word to Messersmith that Mexico wished to make a formal offer of military assistance on the front lines. On March 14, a week after the president had addressed the air force, Foreign Minister Padilla told the U.S. ambassador that Ávila Camacho "was prepared to go ahead with the appropriate arrangements."[83] At the end of the month, therefore, Brigadier General William E. Hall, the deputy chief of the U.S. air staff, traveled to Mexico City to discuss the formation of an air squadron with top Mexican officials. The publicly stated purpose of Hall's trip was to bestow a decoration on the commander of the Mexican Air Force, General Salinas, to whom he also issued an invitation to visit one of the combat fronts as an observer.[84] During his stay, however, Hall met with Padilla and Ávila Camacho as well, securing the president's approval for the organization of a Mexican fighter unit along the same lines as U.S. squadrons that were already in service. The two men also agreed that the Mexican aviators would receive additional training in the United States and that they would be destined for the Mediterranean theater of operations. For the time being, however, "President Camacho stated that he desired that this matter be maintained in its present secret classification." Indeed, the president stated that "even General Salinas will not be notified that the plan has been approved until a later date." Probably because of the personal interest that he took in the matter, but also presumably because he wished to keep his plans secret, the president indicated that "he, himself, planned to pick the personnel" of the squadron and that he would do so within approximately two months.[85]

Ávila Camacho's hesitancy to make public his decision definitely to send an air force unit into combat was influenced in part by the fact that he did not yet have the congressional authorization that would be necessary before troops could be sent overseas. Although the legislature could be relied upon to pass such a measure, Messersmith reported that the president did not want to say categorically that Mexico would deploy an expeditionary force without having the required approval for fear that doing so "would merely raise a storm from certain minority elements here." Ávila Camacho initially hoped that he would be able to secure that approval in a special session to be called in the spring for the purpose of ratifying a water treaty with the United States, but when the finalization of that pact was delayed, the president decided to wait until the regular congressional session began in September. "Although Mexican public sentiment with respect to the war and active participation therein has developed rapidly in a favorable sense," Messersmith wrote, "the President still has a great deal of reluctance in calling a special session for this purpose alone." In the meantime, the government could send soldiers to the United States for training under the terms of a congressional measure passed earlier in the war, which allowed the sending of troops to other countries in the Western Hemisphere, but open talk of sending a unit into combat was temporarily placed on hold.[86] While Ávila Camacho had been preparing the Mexican people for participation in the war "in his usual wise and sound way," and while Messersmith was sure that "the actual announcement, when it is made, will . . . be received here without hardly [*sic*] a dissenting voice," the president still preferred to proceed slowly and cautiously.[87]

The president's reticence with respect to the preparations that were being made for an expeditionary force in the spring of 1944 was probably also connected to tensions that existed within the armed forces. Although soldiers and officers had reacted enthusiastically to Ávila Camacho's statement in March that participation in the war would be seriously considered, many members of the army bristled at the suggestion that the air force, rather than ground units, would have the honor of representing the country on the battlefronts. The U.S. military attaché in Mexico City reported that many of the messages that flooded into the defense ministry "from military men ranking from Generals down to Privates" after Ávila Camacho's speech to the air force expressed not only a desire to go to the front lines but also disapproval of the fact that "'those god-damned aviators are going ahead of us.'" The attaché worried that when news of the organization of an expeditionary fighter squadron and of General Salinas's invitation to the European front became public "the ground forces are going to feel much neglected and slighted."[88]

Mexico's ambassador to the United States, Francisco Castillo Nájera, who was also a general in the army's medical service, and his military attaché, General Luis Alamillo Flores, were apparently among the officers who resented the special role being contemplated for the air force. Castillo Nájera abruptly left Washington for Mexico City on March 16, and U.S. military officials there learned that he was carrying a report from Alamillo claiming that the Mexican Air Force was unprepared for combat and that the U.S. government would prefer for Mexico to provide ground troops. The ambassador allegedly intended to present this document to Defense Minister Cárdenas, to whom both he and General Alamillo had close ties, in an effort "to undermine the Mexican Air Force and prevent its participation as suggested by our President [Roosevelt] and to secure participation of Mexican ground forces instead."[89] Messersmith hastened to assure officials in Washington, who most certainly did *not* want to have to field a Mexican offer of ground troops, that Ávila Camacho was thinking only in terms of sending an air squadron, but he acknowledged that "the Mexican Generals are very anxious to send ground forces" and that "they are very jealous of the air force."[90] Through his March 1944 speech, the president had prepared members of the army for the unwelcome news that it would be the air force that would carry the Mexican flag into action, but given the disappointment that many officers expressed, it is understandable that Ávila Camacho did not yet wish to make his final decision to send only an air squadron into combat publicly known.

Meanwhile, during the months after the president's address to the air force, disturbing signs of instability began to appear on the Mexican political landscape, giving Ávila Camacho an additional incentive to press ahead with plans for participation in the war as a way of stimulating feelings of patriotism and unity. Perhaps the event that most shocked the nation during this period was an April 10, 1944, attempt on the life of the

president. As Ávila Camacho arrived at the National Palace that morning, a military officer approached and fired upon him at close range. The
bullet left a hole in the president's jacket but somehow missed the chief
executive. After the assailant, Lieutenant Antonio Enrique de la Lama y
Rojas, had been subdued, he reportedly told Ávila Camacho that he had
attempted to kill him because he objected to the prohibition on church
attendance by soldiers in uniform. The would-be assassin was then hauled
off to a military base at the former hacienda of Echegaray, just outside
of the capital, where he was shot, supposedly while trying to escape.[91]
With the Mexican public already rattled by the (unrelated) killings of
Sinaloa governor Rodolfo Loaiza on February 20, and of *Novedades* pub-
lisher Ignacio Herrerias on April 3, the attack on the president gave rise
to considerable alarm. A U.S. diplomat reported that "these events have
created a profound impression and are generally interpreted as being at
least an indication of increased uneasiness in the country."[92]

Though some newspapers, such as *Novedades*, called upon Mexicans to
rededicate themselves to Ávila Camacho's policy of national unity in the
wake of the assassination attempt, Lombardo Toledano and other leftist
leaders seized upon the apparently religious motivation for the attack
to denounce the church leadership and Mexican conservatives as fascist
fifth columnists.[93] While this renewal of the ongoing conflict between
the left and the right would have been troubling enough to the administration on its own, the president and his closest advisers might well
have worried, too, about the full range of factors that had prompted the
assassination attempt. Religious fervor was indeed one of the motives
behind the lieutenant's attack on the head of the Mexican regime, and
the available evidence suggested that he was a disturbed individual acting on his own, but in a statement made to military authorities as he
lay dying from the wounds he received while "making his escape," the
assailant insisted that he was "a Catholic but not a fanatic" and that he
had taken action against the president not primarily for religious reasons but rather out of "a vehement desire for a new order of dignity,
of pride, and of honesty." He railed against the "patent immorality of
[Communications Minister] Maximino [Ávila Camacho, the president's
brother] and [Economy Minister Francisco] Gaxiola," both of whom
were reputed to have greatly enriched themselves while in office, and
he cited examples of corruption in the high ranks of the armed forces.[94]
Even State Department officials who generally admired Ávila Camacho

and supported his program acknowledged that corruption within the Mexican government had reached unprecedented heights during the wartime period and that "widespread graft" was, along with inflation and the high cost of living, one of the main factors contributing to "growing disorder and discontent in the country."[95] De la Lama's statement, which was not made public, confirmed that rampant dishonesty and abuse of official positions were breeding resentment in some sectors of society. As the president must have recognized, the stability of the regime could be in danger if such concerns were widespread in the army.

Official concerns about the possible consequences of dissatisfaction within the ranks of the armed forces were heightened on June 22, 1944, when an article in *El Sinarquista* claiming that a communist uprising was planned for July 5 was accompanied by an appeal to the army to join in the resistance to the expected revolution.[96] The UNS publication had become increasingly critical of the administration during the preceding weeks and months, charging the regime with weakness in the face of Stalinist intrigue.[97] Ávila Camacho had long resisted repeated leftist calls for the dissolution of the Sinarquista organization, largely because he saw the group as a useful counterbalance to far-left elements in Mexico. When, shortly after his arrival in 1942, Ambassador Messersmith had asked the president about the potential danger posed by the strength of the UNS, Ávila Camacho had responded that while it was necessary to eliminate the extremists at both ends of the political spectrum, those "fanatics" could be better controlled by allowing the PCM and the UNS to continue to exist rather than by repressing either or both of those organizations all at once. Besides, he noted, "the Sinarquista groups exercised a restraining influence in many communities on the *ejidatarios* and prevented them from taking an arbitrary course."[98]

In the fragile political environment of mid-1944, however, the administration could not abide open calls for the army to take to the streets. Therefore, the federal attorney general's office filed "social dissolution" charges against the individuals responsible for the publication of the "seditious" appeal of June 22. And though it stopped short of meeting demands from the left that it definitively dissolve the UNS, the government also prohibited the publication of its newspaper and imposed an indefinite ban on meetings of the organization.[99] Lombardo Toledano, the CTM, and like-minded individuals and groups rejoiced, sponsoring a July 9 rally in support of Ávila Camacho's decision and flooding the

president's office with congratulatory telegrams.[100] However, the step
was one that the administration took with considerable reluctance, only
after the Sinarquistas had gone too far in their anticommunist fervor by
calling directly upon the army for action.

While euphoric messages from union leaders and left-leaning legislators commending the president for his stand against the Sinarquista
"fifth columnists" continued to arrive at the National Palace, yet
another incident ominously hinted at the existence of dissension and
discontent in the ranks of the army. During the early morning hours
of July 10, Captain Benito Castañeda Chavarría went to the barracks at
Military Base Number One, on the edge of Mexico City, and roused a
group of conscripts. He sought to incite the groggy soldiers to rebellion,
referring to their poor living conditions and—reportedly—to the fact
that the government intended to send them into combat overseas. Upon
leaving the barracks, however, Castañeda was quickly overpowered, and
his ill-conceived mutiny was brought to an abrupt end.[101] He later con-
fessed that he had hatched a plan with five other junior officers to rise
up against the government, but after his coconspirators had abandoned
the scheme for fear of being discovered, the captain had proceeded on
his own.[102]

A court-martial sentenced Castañeda to death, but President Ávila
Camacho, perhaps fearing that an execution would give too much significance to the incident, commuted the sentence to a dishonorable
discharge from the army.[103] The public degradation of Castañeda was
carried out on July 14, and if part of the purpose of holding the ceremony was to demonstrate to other soldiers the importance of loyalty, the
event was effective. The U.S. military attaché, General Harris, reported
that the ritual "made a deep impression on all those who witnessed it"
and that officers to whom he talked "all agree that they would rather be
executed than undergo such a humiliating punishment."[104] In commenting upon this entire episode, the U.S. embassy noted that it had initially
received some indications that the defense ministry was "deliberately
playing down the story and concealing the true facts." The administration certainly would have wanted to minimize the importance attributed
to the incident, but in the end American diplomats concluded that the
brief rebellion was in all likelihood "the work of an unbalanced man."[105]
Nonetheless, Harris observed that "there is considerable discontent
among many of the younger officers," who were frustrated not just by

the slow pace of promotions but also by very low levels of pay.[106] Though Castañeda's plot never posed a serious threat to the government, Ávila Camacho must have been concerned by the signs of dissatisfaction that the captain's actions brought into view, and he likely hoped that moving forward with plans to expand Mexico's role in the war would refocus the attention of the armed forces on military matters while also giving junior officers new hope for upward mobility in the ranks.

As these dramas were unfolding, top officials in the Ávila Camacho administration were quietly completing preparations for the sending of Mexican aviators and support personnel to the United States, where they would receive the additional training that would be necessary before they could be deployed on the front lines. Around the beginning of July, Padilla told the American ambassador that the squadron's personnel had been selected and that the group was ready to depart, and on July 10, a U.S. air corps officer visited the foreign ministry with Messersmith to finalize concrete plans for the training of the Mexican unit.[107] Despite the hints that Ávila Camacho had dropped about the possibility of participation by the air force in combat, however, the true purpose of the new Squadron 201 remained a closely guarded secret. Messersmith had reported in June that "knowledge of the final destination of this Squadron is still confined to the President, the Foreign Minister, the Chief of the Mexican Air Forces, and General Cárdenas."[108] In large part because it still lacked congressional authorization for a deployment outside of the Americas, the administration hesitated to acknowledge that the squadron might eventually see action on the battlefronts, even in July, as the unit prepared to leave Mexico. "The squadron will supposedly be leaving for training purposes only," Messersmith wrote, and he stressed to U.S. officials that it would therefore "be necessary to maintain the same secrecy and reserve we have kept up to now with regard to its ultimate destination."[109]

On July 21, however, when Ávila Camacho reviewed the unit just prior to its departure for Randolph Field in Greenville, Texas, he told the assembled pilots and enlisted men "that he wanted to add a few words" to the official description of their assignment so that they might "carry a clear concept of their mission." The president noted that while "the war has not reached our shores," Mexico had responsibilities as an ally of "belligerent countries that fight for liberty." "We ought to be prepared to respond to any necessity of the war," Ávila Camacho continued, and he therefore informed the personnel of the squadron that after finishing their training, "if it is necessary you will go on to Europe, carrying the representation of the National Army."[110]

This statement did not go far beyond the president's previous utterances on the issue of Mexican participation in the war, and it did not represent a definitive commitment to send troops to the battlefronts, but by speaking openly of the possibility that this particular unit might be destined for combat duty, Ávila Camacho went further than officials who were aware of the plans for the squadron had expected that he would. In doing so, he took another small step toward expanding Mexico's role in the global conflict. The public acknowledgment that Squadron 201 might eventually enter the fight against the Axis was perhaps intended in part to reassert Mexico's claim to a prominent place among Latin American nations after the conclusion of the war. Certainly, when Ávila Camacho remarked to the members of the squadron that "already our brothers from the Republic of Brazil fight on the fields of Italy," he demonstrated an awareness that another country in the region had moved ahead of Mexico in the level of material assistance that it was providing to the Allied cause.[111] Signaling once again that Mexico was willing to do its part on the battlefields of the war could potentially enhance the country's standing in the international arena.

The forthright announcement that it would be Squadron 201 that would "carry the representation of the National Army" to the front lines could also have served to reassure the general public that any Mexican participation in combat would take place on a relatively small scale, through air force units rather than through large divisions of conventional ground forces. Such reassurances would have been welcome in the wake of newspaper reports that had appeared earlier in July claiming that the government was on the verge of sending thousands of troops into battle. Under banner headlines such as "Mexican Troops to the World War" and "We Will Have to Fight Against the Japanese," these July 9 articles cited General Guzmán Cárdenas as saying that the military leadership was prepared to send up to four army divisions into combat. Although the defense ministry's chief of staff stipulated that the deployment of an expeditionary force would take place only at the order of the president and that conscripts would not be sent abroad, the reports raised the prospect of the sort of large-scale participation in the war to which many Mexicans had objected in the past.[112] A U.S. diplomat noted that Guzmán Cárdenas's remarks to the press were perfectly in line with statements the president had made about Mexico's role in the war, but "the newspapers have seized upon them and played them up in an unjustifiable fashion" by making it appear that sizeable infantry units would soon be sent to the front lines.[113] Ávila Camacho's appearance before Squadron 201 on July 21 gave him an opportunity to reiterate the message that he had initially put forward in March: Mexico's military participation would almost certainly be largely symbolic, and it would be the air force that would represent the country on the front lines.

Reaction to the president's revelation that the new Mexican fighter squadron could go into action abroad was generally positive, despite the fact that enthusiasm for participation in the war was still far from universal. Indeed, in a survey of more than a hundred men and women on the street carried out on July 8, the day on which comments by Foreign Minister Padilla on the possibility of Mexican military involvement in the war had been published in the Mexico City press, the PAN's *La Nación* found that 90 percent of respondents opposed such a step.[114] But after months of statements by the president and other officials on Mexico's responsibilities as a belligerent and the limited, symbolic nature of any Mexican military contribution, feelings on the subject no longer ran deep.

Divisions in the press on the question of direct involvement in the conflict had all but disappeared by this time, too. Even *Novedades*, which had previously expressed skepticism about the idea of military involvement in the global conflict, now adjusted its position, asserting that participation in the war was appropriate now that the national territory was secure.[115] "There has not been a single adverse newspaper comment," Messersmith reported to the State Department after Squadron 201 left Mexico for Texas on July 25, "and I think that the Mexicans generally are glad and proud that the plunge has been taken."[116] The ambassador marveled at the change in public opinion on the subject of participation in the war that had been effected by Ávila Camacho's careful management of the issue. "I am sure that up to a few months ago, the President had no idea that he would make such a definite statement" about the probable destination of the squadron, Messersmith wrote. The fact that he did make such a statement and that it was accepted without complaint was "an indication of the increasing consciousness of at least thoughtful persons in Mexico of all the broad implications of the War and what it means for Mexico."[117]

Maintaining that consciousness of the war and of what it supposedly meant for Mexico would be an important objective for Ávila Camacho during the year that followed the departure of Squadron 201 in July 1944, as continuing difficulties with inflation, pre-electoral jockeying for political position, and uncertainty about the shape of the postwar order threatened to undermine the country's stability. News of the exploits of Mexican Expeditionary Air Force in the fight against Japanese forces in the Philippines in the closing months of the global conflict would serve the Ávila Camacho administration well as a useful reminder to the Mexican people that the country was at war.

SIX

Preparing for Peacetime

JULY 1944–NOVEMBER 1945

During the latter part of 1944, it became increasingly clear that the Allies would win the Second World War. The success of the Normandy invasion in June and the steady advance of the Red Army on the Eastern Front after it had turned back the Wehrmacht at Stalingrad guaranteed that Germany would eventually be vanquished, and the defeat of Japan would surely follow. Therefore, even as fierce battles continued to rage in the forests of Belgium and on heavily fortified atolls in the Pacific, officials around the world began to look ahead to the challenges that their countries would face after the conclusion of the global conflict. In Mexico City, as in other capitals, there was considerable uncertainty about the likely shape of the postwar order. Some Mexican commentators wondered whether Washington would maintain its benevolent "Good Neighbor Policy" after the war was over, and there was both enthusiasm (in leftist circles) and apprehension (among conservatives) at the prospect of greatly increased Soviet influence in the international arena.

The primary concern of ambitious Mexican politicians, however, was not the global balance of power but rather the distribution of political forces within their own country. Though presidential elections were still almost two years away, aspirants to the top office were already quietly preparing to vie for the post that the incumbent would be required to relinquish—because of the Constitution's prohibition of reelection—in 1946. Given that the outcome of the war was no longer in doubt, that the high cost of living continued to create economic hardship for most Mexicans, and that political rivalries were threatening to burst out into the open at the beginning of a long campaigning season, it might well have been expected that the Ávila Camacho administration's grasp on the political situation would falter during late 1944 and early 1945. By continuing to insist on Mexico's responsibilities as a belligerent and by emphasizing the now active nature of the country's participation in the fight against the Axis, however, the president was able to maintain at least a facade of national unity during this challenging transitional period between the war years and the atomic age.

★ ★ ★

Announcing in July 1944 that Squadron 201 would be available for combat duty after the completion of its training was one way in which Ávila Camacho reminded his countrymen of Mexico's role in the war, but it would be months before the unit would be ready to proceed to the front lines. In an effort to inspire unity and patriotism in the meantime, the president unveiled plans in August 1944 for a National Campaign Against Illiteracy, and significantly, he presented this program as a war measure, using his emergency powers to launch the initiative by decree. In promulgating a law that would require literate Mexicans between the ages of eighteen and fifty to teach at least one of their countrymen how to read and write, Ávila Camacho argued that "the defense of the country cannot be reduced, in the years of war, to the material organization of the military resources that we have undertaken to face the threats from abroad" and that Mexico's security during wartime required "the profound factor of resistance that is represented by the intellectual, spiritual, and moral preparation of a nation desirous of conserving the vital patrimony of its liberties." The campaign could also be justified as part of the war effort, the president said, because it was consistent with "the purest sense of our participation in the war," which was based on a "true desire not to live in a world divided between the privileged and the oppressed." Moreover, with the global conflict winding down, Ávila Camacho's decree suggested that Mexico would have to remain on a war footing even after the cessation of hostilities, with workers continuing the "battle" of production "in the factories and in the fields" in order to contribute to the development of their country and the reconstruction of a war-torn world. And for those workers to achieve the "intensity of labor" that would be required of them in the postwar era, an educational effort beyond the capacity of the country's school system would be necessary, the decree said.[1]

When the new law went into effect, Ávila Camacho stressed that the literacy campaign that was to run from March 1945 to March 1946 should be understood as an integral part of Mexico's involvement in World War II. In a message to state governors, the president wrote that he had decided to initiate the drive because a situation in which only about half of the population was able to read and write was "incompatible with the necessities of material and moral training that define the wartime conditions of the moment."[2] And in a speech broadcast over the radio on August 21, Ávila Camacho told the general public, "We are at war and we realize that in a total war like the one the world is suffering, any country has two types of enemies: external enemies—in our case, the Nazi-fascist forces—and internal enemies." He went on to say that the latter, in Mexico's case, were "above all the product of grave and secular insufficiencies" and that most of those insufficiencies could ultimately be linked to "the insufficiency of instruction."[3] Education Minister Jaime Torres Bodet echoed this theme in a radio speech on August 27, asserting that "a fatherland is not defended exclusively with the sword and with the rifle," and he told Mexicans that the "law issued this past Monday grants us the highest honor: that of defending the country as instructors of the Mexico of tomorrow."[4] Thus, the literacy campaign was linked explicitly and insistently with Mexico's participation in the war.

The administration also sought to associate the initiative with the drive for "national unity" to which the war had given rise. Although the federal attorney general worried that the campaign could lead to increased agitation by the clergy and other rightists who might take advantage of the program to "influence the youth in a sense contrary to revolutionary postulates," Torres Bodet convinced the president that the law would not "lead to disturbances, alarm, and disorder, but rather, on the contrary, it is to be believed that it will inspire enthusiasm and as a patriotic project it will undoubtedly strengthen the bonds of union that will serve precisely to calm political passions."[5] Therefore, as he concluded his August 21 speech, Ávila Camacho expressed his confidence that the nation would "come out of this experience more bound together and more capable, more Mexican and more united."[6]

The campaign against illiteracy represented an effort to promote national unity by calling for solidarity not just during wartime but also

in the face of the coming challenges of the postwar era. The administration had employed a similar strategy several months earlier, in
February 1944, when it established a National Planning Commission
for Peacetime. This advisory council included prominent citizens from
across the political spectrum. By inviting such disparate figures as PAN
founder Manuel Gómez Morín, conservative national university rector
Rodolfo Brito Foucher, labor leader Vicente Lombardo Toledano, and
El Popular editor Alejandro Carrillo, among others, to come together to
study the issues that the country would have to confront after the war,
Ávila Camacho sought once again to bridge the deep ideological divide
that separated the left and the right in Mexico. The creation of a body
with a mandate to look ahead to the end of the global conflict served as
a reminder to Mexicans that the country was then at war, and it implied
that the economic difficulties and social problems that the country faced
should be understood in the context of the international situation.

However, the profound differences in outlook that existed within
the commission and the selection of a controversial figure as its chairman ultimately undermined the council's effectiveness as a promoter of
national unity. When the commission's membership list was published,
U.S. intelligence analysts called it "an interesting roster of irreconcilable
political figures."[7] The creation of a committee "with such antagonistic,
incompatible points of view" made it unlikely that the group would be
able to reach a consensus on how to address the country's problems, but
it was Ávila Camacho's appointment of Octavio Véjar Vázquez to lead
the commission that made the realization of that goal all but impossible.
As education minister from September 1941 until December 1943, Véjar
Vázquez had earned the bitter enmity of the left by taking a hard line
with the teachers' unions and by firing many employees in a campaign
to rid the nation's schools of communist influence. He had resigned from
the cabinet, ostensibly because of his health, just a few weeks prior to his
appointment to lead the new commission. While the education minister
had indeed been ill during the fall of 1943, it is almost certainly more
than coincidental that he left the department just in time to allow a more
moderate successor to preside over a December 1943 teachers' convention at which rival organizations bitterly divided over Véjar Vázquez's
leadership were to try to reconcile their differences. Indeed, when
Ávila Camacho informed poet and diplomat Jaime Torres Bodet that he
intended to appoint him to serve as education minister just three days

before the convention was scheduled to begin, the president explained that such a move was necessary because Véjar Vázquez's continuing presence "at the head of the Secretariat of Education would without doubt pose serious obstacles to the success of the congress."[8]

The change in ministers apparently caught outspoken teachers who had planned to use the meeting to denounce Véjar Vázquez off guard: "It was said that many kilos of [anti–Véjar Vázquez] flyers had to remain in the shadows of who knows what printing establishments or warehouses," Torres Bodet later wrote.[9] When the National Congress for the Unification of the Teachers opened on December 24, a few hours after the new minister had been sworn into office, Torres Bodet stressed Ávila Camacho's calls for national unity, placing a special emphasis on the fact that the country was at war. With the country "living through hours of unusual gravity" while "the whole world finds itself at war," "the teachers of Mexico with good reason are trying to unify themselves more firmly to defend Democracy," he said.[10] The delegates to the meeting responded, after several days of sometimes acrimonious discussions, by joining together in a consolidated union, the Sindicato Nacional de Trabajadores de la Educación (SNTE).[11]

Véjar Vázquez's appointment to head the postwar planning commission was perhaps a reward for his quiet departure from the cabinet and for his willingness to be the focus of leftist attacks on the administration's education policy during his tenure there. His enemies were not disposed to forgive and forget his role as their nemesis, however, and they continued to be annoyed by Véjar Vázquez's apparent intention to place a conservative slant on the commission's findings. In June 1944, the prominent socialist Victor Manuel Villaseñor resigned from the committee, saying that he had been doubtful from the beginning that it would be able to accomplish anything under Véjar Vázquez's leadership and that he objected to the chairman's practice of speaking in the name of the commission without necessarily consulting or taking into account the views of its members.[12] The commission continued to sponsor lectures and issue publications through the fall, but Véjar Vázquez ran into further trouble after a November 1944 speech in which he "gave a gloomy picture of agricultural, financial, social and educational conditions in present-day Mexico and thus indirectly criticized the achievements of the Mexican Revolution." Cristóbal Guzmán Cárdenas, the defense ministry chief of staff, subsequently gave a more positive assessment of the progress Mexico had made during the preceding decades in a speech that was widely interpreted as a cardenista rebuttal to Véjar Vázquez's presentation.[13] Rather than facilitating the establishment of a consensus on the proper approach to Mexico's social and economic problems, the chairman of the postwar planning commission was only succeeding in exacerbating tensions between the left and the right.

To avoid further controversy, Ávila Camacho decided to disband the commission.[14] A December 14 presidential decree said only that the commission was being dissolved because it had fulfilled its mission, but an earlier draft of the document had conceded that decisions about national policy in the postwar period needed to be made with a "rapidity incompatible with the complex structure of the Commission." Ávila Camacho's staff deleted this phrase, however, because they read it as a tacit admission of the failure of "the idea of a national policy" that had inspired the president to form the committee. While the consultative body had been envisioned as a forum in which "the distinct representative tendencies of public opinion would collaborate," the president's advisers wrote, its work had been frustrated by the inability of its members to overcome their political differences "even in the presence of a high common interest."[15] Although this particular initiative failed to advance the cause of national unity, it was typical of the Ávila Camacho administration's efforts to overcome political divisions by appealing to "a high common interest" arising from the tumultuous international situation that existed during the early 1940s.

Moving ahead with preparations for military involvement in the war must have seemed like an obvious way to remind Mexicans of the "high common interest" that should unite them during wartime. Therefore, on December 27, 1944, as Squadron 201 entered the final stages of its training in the United States and as the 1944 congressional session was drawing to a close, Ávila Camacho finally sent a message to the Senate, seeking its authorization "to send from the national territory troops and elements of war [*elementos bélicos*] in the amount and at the time [*en la medida y oportunidad*] that [the executive branch] might judge to be convenient." Although the president had pledged in his May 1942 message to Congress seeking a declaration of a state of war that no Mexican soldiers would leave the country, he now argued that "upon adhering to the cause of the United Nations, Mexico expressed not only the purpose of defending the material integrity of its territory, but also the firm resolution to contribute through all possible means to the final victory of the Democracies." While the participation of Mexican units in combat had not been required by the country's allies, Ávila Camacho said, "Mexico feels the moral commitment to assist in the achievement of the common triumph against the Nazi-fascist dictatorships with forces that act under their own Flag and in the site that the circumstances demand." Even if this contribution was "modest" in numerical terms, the president concluded, "its symbolic importance would be great."[16] The text of Ávila Camacho's request for permission to send forces abroad did not contain any limit on the number or type of troops that he would be able to deploy overseas, but the Senate's presiding officer, administration ally Eugenio Prado of Chihuahua, assured his colleagues that the president's initiative was intended to apply only to the men of Squadron 201, whose possible participation in combat had already been announced. Armed with this reassurance, the Senate unanimously approved the measure on December 29.[17]

Inasmuch as the likely final destination of Squadron 201 had been revealed in July, when the group left the country for its training, Ávila Camacho's request to the Senate did not generate much surprise or controversy, but because little had been said about the unit during the preceding months, the press gave prominent coverage to the news that the president had been given authorization to send the aviators into combat. The afternoon newspaper *Últimas Noticias*, published by *Excélsior*, used banner headlines to report on the 43–0 vote in the Senate that allowed Ávila Camacho to send Mexican forces overseas.[18] A handful of conservative voices in the media expressed dismay at the move. *Novedades* observed with obvious distaste that the most consistent and enthusiastic proponents of direct Mexican participation in the war had been "communists and creole and mestizo fellow-travelers [*comunizantes*] animated, without a doubt, by patriotic ardor . . . for the U.S.S.R." The newspaper questioned the motives of the "pseudo-marxists" who advocated the deployment of a large expeditionary force, wondering if they perhaps wanted the security of the country to be in the hands of inexperienced conscripts during the upcoming electoral season. *Novedades* was willing to grant, however, that "the consensus of all good citizens has pointed toward a symbolic participation for Mexico in the armed conflict." As long as the country's presence on the front lines remained a merely symbolic one, with the bulk of the armed forces available at home to maintain order, the nation should be secure, the *Novedades* editorial grudgingly concluded.[19]

The PAN also worried that Mexican participation in combat would not ultimately be limited to a token air force unit. Its weekly magazine, *La Nación*, darkly hinted that the deployment of Squadron 201 was just a first step toward the mobilization of a much larger expeditionary force. "Public opinion" believed that "not less than 50,000 men would depart for the battlefronts," the publication asserted. Noting that U.S. officials had expressed great satisfaction at the Mexican move toward direct participation in the war, the magazine asked, "Can the jubilation in Washington be explained by the sending of just one squadron?"[20] *La Nación* also mocked the official conventional wisdom which held that it was "logical" for the country to send its troops to the front lines since Mexico was officially at war with the Axis. Seeking to apply the same standards of "logic" in a broader examination of Mexican political realities, the magazine asked, "Is it completely logical that a country at war for democracy and for liberty has not a single deputy nor a single municipal president who has been truly elected?"[21] The PAN thus implicitly objected to the rhetorical use that the government was making of the war. Gómez Morín and his followers recognized that the administration was capitalizing on the global conflict by presenting itself as an honorable and active supporter of the democratic cause, and through *La Nación*, their organization sought to expose the obvious contradictions underlying the regime's position. The Sinarquista movement might well have been inclined to raise similar issues, but its publications and most of its operations had been banned since July, after *El Sinarquista* had published an appeal to the army that was judged to be seditious. Thus, when the Senate voted to allow Ávila Camacho to send troops into battle, the PAN stood out as the opposition group most vocally opposed to direct participation in the war.

In general, though, editorials supported the president's decision to seek a more active role for Mexico in the conflict. *El Universal* advised its readers that sending Mexican forces into combat should be seen as "a logical action, an unavoidable consequence of the situation in which the gratuitous and unjustified aggressions of the totalitarian powers placed the country." Although Mexico had been contributing to the fight against the Axis in a variety of ways, the newspaper argued, the nation "cannot avoid its responsibility to intervene in the most relevant aspect of [the war], which is the military [aspect]." Moreover, with Squadron 201 on the front lines as a symbolic Mexican contribution to the Allied cause, not even those "least able to value the importance of the cooperation that the Republic has been giving to the war effort of the democracies will be able . . . to deny that the Mexican people has been a factor in the realization of the ever-closer victory."[22] Naturally, *El Popular*, which had long advocated active Mexican involvement in the struggle against fascism, also praised the administration and the Senate for taking another step toward direct participation in the war. "For a long time, since the country declared war on the Axis, the country has been waiting for this resolution," the Lombardo-controlled CTM newspaper said, blaming resistance to such a move on "the passive part of the Nation, the fifth column, the myopic conservatives." In contrast to the recalcitrant attitude of the Sinarquistas and other elements of "the reaction," the editorial went on, "the sentiment of the democratic masses in relation to the conflict has been clear: honest Mexicans desire the effective participation of Mexico in this struggle."[23] To be sure, *El Popular*'s interpretation of Mexican public opinion was undoubtedly colored by its ideological leanings, and the positive tone of the mainstream press's coverage of the subject may well have been encouraged in subtle ways by the administration, but the lack of a serious outcry over Ávila Camacho's request to send forces abroad reflects the success of the president's efforts to prepare the groundwork for such a move slowly and cautiously over the course of many months.

The president had also been prudent and cautious in his handling of the army's continuing desire for even deeper involvement in the war. Ávila Camacho recognized that the excitement that many generals felt about direct Mexican participation in the war was tempered by disappointment that aviators rather than ground forces were being sent into action. Therefore, on July 24, 1944, as Squadron 201 prepared to board the train that would carry the unit to the United States for its training, the Mexican embassy in Washington asked U.S. military authorities to accept six Mexican staff officers who would serve with Allied forces in Europe.[24] Such an opportunity would allow at least a select few Mexican officers to gain the firsthand experience of modern warfare that they craved. From Ávila Camacho's perspective, the arrangement would be perfect inasmuch as the relatively junior staff officers would be performing important but unglamorous duties in the headquarters of an American general rather than leading troops into battle. Thus, it was unlikely that they would be able to return to Mexico as conquering heroes who might use their renown as a platform for political adventures. The U.S. War Department did approve the Mexican request, offering to attach six officers to the Allied headquarters in Caserta, Italy.[25]

The initiative did not immediately go forward, however, possibly because the Mexican officer who was handling the matter, military attaché Luis Alamillo Flores, was still holding out hope that a larger Mexican force might be sent to the fronts. As the highest-ranking member of the military mission that had traveled to North Africa in 1943, the ambitious and relatively young General Alamillo likely hoped that he would be given a prominent place in an expeditionary ground force. In an August 8 conference with an influential U.S. general, he had "discussed unofficially" the possibility of employing about five thousand Mexican ground troops in the Philippines.[26] Two months later, in another conversation with an American officer, Alamillo again pitched the idea "that there might be an opportunity for Mexican forces to participate in the Pacific war," adding that "Mexican elements could very well operate in the Philippines where they would find the terrain and the environment similar to their own." This time, he suggested that his country "could probably equip three divisions"—about fifteen thousand men—"to participate in the Philippine campaign."[27] Alamillo's lobbying efforts failed to bear fruit, but they reflected the continuing enthusiasm that many Mexican military men felt for the idea of direct participation in combat.

Though Alamillo was apparently acting on his own initiative, during the days after Squadron 201 left Mexico City, Ávila Camacho was at least considering the possibility of sending ground troops into action. According to General Guzmán Cárdenas, the president had "been so pleased with the reception by the public" of the news that the fighter unit might be sent into battle that he had given him secret instructions to draw up plans for the organization of an infantry division that could join the air force detachment overseas.[28] Whether or not Ávila Camacho seriously intended to follow through on these plans, charging the defense ministry's chief of staff with the task of preparing for the possible involvement of ground forces in combat was a good way of placating one of the army's leading proponents of direct participation in the war.

Ultimately, the only representatives of Mexico's ground forces who reached the battlefronts during the final year of World War II were three generals who toured the European theater of operations at the invitation of the U.S. government during the very last days of the conflict on that

Figure 18: Mexican officers touring the ruins of Berchtesgaden, in the German Alps, as part of an observer mission at the end of World War II. (National Archives and Records Administration)

continent. Eulogio Ortiz of the Monterrey-based Seventh Military Zone, Director of Artillery José Sebastián Beltrán Moreno, and Subdirector of Personnel Ramón Rodríguez Familiar arrived in Paris at the end of April 1945 and subsequently spent a month in Europe, traveling to the headquarters of Generals Eisenhower and Patton and, after the German surrender, visiting Hitler's retreat at Berchtesgaden and flying over the liberated concentration camp at Dachau.[29] By allowing these generals to take part in this observer mission, the Mexican government found a way to give some of the army's strongest advocates of participation in the war an inside look at the results of the conflict without having to expand greatly the scope of Mexican involvement in combat.

Through the latter part of 1944, while many army officers continued to seek some sort of role for themselves in the war, the members of Squadron 201 spent several months at bases in the United States receiving instruction in their respective specialties before reassembling in Texas at the end of the year. Although Ávila Camacho had told them before they left Mexico that they might well be sent into battle, it was not until December 27, 1944, that the pilots and enlisted men of the unit received any further official indication that they would be moving on to the front lines after the completion of their training. On that date, as the president sought congressional approval for the overseas deployment of Mexican forces, the defense ministry issued an order designating the squadron as the Mexican Expeditionary Air Force (FAEM). "It was not until we received" this order, the unit's commander later wrote, "that we were able to infer the possible decision taken by our Government."[30]

Shortly thereafter, the aviators learned that they would be assigned to the Pacific theater. U.S. and Mexican officials had initially agreed that the squadron would be deployed in Europe, but Ávila Camacho himself requested in December 1944 that the unit be assigned to the command of General Douglas MacArthur. Citing his personal admiration for the Allied commander in the Pacific and a pledge he had made to the late president Manuel Quezon of the Philippines during a joint radio broadcast in 1942 that Mexico would do what it could to assist in the liberation of the archipelago, Ávila Camacho told Messersmith that his country had "sentimental reasons for wanting to fight in the Pacific theater" and that it would "mean a tremendous lot to the Mexican people to have their Squadron fight" there.[31] "Sentimental reasons" aside, the president probably judged that his countrymen's response to the participation of its forces in the struggle to free a partially Spanish-speaking population in the Philippines from foreign occupation would be more favorable than its reaction to the involvement of its troops in the invasion of the Third Reich and in attacks on German cities. In order to derive maximum political advantage from Mexican participation in the war, Ávila Camacho had to consider such matters very carefully. In any event, U.S. officials were happy to grant this request, especially since Allied forces in Europe were struggling with the challenge of coordinating the operations of the many different national forces that were already there. By contrast, incorporating a single Mexican unit into an overwhelmingly American force in the southwest Pacific would be relatively easy.[32]

When the FAEM completed its training in February 1945, Undersecretary of Defense Francisco L. Urquizo traveled to their base at Randolph Field to present the squadron with its battle flag before it shipped out for the Philippines. Prior to making the trip to Texas, Urquizo had told U.S. officials of his hope that "this would be the occasion for a really big ceremony which would focus the light of public attention on the fine collaboration between the two Air Forces," suggesting that the Ávila Camacho administration wished to play up the fact that Mexico was taking an active part in the war. The government likely calculated that a grand program in which the country's fighting men would be charged with carrying the nation's tricolor banner into battle could do much to inspire patriotism at home. Moreover, by "making this a really big and important milestone in Mexican-U.S. military cooperation," the administration perhaps hoped to consolidate public support for the more collaborative relationship with Washington that it had developed during the war years.[33] In a speech that was broadcast over the radio in Mexico, Urquizo told the members of the squadron on February 22 that they would be contributing to the liberation of "a land united to the traditions of our history" through a common cultural background and that they would be fighting both for their fatherland and for humanity itself. Speaking in the name of the president, he added, "Between battle and iniquity our people has never hesitated."[34]

The event, and the subsequent departure of the FAEM for the front lines captured the imagination of the press and of much of the Mexican public. "Upon putting their own flag in the hands of the young soldiers of Squadron 201, the Fatherland trusts in them and is sure that they will exalt it with glorious deeds," *El Universal* gushed on the day of the ceremony.[35] On his daily radio program, commentator Félix Palavicini told his listeners that "the historic Squadron soon will have the opportunity to demonstrate the courage, the valor, and the heroism of Mexican soldiers" and that they would be fighting "for the moral interests of all of humanity."[36] At the same time, the archbishop of Mexico City presided over a Mass at which prayers were offered for the success and for the safe return of the Mexican fighter unit. While high-ranking officials of the secular government studiously avoided attending the service, the church hierarchy clearly saw the departure of Squadron 201 for the battlefields of the Pacific as an occasion on which it might usefully offer a sign of its commitment to a policy of national unity and to a continuation of the rapprochement with the state that had taken place during the war years.[37] *La Nación*, which had been so suspicious of the move toward direct participation in the war after the Senate approved it in December, now provided ample coverage of the religious ceremonies that had been staged on behalf of the squadron. "Mexico is sending her best sons to defend her," the PAN publication said. Putting aside its objections to the government's policy of seeking a deeper role in the war, *La Nación* expressed the hope that the men of the FAEM would "return to the Fatherland safe and sound and triumphant, for the good of all."[38]

Some editorialists went beyond praise for the brave men of Squadron 201 to call for unity and discipline among the population at home while the aviators were overseas. For example, *El Universal Gráfico* argued that "with our young eagles [*aguiluchos*, a term often used to refer to members of the squadron] at the front, a commitment of honor and of effort that we ought to fulfill loyally falls to the civilian population of the country." In a call for national unity that echoed appeals frequently made by President Ávila Camacho, the editorial urged Mexicans "to work intensely and enthusiastically," "to place the supreme interest of the fatherland before the particular interests of groups," and "to forget hatreds and quarrels, in order that a true unity of the Mexican family might shine forth." In short, *El Universal Gráfico* concluded, "our mission is to be, in all senses, worthy of the sacrifice that our pilots make and embody."[39] Ambassador Messersmith reported that the only slightly negative note in the coverage of the ceremony in Texas was sounded by *Novedades*, which stated that it "would have desired that it would never have been necessary for Mexican soldiers to be present on any front," but even the editors of that conservative newspaper used the occasion to call for a constructive approach to domestic problems, "in order that the aviators may have a country worth fighting for."[40] As Squadron 201 carried the national flag into battle, *Novedades* concluded, "All of us who are left behind ought to be conscious of a double responsibility to honor that same flag, but also to render a practical and real tribute to the men who bear it."[41] Just as the administration had intended, the organization of a symbolic force that would represent Mexico on the front lines thus helped to focus the attention of at least a part of the Mexican public on the place of their country in the global conflict and on the need for unity during wartime.

Ávila Camacho was no doubt particularly eager to convince his countrymen "to place the supreme interest of the fatherland before the particular interests of groups" during the early part of 1945, as it was becoming increasingly difficult for him to prevent his would-be successors from launching potentially divisive political campaigns in advance of the July 1946 presidential elections. Aspirants to the presidency had already spent years positioning themselves for a run for the top office, while also attempting to discredit possible rivals. By the latter part of 1944 and the beginning of 1945, many were eager to begin seeking support for their candidacies openly rather than behind closed doors and through veiled attacks on their competitors. As early as September 1944, Ambassador Messersmith lamented "that this pre-electoral activity has become so evident so long before the elections in Mexico, for it is most disturbing in the picture here."[42]

Because overt electoral maneuvering could undermine the president's authority and effectiveness and threaten his policy of promoting national unity, Ávila Camacho repeatedly called on potential candidates to continue to abstain from political activities in order that Mexicans might continue to devote their energies to the betterment of the country during a difficult period. When the president received a delegation of senators in his office on December 1, 1944, the fourth anniversary of his inauguration, he told them that campaigning for the 1946 elections should not begin for at least another year. A longer season of electoral agitation "will not benefit anyone," he said.[43] Later in the month, almost every senator dutifully signed a statement in which the legislators pledged "not to begin prematurely any political electoral activity regarding the change in the Executive," inasmuch as such disruptive *futurismo* "could obstruct even the great work of the reconstruction and the defense of Mexico, as well as plans for the postwar period, which with unquenchable patriotism, the Chief Executive has been undertaking."[44]

In his annual New Year's Eve speech to the Mexican people on December 31, 1944, Ávila Camacho again warned against pre-electoral agitation, denouncing not just open electioneering that might disturb public order but also the "subterranean politics" of those who were preparing their campaigns. Such activities "would hinder those who want to continue working with efficacy" for the good of the nation and "would add to the picture of our life an inconvenient motive of mistrust and an obscure factor of social anxiety," the president said, and he expressed the hope that "in 1945, as in 1944, the ideal of our unity will prevail."[45] Though the poll that would be held on July 7, 1946, loomed ever larger on the horizon, as 1945 began Ávila Camacho hoped for at least a few more months during which it would be possible for him to set the national agenda.

Even without any open campaigning under way, however, several events during the early part of 1945 had obvious implications for the upcoming electoral campaign. When Foreign Minister Ezequiel Padilla delivered a strident speech on January 7 defending his conduct of Mexico's international relations, it was clearly understood in political circles as an attempt to shore up his position in the face of attacks by detractors who had labeled him as an *entreguista*, a lackey of the United States. Those attacks, in turn, had been largely engineered by rivals who were less concerned with the foreign minister's policy of collaboration with Washington than they were with the possibility that Padilla could make a strong run for the presidency. Observers had long attributed presidential ambitions to the foreign minister, and certainly, because of the prominent role he had played as an outspoken advocate of Pan-Americanism and of the Allied cause during the war years, he stood out as a leading member of Ávila Camacho's cabinet.

Although he lacked a significant political following in Mexico, Padilla had been subjected to bitter criticism in the press at moments when he seemed to be gaining credibility as a possible contender for the presidential chair. When he earned glowing reviews in the North American press for his rhetorical efforts at the Rio de Janeiro conference in January 1942, some Mexican commentators blasted Padilla as a grandstanding U.S. stooge, especially after the foreign minister received extensive publicity during a visit to the United States in April and May of 1942. Critics then charged that he was promoting himself as an indispensable interlocutor rather than quietly representing the policies of his government.[46] In the months that followed, Padilla absorbed further criticism after making statements hinting that Mexico might become more actively involved in the war and announcing that Mexican citizens living in the United States could be drafted for military service there. Though these attacks on Padilla reflected legitimate nationalist sentiment to a certain extent, commentators generally agreed that the primary purpose of the criticism was to weaken the foreign minister politically.[47]

Padilla faced another round of denunciations during the latter part of 1944. This time, his leading detractor was J. Rubén Romero, a noted writer and poet who had served as ambassador to Cuba until Padilla dismissed him for publicly advocating a more assertive, nationalistic stance toward the United States.[48] When Padilla finally set out to answer his enemies in his January 1945 speech, Messersmith, a friend and admirer of the foreign minister, hailed his remarks as "magnificent," adding that they exposed the "insidious and dastardly" nature of the ongoing attacks on Mexican foreign policy. However, Romero and other critics simply called the speech "the first step of his electoral propaganda," and they continued to denounce his conduct of the country's international relations.[49]

U.S. analysts were sometimes puzzled by the apparent zeal with which Padilla's rivals sought to discredit him, given that he lacked the kind of mass following that would be necessary for a successful run for the presidency. For example, when the foreign minister was being subjected to a round of attacks in late 1942, one observer reported to the OSS that "Padilla never has been a popular man with the Mexican public, probably never can be," and he "would have a hard time building himself as presidential timber." Thus, "it seems odd that his opponents are fearfully paying so much attention to him as a competitor," the informant concluded.[50] However, largely because it was believed that support from the United States might make the foreign minister a strong candidate, Padilla continued to attract the wrath of his opponents through the first half of 1945, as he took on prominent roles as the host of the inter-American foreign ministers' meeting that was held at Chapultepec Castle in February and March and later in the spring as the Mexican delegate to the San Francisco Conference that resulted in the creation of the United Nations.[51]

The constant criticism took its toll on Padilla's viability as a presidential candidate, but it is worth noting that his credibility as a contender for the office was entirely a product of Mexico's involvement in World War II. The fact that he was charged with managing the country's ties with the rest of the world during a period of international crisis arguably gave him a higher profile in domestic politics than any Mexican foreign minister has enjoyed before or since. The foreign ministry was not then and is not now seen as a springboard to the Mexican presidency, but Padilla's aspirations to succeed Ávila Camacho were taken seriously by his rivals because the international situation had allowed him to play such an important part in the nation's life under Ávila Camacho.

Another development that would influence the pre-electoral political landscape was the sudden death of Maximino Ávila Camacho in February 1945. During the first half of Manuel Ávila Camacho's term in office, it was widely rumored that the volatile communications minister intended to succeed his younger brother as president. The elder Ávila Camacho was a political force in his own right, having served from 1937 until 1941 as governor of Puebla, where he continued to cast a long shadow over local politics. When a delegation of senators informed Maximino that Manuel would be the official candidate for president in 1940, he reportedly exploded at the news that he had been passed over in favor of his less politically experienced sibling. In a rage, Maximino was said to have called his portly brother a "steak with eyes," while asserting his own claim to the presidency as "the governor of a state as important as Puebla which before was a nest of scorpions and which now I have perfectly controlled."[52] Maximino soon calmed down, but even after he accepted the lucrative post of secretary of communications and public works in his brother's cabinet, reports continued to circulate that he still hoped to reach Los Pinos. His efforts in late 1942 and early 1943 to engineer favorable coverage of himself and negative coverage of potential rivals, such as Padilla, in the pages of the weekly magazine *Hoy*, which he subsidized, and his interest in setting up a newspaper of his own fuelled these reports, as did his failure to disavow an intention to run for president.[53] By early May 1943, Ambassador Messersmith, along with many other observers within Mexico, took it as "very certain that General Maximino has presidential ambitions."[54]

However, even if the Mexican political class could be convinced to allow one brother to succeed another as president, Maximino's candidacy would have been fraught with difficulties. He had no chance of winning the support of the left, which he had alienated through his harsh treatment of labor unions in Puebla and through his continuing references to figures such as Lombardo Toledano as "professional agitators."[55] His presidential hopes were also not helped by the fact that he was known as an unbalanced man with a violent temper; Messersmith at one point worried "that he is really in some respects quite a psychopathic case and not quite responsible."[56] Moreover, he had distinguished himself as the most visibly corrupt government official in a period of rampant corruption. "It can hardly be denied that the public and private actuation of don Maximino is little short of scandalous," a U.S. embassy analyst wrote in 1943, adding that the "Ávila Camacho nest is being feathered in a large and imposing way."[57] In May 1943, perhaps recognizing that his political maneuvering was futile or at least premature, Maximino told the press that he would "not be a candidate for the presidency of the Republic," but he added that he would "be in a position where I can see to it that the general interests of the country remain in the hands of men whose ambition is the national welfare, who are not professional politicians and who do not have merely personal interests."[58] In light of this declaration that he would seek to influence the selection of the next president, and in light of the possibility that he might ultimately jump back into the fray himself, the communications minister's death on February 17, 1945, worked to the advantage of other aspirants to the presidency whose candidacies Maximino had opposed.[59]

One such individual was Manuel Ávila Camacho's powerful interior minister, Miguel Alemán Valdés. Rumors that Maximino and Alemán were at odds had been heard since at least 1943, and Finance Minister Eduardo Suárez later wrote that in his opinion Alemán might not have prevailed as the official candidate if the president's brother had lived.[60] When San Luis Potosí governor Gonzalo Santos sought—at Manuel Ávila Camacho's request—to convince Maximino to abandon any remaining presidential aspirations around the beginning of 1945, the communications minister said that he would, but he angrily swore that "the bandit Miguel Alemán" would "not become president of the Republic, because I am going to kill him."[61]

Maximino might have created problems for Alemán on the campaign trail, to be sure, but it is likely that the young Veracruz politician would have been in a strong position to make a bid for the presidency in any event, in part because of his close relationship with the incumbent— he had served as Ávila Camacho's campaign manager in 1940—but also because of the keen understanding of the country's political landscape that he had been able to develop as interior minister. His control over the government's intelligence services gave him an insight into political trends in Mexico that no other aspirant to the presidency could have. Moreover, because the official internal security apparatus grew during the early 1940s in response to the possibility of wartime subversion and espionage, Mexican participation in World War II served to enhance Alemán's clout and authority. With the country at war, many intelligence and law enforcement functions that had previously been spread among different agencies were placed under the control of the interior minister. For example, a secret service bureau that had been established to combat smuggling was transferred from the treasury ministry to Gobernación.[62] Moreover, the interior ministry's own relatively small Office of Political and Social Information grew to become a more active General Directorate of Political and Social Investigations (DGIPS), and Alemán later recalled that "a special security group was created to respond to the necessities derived from the war, specifically with respect to the protection of the president of the Republic and the investigations intended to prevent possible acts of sabotage." This office would later be converted into the Federal Directorate of Security, which became notorious for its involvement in the repression of guerrilla and other opposition groups during the 1960s, 1970s, and 1980s.[63]

The need to monitor and control the movements of enemy aliens who lived in Mexico also contributed to an expansion of the scope of the interior ministry's functions during the Second World War. Much to the consternation of the U.S. embassy, ministry officials, presumably including Alemán, found that they could build war chests with which to finance future political endeavors by accepting bribes in exchange for permits allowing Axis nationals to avoid resettlement in Mexico City or detention in a concentration camp at Perote, Veracruz.[64] In this respect, too, the war strengthened Alemán's political position. Furthermore, the fact that his ministry oversaw the country's electoral machinery meant that many recently installed legislators and state governors owed their positions in part to Alemán's assistance. The particularly active role taken by the Ávila Camacho administration in screening candidates for lower-level office and in insisting on "single candidates" for such positions in order to maintain a calm political atmosphere during wartime meant that these officials were even more beholden to Alemán than they would have been if the international situation had not created the perception that a state of emergency existed in Mexico.[65] The interior minister therefore would be able to rely on their support if he were to seek higher office.

Alemán's chances of emerging as the official candidate for president in 1946 were greatly enhanced by a sense in political circles that it was time for a civilian to take power in Mexico. But despite the growing consensus that the next president should not be a military officer, which arose largely as a result of Ávila Camacho's wartime drive to professionalize and depoliticize the armed forces, many still believed that power would remain in the hands of a general, as it had been since the Mexican Revolution. Some military leaders favored Undersecretary of Defense Francisco Urquizo as a possible presidential candidate, but the officer who appeared to have the greatest chance of making a successful run for the presidency was the commander of the Guadalajara-based Fifteenth

Military Zone, Miguel Henríquez Guzmán, who was seen as the preferred candidate of the left wing of the PRM.

Speculation about Henríquez Guzmán's possible presidential ambitions had been rampant since at least November 1943, when the general
found it necessary to deny rumors that the war games he had then organized in Jalisco represented an effort to draw attention to himself and
to enhance his political prospects. The zone commander told the press
then that he had no intention of "mixing myself up in untimely political
agitation," as doing so would constitute "treason against the President of
the Republic and against my duties."[66] Nonetheless, insiders continued
to view Henríquez Guzmán as the figure most likely to win the backing
of Cárdenas and his allies in the upcoming elections. Therefore, when
the general embarked on a three-month-long goodwill tour of Central
and South America in August 1944, the trip was widely seen as having
been intended to raise his profile as a possible candidate for the presidency.[67] Upon his return to Mexico in November, Henríquez Guzmán
declined to offer any indication that he intended to seek public office,
saying simply that he was "a soldier in the service of the President of
the Republic" and that it was his duty "only to observe and to obey."
But reports in the press openly referred to the general as a "possible
presidential candidate," and they devoted more attention to his refusal
to discuss political matters than to anything he said about his travels.[68]

Despite Ávila Camacho's best efforts to keep pre-electoral political
agitation to a minimum for as long as he could, it became impossible to
prevent the initiation of open campaigning for the presidency as World
War II came to a close. Early in June 1945, less than a month after
Germany's unconditional surrender had ended the fighting in Europe,
Alemán left the cabinet in order to launch his candidacy.[69] Behind the
scenes, the interior minister had already secured the backing of key
sectors within the official party by the time he submitted his resigna-
tion on June 4. In a private meeting in Cuernavaca on April 23, Alemán
had spoken with Cárdenas about his political plans, and although the
influential ex-president reportedly was sympathetic to the candidacy of
General Henríquez Guzmán, he gave the interior minister an oblique
blessing. After Alemán told the defense minister of the expressions of
support that he had been receiving, Cárdenas replied that he "was doing
well by not acting rashly and by keeping a serene attitude, waiting for the
national feeling to manifest itself, taking care to maintain revolutionary

unity for the good of the social interests of the country, in a form that will permit the international problems that the war presents to be confronted."[70] While Cárdenas might well have favored Henríquez Guzmán over Alemán, his interest in "revolutionary unity" meant that he would not stand in the way if "the national feeling" were "to manifest itself" in his favor.

Meanwhile, Vicente Lombardo Toledano was working to build up the appearance of strong "national feeling" in favor of Alemán by lining up support for the interior minister among the heads of labor and agrarian organizations. The labor leader reportedly told those of his colleagues who were reluctant to commit themselves to a candidate more than a year before the 1946 elections that they had little choice but to back Alemán if they did not want to lose prestige and clout during the next sexenio, inasmuch as the interior minister already had the support of twenty-two of the country's thirty-one state and territorial governors.[71] The labor sector therefore sought to ingratiate itself with Alemán by proclaiming him as their candidate for the presidency at the Third Extraordinary National Council of the CTM on June 6, thereby initiating his campaign. Not wanting to be left behind, the federation of public sector labor unions (the FSTSE), the agrarian sector of the official party (the CNC), and its recently formed "popular" sector (the CNOP, incorporating bureaucrats, students, professionals, and other groups) soon added endorsements of their own.[72]

As much as Ávila Camacho might have wished for a few more months free from the distractions of political campaigning, when the leaders of these organizations informed him on June 4 that they had all agreed on Alemán as their candidate, the president told them that he was pleased by the unity of the revolutionary sectors.[73] His pleasure was no doubt sincere, inasmuch as a strong consensus behind a single candidate would likely diminish the intensity of electoral agitation, which might otherwise be quite disruptive. Moreover, unity in the ranks of the official party diminished the likelihood of a strong showing by rightist groups. As a U.S. intelligence analyst noted, the anointment of Alemán was "the result of a general effort by pro-government elements to avoid internal party conflicts on which the opposition could capitalize," inasmuch as a "conflict between President Avila Camacho and ex-President Cárdenas over the candidacies of Miguel Alemán and General Henríquez Guzmán (the latter reported to have been the initial choice of Cárdenas), would undoubtedly have strengthened the right." Furthermore, by settling on a "mildly liberal," pragmatic figure like Alemán, who was not seen as a radical leftist, the party could assure itself of some measure of support from Mexican industrialists and businessmen as well as from the labor, agrarian, and popular groups that were pledging themselves to him.[74]

The strong momentum with which the Alemán campaign got under way surprised many observers. Certainly some of his potential rivals were caught off guard. The governor of the Federal District, Javier Rojo Gómez, who had been lining up support for a presidential bid among certain left-leaning elements, quickly abandoned the field in the name of party unity. Miguel Henríquez Guzmán also reacted to the surging *alemanista* juggernaut by renouncing his presidential aspirations, but he made it clear that he was not leaving the race entirely of his own accord. Having been told by Ávila Camacho that "as a functionary he would ensure that the rights of all candidates are respected [*hará que se den ganantías a todos los candidatos*] but that as the friend of his that he is, he advises him not to contend in the political struggle," Henríquez Guzmán withdrew from the race, saying that he did not intend to go against the wishes of the president, especially with "the country finding itself in a state of war." He also told the press, however, that he would not run for president because official pressure was being exerted on behalf of Alemán, making a democratic contest impossible.[75]

The withdrawal of Rojo Gómez and Henríquez Guzmán from the campaign trail left Padilla as the only figure within the ranks of the administration who could be considered a likely challenger, but the foreign minister found himself in a difficult position after it became clear that Alemán had established such a formidable base of support. In June 1945 Padilla was serving as the Mexican delegate to the San Francisco Conference, at which talks to determine the structure of the new United Nations organization were being held. To be sure, his role at the forum in which the postwar order would be defined raised his profile in Mexico, and Alemán later admitted that "he had feared that the President would be so impressed by Padilla's international prestige that he would switch" his support to the foreign minister.[76] However, when Alemán responded to the threat posed by Padilla's perceived ascendancy by taking the initiative in declaring his candidacy—with the support of Lombardo Toledano, who might also have been reacting in part to signs of Padilla's high standing abroad that he observed while attending an international labor convention in Oakland that was running parallel to the intergovernmental conference across the bay—Padilla's absence from Mexico limited his ability to mobilize political support and to stem the alemanista tide at home.[77]

Moreover, Padilla's pro–United States stance at the international conference left him open to bitter criticism from the Mexican left, which was becoming markedly more willing to denounce U.S. "imperialism" as World War II wound down and as early signs of tension between Washington and Moscow began to appear. When Padilla backed a motion that would have given the chairmanship of the conference to the United States as the meeting's host country, he was drawn into a sharp exchange with Soviet foreign minister Molotov, who insisted that the chairmanship rotate between the leading Allied powers. General Guzmán Cárdenas, who was at the conference as a Mexican military representative, was evidently disgusted that the incident had made his country appear to be a servile instrument of the United States. Although he himself had long favored close cooperation with Washington, Guzmán Cárdenas shared a left-leaning, nationalist political outlook with his boss at the defense ministry, and he reported to Cárdenas that the matter had been handled in a way that was contrary to Mexican interests.[78] Later in the conference, Padilla advocated the admission of Argentina to the United Nations, which gave another vote to a U.S.-led bloc of Latin American countries in the new world body. With the Soviet Union opposing the inclusion of the Buenos Aires regime on the grounds that it had fascist leanings and had failed to break with the Axis until the final months of the war, Mexican leftists attacked the foreign minister for supporting the proposal for Argentine membership.[79]

Disillusioned by Alemán's strong early showing as a presidential candidate and by Ávila Camacho's failure to support him in the face of the withering attacks to which he was being subjected, Padilla resigned from the cabinet upon his return to Mexico in early July, citing a need "to disconnect himself from all official positions in order to explain and defend the international policy of Mexico against its detractors."[80] At the time, he disavowed any intention of running for the presidency, though he remained watchful for any opening that might allow him to enter the contest against Alemán.

The U.S. embassy was also taken by surprise when Alemán quickly emerged as a prohibitive favorite in the race to succeed Ávila Camacho.

In April, Messersmith had written that Alemán's candidacy "does not seem to be viewed with much favor, because he is considered too political by many people and not fixed enough in his convictions and one who would be swayed too much by opportunistic considerations." While the president might have "given certain encouragement to Alemán," Messersmith said, the interior minister knew "that he cannot have the support of Cárdenas and Lombardo Toledano," as they were supposedly committed to Henríquez Guzmán.[81] When Lombardo Toledano and the CTM kicked off Alemán's campaign, the U.S. ambassador reported that news of their endorsement "came as a bombshell," since leftist support for the former interior minister "was one of the most unexpected developments which could have taken place."[82] Messersmith was deeply troubled by the fact that Alemán already appeared to be assured of victory in 1946. Though he claimed to have "no fixed views" on Alemán, the ambassador clearly had been unimpressed with his record as interior minister.[83] Messersmith recalled that Alemán had been "very obstructive" in certain areas and that "his attitude towards Germans has been a very questionable one from the beginning."[84] Moreover, he worried that Alemán—whom he considered to be a person "of mediocre qualities with little knowledge of Mexico's internal problems and no knowledge really of foreign relations"—would be subject to the influence of Lombardo Toledano and other untrustworthy leftists.[85] "Irrespective of Alemán, and whatever capacities he may have," Messersmith wrote in July, "when one considers who his fellow-travelers are and what they represent, one cannot but have misgivings for the future."[86]

Despite the ambassador's increasing despair at the prospect of an Alemán presidency, however, State Department officials in Washington concluded that his election would not pose a serious threat to U.S. interests. The head of the department's Mexico desk wrote that while his office "has no illusions concerning Alemán's integrity, it is not of the opinion at this time that, should Alemán win out, he would make a poor President from the point of view of our national interest," in part because "he is too astute a politician not to 'play ball' with us."[87] On the other hand, while Messersmith was clearly sympathetic to the presidential aspirations of his friend Ezequiel Padilla—and those sympathies certainly played a major role in his efforts to discredit Alemán—the ambassador's superiors at Foggy Bottom wondered if the foreign minister's "somewhat austere lack of mob appeal" would make it impossible for him to be a successful, popular president. Although Padilla had been "friendly" and "loyal" to the United States, "if his administration were unpopular, it would not turn out as much to our advantage as a popular administration which might be somewhat less friendly toward us," the Office of Mexican Affairs concluded.[88]

In any event, both Messersmith and the State Department bureaucracy in Washington agreed that no effort should be made to influence the course of the Mexican election campaign, whatever their preferences might be.[89] This determination constituted a major setback for Padilla. Since the foreign minister lacked a significant domestic following, his connections to the U.S. government were among his most important political assets, and he tried his best to use them to his advantage. Indeed, when Padilla visited Washington after the conclusion of the San Francisco Conference, State Department officials reported that "he was determined to discuss politics with the President." Since the department had decided to maintain its policy of noninterference in the Mexican electoral process, however, Assistant Secretary of State Nelson Rockefeller dissuaded him from raising such topics in his meeting with Truman.[90]

On the other hand, the U.S. government's decision to remain on the sidelines surely came as a great relief to Alemán, though he was never quite convinced that Washington really would remain neutral. In a September 1944 conversation with U.S. diplomat Guy Ray, Alemán had demonstrated his concern that the United States might effectively block his candidacy. During that encounter, the interior minister had referred to "speculation as to what candidate the United States would pick as its favorite," prompting the U.S. embassy official to state "that the United States has no favorite and will not have one" and that "Ambassador Messersmith believes firmly in refraining from interfering in Mexican politics." Though it was hardly to be expected that Ray would characterize his government's policy toward Mexico's internal affairs in any other way, Alemán reportedly "was delighted" that Ray "had made such a categoric statement," since he apparently "feared the United States did not look upon him with favor as a possible presidential candidate."[91]

In another conversation with Ray a year later, with his campaign under way, Alemán admitted that he still believed that "the United States would prefer to see Padilla elected." During their discussion, the candidate "seemed to be strongly desirous of receiving assurances that the United States would not intervene either directly or indirectly,"

Figure 19: Members of the Mexican Expeditionary Air Force are met by the daughter of the Mexican consul in Manila, in traditional Mexican dress, upon their arrival in the Philippines. (National Archives and Records Administration)

Ray reported. In an effort to convince the U.S. government not to take sides, Alemán told Ray that he would maintain friendly relations with Washington, and he pledged that figures such as Lombardo Toledano would play no significant role in his administration, despite their prominence in his campaign.[92] As the East-West tensions deepened in the months that followed, Alemán went further, promising that "under no conditions would he accept in his Government any Communists" and that "Mexico would immediately declare war against Russia" if a conflict were to break out between the United States and the Soviet Union.[93] Alemán's repeated efforts to get across to the U.S. government "that he is friendly to us, that he will not side with Russia, and that the elections in July will be free and honest" demonstrate the importance of the international environment to the political transition that was occurring in Mexico as World War II ended and as the postwar period began.

Fortuitously for President Ávila Camacho, open campaigning for the 1946 presidential election began almost precisely at the same time that the Mexican Expeditionary Air Force flew its first combat missions in

Figure 20: The Mexican flag is raised over Clark Field, Squadron 201's base in the Philippines. (National Archives and Records Administration)

the Philippines. Just as political passions began to rise in Mexico, the exploits of Squadron 201 gave the government another opportunity to insist on unity and solidarity. On June 11, 1945, Mexico City newspapers published a message from General Douglas MacArthur reporting that the Mexican aviators in the Far East were actively engaged in operations against Japanese forces. Thus, within a week after Alemán had announced his candidacy for the presidency and his rivals Rojo Gómez and Henríquez Guzmán had dropped out of the running, the Mexican people received a timely reminder that their country was at war. Hailing the heroism and sacrifice of the airmen on the front lines, *El Universal* called upon Mexicans to "make our Fatherland—which is their Fatherland—a place where concord and brotherhood reign" and to "make a supreme effort—above all passions and baseness—in order that all our works might be directed, above all things, toward the greater glory of Mexico." In what must have been read as a clear reference to the political machinations then under way, *El Universal*'s editorial concluded that by doing otherwise, "continuing in our sterile conflict, moved by low appetites and mean interests, we would be defrauding those who carry in the war the weight of fatigue and the honor of our flag."[94]

Figure 21: Pilots of the Mexican Expeditionary Air Force in front of their P-47 fighter planes. (National Archives and Records Administration)

Two days later, after word reached Mexico of the squadron's first casualty—Sub-Lieutenant Fausto Vega Santander, killed when his plane went down during a June 1 dive-bombing mission—the official government newspaper, *El Nacional*, cited the sad news as "a formidable alert, in order that we might at every moment keep the state of war present and burning" in our minds. The organ of the administration then sought to use the tragic incident to inspire patriotism, comparing the sacrifice of Vega Santander to that rendered by the famous "Boy Heroes" (Niños Héroes) of 1847 and reminding its readers that Squadron 201 was fighting for "the honor, the dignity of Mexico," in fulfillment of the decision made by the Mexican "government and people, to fight, to defend itself, to make common cause with our democratic brothers and friends of the world."[95] A commentator in *El Universal* added that with the death of Vega Santander, Mexico "begins to be indebted to our brave aguiluchos," expressing the hope that the pilot's actions and those of his comrades might serve as a "severe, but magnificent and luminous" example to their compatriots at home.[96]

Mexican newspapers and radio broadcasters provided strongly favorable coverage of the actions of the squadron in the weeks that followed.

The media emphasized that the Mexican aviators were being entrusted with difficult assignments requiring considerable skill and that they were performing successfully.[97] Positive reports continued to appear even as word of additional deaths reached the country. After another pilot was killed in June and three more were lost in July, the U.S. military attaché's office noted with some surprise that despite the grief felt by the public, the general reaction to the news had been "more or less fatalistic" and "stoical." There had been "an acceptance of losses comparable with a people who have long been engaged in an extended war," the report concluded, and the public manifested an "obvious pride" in the fact that Mexican blood had been shed "as proof of their participation and engagement as an Allied Nation of a victorious and powerful coalition."[98] The participation of Squadron 201 in the fighting in the Pacific theater apparently gave many Mexicans a consciousness of their country's role in the war that had largely been lacking before the unit went into action.

While the FAEM was still flying combat missions during the final weeks of the war, Ávila Camacho took the opportunity to make another push forward in his efforts to modernize the country's armed forces and to remove them from the political sphere. Speaking at the graduation ceremony of the Escuela Superior de Guerra on July 2, 1945, the president declared an end to the era of the caudillo, the military strongman, in Mexican politics, and he announced plans to introduce a bill that would reorganize the army, eliminating hundreds of generals and colonels from the ranks. Such a move would allow upward mobility for younger officers with professional military training while older, more politically active generals, many of whom had joined the army during the Revolution, would be retired. Reporting on Ávila Camacho's speech, Messersmith noted that under Ávila Camacho there had been "a constant tendency to divorce the Army from politics," which had been driven by the president. While the administration's efforts to diminish the political clout of the armed forces had not been widely remarked upon by the population at large, "the President has now made it clear to the nation that the Army will abstain from politics and that the point has been reached where this can definitely be said by the head of the State." The U.S. ambassador concluded that "the fact that so thoroughgoing a reform and reorganization can be carried through peacefully and without reactions in this country . . . is perhaps the most striking proof of the fundamental changes which have been taking place in the country in

Figure 22: Members of the Mexican Expeditionary Air Force inspecting their weaponry in the Philippines. (National Archives and Records Administration)

recent years."[99] Indeed, it is difficult to imagine that it would have been possible for Ávila Camacho to propose such a radical restructuring of the Mexican military establishment if the country's participation in World War II had not already given impetus to reorganization initiatives and to a reorientation of the army's priorities, with a greater emphasis being placed on mastery of modern equipment, strategy, and tactics.

Ávila Camacho ultimately refrained from sending a military reorganization bill to Congress after its session began in the fall, however. With the political landscape already complicated by pre-electoral campaigning and maneuvering, he apparently judged it unwise to introduce such a significant piece of legislation. He might also have feared nationalist criticism of the reorganization plans drawn up by a defense ministry commission, which called for a restructuring of the armed forces such that their components would correspond more closely with those of the U.S. military. Nonetheless, the president's call for a more modern army and his public advocacy of the complete removal of the military from politics had their intended effects. Even many of the generals and colonels who faced forced retirement as a result of the reorganization initiative did not openly oppose the plan. An interior ministry investigator charged with gauging the reaction in military circles to Ávila Camacho's speech found that many senior officers accepted that fact that those of them who "are already veterans need to be replaced and to rest, leaving our places to those who arrive full of vigor and energy."[100] Ambassador Messersmith also observed that the "so-called political Generals" realized that "a new phase in the development of the Mexican Army" was under way and that "they had to conform."[101] World War II thus brought about a change in the structure and outlook of the Mexican armed forces that was not reversed even after the conflict ended.

When the war did come to an end in August 1945, the Ávila Camacho administration hailed the Allied victory as a great triumph for Mexico and for the democracies of the world. Ceremonies marking the conclusion of the global conflict sought to inspire patriotism and loyalty to the government by reinforcing the message that Mexico had played an important part in the war and by stressing that national unity would continue to be needed to confront the challenges of the postwar era. On August 15, one day after President Truman announced the Allied powers' acceptance of Japan's unconditional surrender, Ávila Camacho reminded the public once more of Mexico's direct role in the defeat of the Axis powers by releasing the text of a telegram he had sent to the Mexican squadron in the Philippines. In that missive, Ávila Camacho commended the FAEM for uniting "the name of Mexico forever with the great victory of liberty that is celebrated today," and he noted "the gratitude with which the Mexican Government and people have received the pages of glory which your heroism and your blood wrote upon the skies of the Pacific."[102]

That same day, Ávila Camacho directed a congratulatory message to the Mexican people and to the country's allies at a large public rally, and in the evening, he reviewed a parade of thousands of students, conscripts, and workers who marched through the streets of the capital to celebrate V-J Day.[103] Speaking to the crowd assembled at the end of the parade route, in the Zócalo, the president announced that new tasks would require the same dedication, perseverance, and solidarity that had been necessary during wartime. Mexicans would now have to take up a "more arduous, more beautiful assignment," he said. They would have to contribute to the struggle to build a better society "with the same courage and the same firmness" that had been shown by the fallen "heroes, whether anonymous or famous, who made possible the triumph that we celebrate."[104]

When he delivered his annual report to the legislature a fortnight later, on September 1, Ávila Camacho again cited the need for continued discipline and adherence to the program of his government. Although he could no longer justify his insistence on unity with references to any clear and present danger associated with wartime, the president asserted that any failure to remain loyal to the principles of the Mexican Revolution— as defined by his regime—would constitute a betrayal of the principles for which the Second World War had been fought. "To interrupt the program of the Revolution would be not only to erase thirty-five years of our life and more than a century of our history," he said, "but also [it would be] to lose the war that the democracies won and to lose it in our country, to lose it ourselves," for the Revolution, like World War II, had been based on "the purest universal principles." Not only was unity still necessary, he argued, but also, "our union, in order to be Mexican, must be revolutionary," because in a country in which "the great majority still suffers from ignorance and hunger," the Revolution represented "a collective and ardent thirst for redemption." Jaime Torres Bodet, who had drafted the concluding section of Ávila Camacho's speech, later reflected on the purpose of this passage. "It was indispensable," the education minister wrote, "to remind Mexicans that, if the war had ended, the revolutionary process, within an institutional regime, had not."[105]

These calls for solidarity and a recommitment to the ideals of the Revolution as a continuation of Mexico's commitment to the Allied cause came as the facade of national unity began to crack in the weeks after the close of the war. Lázaro Cárdenas, who had subordinated himself to his successor's policies during wartime despite his own opposition to Mexican participation in World War II, left the cabinet as soon as the fighting ended, handing the defense ministry over to his deputy, General Francisco L. Urquizo, on August 31. It had long been rumored that the former president wanted to step down from his post so that he would be able to enjoy greater political independence. As early as September 1943, Cárdenas had confided to his friend Francisco Castillo Nájera that he wished to leave the defense ministry, inasmuch as he found his position there "very uncomfortable." Cárdenas told Castillo Nájera that he considered himself a political liability to the administration, but Ávila Camacho clearly did not share this view; when told of Cárdenas's desire to give up his cabinet portfolio, the president "did not hide his annoyance," and he said that would convince his predecessor to change his mind.[106] Cárdenas also recorded in his diary that he had attempted to resign in October 1944.[107] As long as Mexico remained a belligerent at war with foreign powers, however, Ávila Camacho was able to prevail upon the dutiful defense minister to remain in his cabinet.

When Cárdenas took the opportunity provided by the end of the war to return to private life, his old friend Francisco Múgica, a fellow left-leaning nationalist then serving as governor of the territory of Baja California Sur, congratulated him "because you return to being a free man," and many wondered if he would become active in the pre-electoral political machinations then taking place.[108] Rumors also circulated that Miguel Henríquez Guzmán would revive his aborted bid for the presidency now that the war was over, since he had cited the fact that the country was at war as one of the reasons he had decided to abandon his candidacy in June.[109] By stressing the need for revolutionary unity and emphasizing the regime's continuing concern with those who "still suffer from ignorance and hunger," Ávila Camacho aimed to limit the intensity of the pressure that his administration and the official party might face from leftists led or inspired by Cárdenas or Henríquez Guzmán.

A more direct threat to Ávila Camacho's vision of postwar national unity behind an institutional revolutionary regime emerged on September 2, when Ezequiel Padilla revealed his intention to run for the presidency. The former foreign minister seized upon the president's vague but favorable references to Mexican international policy during his annual report to the legislature as a vindication of his work in the cabinet, and he let it be known that he was prepared to stand against the official machinery that was being mobilized on behalf of Miguel Alemán. The recently concluded global conflagration served as the backdrop for Padilla's announcement, just as it had for Ávila Camacho's address to Congress. But while the president had argued that the nation should build upon its wartime experience by rededicating itself to the principles of its revolution—and, he implied, by rejecting political alternatives that did not represent "revolutionary" values—Padilla asserted that Mexico, as a victorious Allied power, should strike a blow for democracy by thwarting the efforts of the ruling party to "impose" the former interior minister upon the country as its next president.[110] "Democracy victorious in war cannot be defeated in peace," he said, adding that "it would be ironical for Mexico, which fought for democracy, not to know how to consecrate itself by putting it into practice."[111]

Recognizing that Alemán had essentially locked up the support of the official establishment and its mass organizations, Padilla had little choice but to launch his campaign as an opposition figure. He therefore lashed out against the corruption and fraud that helped to sustain the PRM in power, courting the support of conservative groups that had long reviled him for his anticlericalism in the 1920s and his pro-Americanism as foreign minister.[112] These groups remained suspicious of him, however. The PAN noted that while Padilla was now telling the truth about the nature of the regime, it was not eager to back "a man who during so many years has lived and acted within that regime and within that system."[113] As a U.S. analyst reported, the former foreign minister unveiled a platform in late September that "essentially opposed continuation of the Mexican Revolutionary regime and invited the support of conservative commercial and landed interests" by putting "greater stress on the importance of private initiative for industrial development" and strongly opposing "excessive government intervention in the economy."[114] The Partido Democrático Mexicano that coalesced around his candidacy, formally nominating him at a convention in November, was made up of a disparate group of rightist ex-almazanistas (such as former PAM head Pedro Julio Pedreto) and individuals who had been on the losing side of some of the revolutionary infighting of the 1920s (such as former the *delahuertista* and *escobarista* Jorge Prieto Laurens). These groups were joined by a small number of former diplomats and prominent legislators, such as Senators Emilio Araujo of Chiapas and León García of San Luis Potosí, who backed Padilla's campaign out of personal loyalty to the former foreign minister or because they were dissatisfied with the political opportunities then available to them within the PRM.[115]

While this fragmented coalition was unlikely to prevail in the upcoming elections, its strident criticisms of the Mexican political system could potentially have undermined Ávila Camacho's efforts to promote national unity and social peace. Fortunately for the president, even after World War II was over he had one last chance to use Mexican participation in the conflict to rally his countrymen around the flag. When the men of FAEM returned home in November 1945, the government received them as conquering heroes, and by incorporating the aviators' arrival in the capital into the festivities surrounding the Anniversary of the Revolution holiday on November 20, the administration forged a significant symbolic link between Mexico's contribution to the defeat of the Axis and its commitment to the "revolutionary" project represented by the official party.

In the weeks and months between the end of the fighting in the Far East and the return of Squadron 201 to Mexican soil, there were many signs that a substantial portion of the population was proudly looking forward to welcoming the members of the unit home. The Mexico City tabloid *La Prensa* announced its intention of staging a grand tribute of its own to the men who had represented the country in combat when they arrived in the capital, and for several weeks beginning in mid-August, the newspaper collected and published statements expressing admiration for the squadron from many sectors of Mexican society.[116] *La Prensa* also received from schoolchildren unsolicited pieces of artwork that celebrated the upcoming return of the aguiluchos to Mexico.[117] At the same time, individual citizens whose imaginations had been captured by the exploits of the fighter unit were sending directly to President Ávila Camacho poems, ballads, and, in one case, a design for a commemorative coin in honor of the squadron.[118] By the end of October, it was clear to U.S. analysts and to all other observers that the misgivings that many Mexicans had once felt with regard to participation in the war had disappeared and had been "replaced by outspoken and obvious pride."[119] It was upon these feelings of pride and patriotic enthusiasm that the administration hoped to build by staging a grand ceremony for the men of the FAEM upon their return.

To ensure that the reception accorded to the members of Squadron 201 would be sufficiently rapturous to inspire a burst of patriotism and to enhance the prestige of the government, the president instructed his defense minister to coordinate celebrations in honor of the unit throughout the republic. As the Mexican airmen traveled back to the United States en route to their homeland, General Urquizo sought the cooperation of the foreign ministry, the interior ministry, the navy ministry, and the indigenous affairs agency as preparations for the squadron's arrival were made, and he invited state governors to organize "commemorative festivities of patriotic exaltation which, besides stimulating civic virtues, might serve to strengthen the ties of unity between the Army and the civilian population."[120] In a letter to the governor of the Federal District, the defense minister asked that his department "participate intensely"

Figure 23: Admiring crowds greeted the train carrying members of Squadron 201 upon their return to Mexico. (Fototeca Nacional, Instituto Nacional de Antropología e Historia; © 202021 CONACULTA.INAH.SINAFO.FN.MÉXICO)

in the homage that was being prepared for the FAEM in the capital and that the city's buildings and public transportation vehicles be decorated on the occasion of the aviators' return.[121] Javier Rojo Gómez accordingly published "a kind invitation to the inhabitants of the city," asking them to "adorn the facades of their houses with the national colors" on the day the squadron was due to arrive.[122]

Defense Minister Urquizo also suggested to his counterpart at the education ministry that ceremonies in honor of the squadron be held at every public school in the country on the day of the unit's return to Mexico, "highlighting the transcendent nature of this historic step for our country, with the object of fomenting the civic spirit of the new generations."[123] The education ministry later reported that a large number of schools had organized programs to pay homage to the Mexican combat unit, and it sent to the defense ministry many of the speeches, poems, and songs that had been written for the occasion by schoolchildren and teachers.[124] And in case some Mexicans somewhere in the country somehow managed to miss the opportunity to have their civic virtues stimulated in person at one of the many events marking the return of Squadron 201 to Mexico, they could view a new motion picture

Figure 24: The return of the Mexican Expeditionary Air Force to their homeland generated real excitement and enthusiasm. "One does not hear or read of anything but the arrival of Squadron 201," wrote Salvador Novo. (Fototeca Nacional, Instituto Nacional de Antropología e Historia; © 202056 CONACULTA.INAH.SINAFO. FN.MÉXICO)

celebrating the unit's participation in the war. The film *Escuadrón 201*, produced by a private studio with the full cooperation and support of the defense ministry, premiered in Mexico City on November 26, 1945.[125]

Naturally, the most elaborate festivities celebrating the heroism of the FAEM were those that took place along the route of the squadron's triumphal return. The unit arrived by ship in the port of San Pedro, outside Los Angeles, California, on November 13, and it traveled by train to the U.S.-Mexico border at Laredo, Texas. After the crossing the Rio Grande on November 16, huge crowds greeted the aguiluchos in Nuevo Laredo, Saltillo, San Luis Potosí, and Querétaro as they slowly made their way toward Mexico City.[126] On the eve of the unit's arrival in the capital, the prominent *Novedades* commentator Salvador Novo wrote in his diary, "One does not hear or read of anything besides the arrival of Squadron 201," and the next day, as the airmen marched through the streets of the city, he remarked, "Interest in the 201st is at its peak."[127]

When the men of the squadron reached Mexico City's Buenavista Station on the morning of November 18, 1945, some twenty thousand

Figure 25: The Mexican Expeditionary Air Force on parade through the streets of Mexico City, November 1945. (Fototeca Nacional, Instituto Nacional de Antropología e Historia; © 117505 CONACULTA.INAH. SINAFO.FN.MÉXICO)

people were on hand to receive them, and thousands more cheered them as they proceeded to the Zócalo, where they symbolically returned their battle flag to the president. The official newspaper marveled at "the homage that thousands and thousands of people of all social classes paid to the valiant aguiluchos upon their arrival in the metropolis," concluding that the size and enthusiasm of the crowds had only been matched during "the historic events of the greatest significance that have [ever] occurred in this capital."[128] Though *El Nacional* might be suspected of exaggerating the excitement generated by the squadron's return, its reporters' account of a celebration that was a display of "overwhelming and affectionate joy" is confirmed by photographs showing large crowds showering streamers and confetti upon the men of the expeditionary force as they passed underneath arches erected for the occasion in downtown Mexico City.[129]

Two days later, at the official ceremony marking the anniversary of the start of the 1910 Revolution, Ávila Camacho bestowed medals on the members of the squadron before a large multitude in the National

Stadium. General Leobardo Ruiz, a senior official at the defense ministry, spoke in the name of the army, telling the aviators that they had had "the power to fulfill the fervent wish of the Head of the Nation: 'To make stronger the Unity of the Fatherland.'"[130] With Mexicans again momentarily unified by the pride they felt in their symbolic contribution to the Allied victory in World War II, the administration and the official party took advantage of the opportunity to call once more for a continuation of that unity in the postwar period. At the same time that the members of Squadron 201 were receiving their decorations from the president, the Partido de la Revolución Mexicana issued a statement calling on the people to "continue working in an untiring form with General Manuel Ávila Camacho, the President of the Republic, in the same form in which they have been doing to date inasmuch as the end of the war has not resolved the problems of an economic character that the second worldwide conflagration brought as a consequence."[131]

The regime was thus able to carry into the postwar period its insistence that Mexicans rally behind it to confront the challenges facing the country. After the FAEM was formally dissolved at the beginning of December 1945, official references to the country's role in the war became less frequent as Mexico settled into a new era, in which a new set of international conditions would help to shape the options available to Mexican administrations. However, the political and structural consequences of Mexican involvement in the Second World War had a significant long-term impact on the subsequent development of the country.

On July 7, 1946, less than eight months after the triumphant return of the men of the Mexican Expeditionary Air Force to their homeland, Miguel Alemán Valdés won election as president of Mexico for the 1946–1952 term. For the first time since the Revolution, the contest for the presidential chair had been between two civilian candidates. That fact, along with the contrast between the chaotic and bloody election day that Mexico had experienced in 1940 and the peaceful, orderly atmosphere that prevailed in 1946, seemed to confirm the extent to which Mexico had changed during the war years. Claims by supporters of Ezequiel Padilla that fraud had taken place and that they had been subject to intimidation were not entirely without foundation, to be sure, but the scale of the alleged irregularities was relatively small, and Alemán's margin of victory was substantial and convincing.[1]

The transfer of power from Ávila Camacho to Alemán on December 1, 1946, marked the beginning of a new era in Mexican history. For the rest of the century, Mexico would be led by civilian politicians representing the Partido Revolucionario Institucional (PRI). The fact that the Partido de la Revolución Mexicana had reconfigured itself as the PRI in January 1946 was another sign of the completion of a significant shift; the reconstituted party's name suggested that the Revolution was entering a new phase, one in which reform would occur in a more measured, gradual way, through institutional channels.

In the years that followed, the Mexican regime became more markedly conservative and authoritarian, even as it presided over a period of rapid industrialization and explosive economic growth. Alemán and his successors went further than Ávila Camacho in limiting the influence and independence of the once powerful labor unions, the expanded intelligence services took a more active role in monitoring and stamping out dissent, and those who dared to protest against the increasingly repressive character of the state often found themselves facing charges of "social dissolution." International conditions played a part in making possible this more open shift to the right; Cold War tensions between East and West created an environment in which crackdowns on leftist activity could be framed in terms of the alleged need to counter the threat to national sovereignty posed by global communism. To be sure, the regime faced significant challenges during the postwar decades: from an opposition presidential campaign by Henríquez Guzmán in 1952, from major strikes by teachers and railroad workers in the late 1950s and by doctors in the mid-1960s, and from guerrilla groups in the countryside, to name a few examples. However, with the "Mexican miracle" of sustained economic expansion bringing improved standards of living for many during these years, successive PRI administrations were generally able to maintain stability by continuing to claim the mantle of the Mexican Revolution, by dispensing patronage through clientelistic networks, by co-opting potential opponents, and, at times, by forcefully repressing dissent. It was only after the regime violently suppressed a student protest movement calling for reform in 1968, and after episodes of economic mismanagement and crisis in subsequent decades, that the PRI regime's claims to legitimacy were increasingly called into question.

As historians, political analysts, and individual citizens have reflected on the Mexican experience during the second half of the twentieth century, they have often not fully recognized the importance of the World War II era as the period in which the foundations of the PRI regime were laid. This tendency to underestimate the significance of the war years can be understood in part as a consequence of the subtlety with which Ávila Camacho managed Mexican political life during the early 1940s. While he was in office, "the gentleman president" was happy to cultivate a rather dull image of himself. After visiting Mexico in 1941, American journalist John Gunther described the president as being "about as colorful as a slab of halibut," calling him "steady, cautious, and efficient," and adding that the "key to his character is sobriety."[2] The contemporary Mexican press commented not on his charisma, his ideological dogmatism, or his personal magnetism, but rather on his "serenity."[3] Ávila Camacho himself once told a political associate that he had learned "that the president of the Republic does not have the right to become angry."[4] The president's reputation as a placid, reasonable man helped him to avoid open political conflict during the tumultuous years of his administration, even as he slowly and steadily steered the country in a more conservative direction. While Ávila Camacho's colorless persona thus served him well, his avoidance of dramatic political gestures has contributed to the neglect of his sexenio in the historical literature on modern Mexico.

It does not help that Ávila Camacho's predecessor and his successor were both dynamic, larger-than-life figures who have attracted far more attention. Cárdenas is widely remembered by Mexicans from all walks of life for nationalizing the country's oil industry in 1938 and for dramatically expanding the government's agrarian reform program, while Alemán also maintained a high profile as president, placing his name and his image on projects throughout the country and taking a leading role in the so-called *charrazo*, through which an independent labor movement was crushed. Furthermore, while Cárdenas, who died in 1970, and Alemán, who died in 1983, both remained towering figures in Mexican politics for decades after they left office, Ávila Camacho essentially withdrew from public view after giving up the presidential sash, and he died on October 13, 1955, less than nine years after completing his term. And while children and grandchildren of Cárdenas and Alemán have remained active in Mexican public life for decades after their forebears passed from the scene, the once formidable Ávila Camacho clan is no longer a highly visible political force, further limiting the amount of attention that is given to the war years relative to the immediate prewar and postwar periods.[5]

Another reason that the impact of World War II on Mexico has been largely forgotten is that Mexicans came to see their country's symbolic participation in the conflict as a somewhat ridiculous episode, rather than as part of a larger process that had a significant effect on the country's history. While the small role played by the FAEM in the fighting in the Philippines was a source of great national pride when the unit returned to Mexico in 1945, within a few years many had concluded that the once-celebrated exploits of Squadron 201 were of little consequence. Indeed, in 1949, when the commander of Mexico's air force proposed the erection of a monument to the pilots who died while serving overseas, the defense ministry general staff rejected out of hand the suggestion that the aviators should be designated as national heroes. Noting that a number of the fallen aguiluchos had perished in accidents, the ministry ruled that none of pilots had died "carrying out an act of extraordinary valor," and it scolded the air force leadership for having the audacity to compare the casualties of the FAEM with the revered Niños Héroes, the cadets who had died while defending Chapultepec Castle during the Mexican-American War in 1847. It was the Mexican "people who have consecrated them as national heroes," the general staff wrote, and the people had not given the same level of recognition to the men of Squadron 201. Moreover, the general staff's legal adviser added that the pilots who lost their lives in the Far East could not really be designated as having "died for the Fatherland," given that while "those who perished fighting against the totalitarianism of the powers of the Axis offered their lives for human liberty, it could be argued in [outlets of] public opinion that they did not die in defense of national sovereignty, that is, for the Fatherland."[6]

Meanwhile, the FAEM members who had been cheered in 1945 were ignored in later years. The government of the Federal District did grant land after the war to a group of enlisted men from the unit, but the area, still known today as Colonia Escuadrón 201, was occupied instead by squatters.[7] In 2003 a small number of aged FAEM veterans marched to the Zócalo in Mexico City, asking that the government set aside a day each year to commemorate their service and decrying the fact that they had been forgotten for nearly sixty years, with only the names of a neighborhood (Colonia Escuadrón 201) and a metro station (located in the colonia) serving as official reminders of their contribution to the fight against the Axis.[8]

Indeed, for decades the government did little to promote the memory of Mexico's role in the Second World War, perhaps because it did not wish to draw attention to the high level of cooperation with the United States that had characterized that period. While PRI administrations in the postwar period privately assured the United States of their steadfast anticommunism and welcomed U.S. investment within the framework of their import-substituting industrialization development strategy, they also reclaimed nationalist rhetoric as a political tool, stressing their independence from Washington rather than celebrating the closeness of their relationship with U.S. officials, as Ávila Camacho and Padilla had done. Miguel Alemán signaled that such a shift would take place when he told U.S. diplomat Guy Ray in September 1944 that "he was getting somewhat tired of the 'sugary' propaganda which had been distributed trying to convince Mexicans that they should love the United States." To be sure, Alemán hoped for a friendly relationship with the U.S. government; after all, he added, "we are geographically side by side and [I do] not know of any cure for such a situation." But Ávila Camacho's chosen successor would not spend time trying to convince the Mexican people they should like their neighbors. The key to good relations, he said, was not convincing Mexicans they should love the United States but rather it was "convincing both Mexicans and Americans that it was in their interest to cooperate."[9] With Alemán and his successors less eager to highlight Mexico's role as an ally of the United States during World War II, the country's participation in the conflict was largely forgotten, making it easy for analysts to overlook the significant effects that the war had on the Mexican political landscape.

But as this study has shown, the Second World War did bring important changes to Mexico. Most significantly, the delicate international situation gave increased political leverage to the chief executive, allowing him to strengthen the powers of the presidency and of the state more generally. The war permitted Ávila Camacho to call repeatedly for national unity, making it possible for him to paper over long-standing rifts within the official establishment. While factional infighting between members of the "revolutionary family" had been tamed somewhat by the establishment of the Partido Nacional Revolucionario in 1929 and the Partido de la Revolución Mexicana in 1938, it was only as a result of the global conflict in the early 1940s that a Mexican president was able to rally the full spectrum of actors within the ruling party behind his leadership. Important figures who might otherwise have commanded a potentially destabilizing independent political following, such as Lázaro Cárdenas, Plutarco Elías Calles, and Abelardo L. Rodríguez, were incorporated into the regime, ostensibly because the nation needed their services during wartime. The policy of national unity also helped the president to fend off the calls of the left and right for the destruction of their political adversaries, as he steered a middle course between the two ideological extremes.

Moreover, with Mexico formally taking part in the war as an Allied belligerent, Ávila Camacho had been able to insist upon the removal of the armed forces from the political sphere and the creation of a more professional military establishment. Paradoxically, the physical strengthening of the army actually diminished their political clout; with the latest implements of war arriving from the United States, Mexican officers increasingly abandoned their political ambitions, turning their attention instead to the technical challenges involved in organizing a modern military force. The war also helped to accelerate a generational shift that was under way within the military, as younger, professionally trained officers began to displace an older group of revolutionary generals who had traditionally been more heavily involved in political affairs. The isolation of the armed forces from politics facilitated the historic transition that took place in 1946 as a civilian, rather than a general, took office as president. A wartime concern with internal security had also greatly increased the size and clout of the interior ministry and of its intelligence apparatus. The strengthening of Gobernación helps to account for the fact that four of the next five Mexican presidents had served previously as interior minister.

Furthermore, Mexican participation in the war had prompted the country's labor movement to commit itself to a less adversarial relationship with industrialists and other employers, so that vital war production would not be slowed. Unions would find it difficult to escape this commitment even after the war was over. Indeed, in a "Labor-Industry Pact" engineered by Vicente Lombardo Toledano in September 1945, supposedly to ensure that the country's industrial development would continue at a rapid pace after the end of World War II, the CTM pledged "to renew, during the stage of peace, the *patriotic alliance* which we Mexicans have created and maintained during the war for the defense of the nation's independence and sovereignty, under the policy of national unity eulogized by the President General Manuel Ávila Camacho."[10] During the late 1940s, Ávila Camacho's successor would bring the labor movement even more firmly under control, subordinating its interests to the all-important goal of rapid economic growth.

Because Mexico was so far from the battlefields of World War II, and because its symbolic, direct contribution to the Allied cause was militarily so inconsequential, the importance of the conflict in the political history of the country has not been fully recognized, but as in other periods of Mexican development, the international situation during the early 1940s played a pivotal role in shaping political trends there. As *El Universal* had noted in 1942, the war brought a degree of peace to Mexico. Though ideological differences and internal political conflicts did not disappear during the war years, the global conflagration contributed to the consolidation of a stable regime that would dominate the country for decades to come. The relative stability and tranquility that Mexico enjoyed during the postwar period set the country apart from many of its Latin American neighbors, but the price paid for this peace was substantial, as Mexico would have to wait until the end of the century for the development of a political culture that could reasonably be described as democratic. To a greater extent than has been acknowledged, both the stability of the mid- to late twentieth-century Mexican political system and the authoritarian character of the PRI regime are legacies of the Second World War.

Introduction

1. "Seis frases para la historia," *El Universal*, September 16, 1942.

2. Diego Arenas Guzmán, "La guerra ha traído la paz a México," *El Universal*, September 16, 1942.

3. See "Brillantemente fue conmemorado el XXXV aniversario de la Revolución," *El Nacional*, November 22, 1945; "El P.R.M. hace un llamado," *El Nacional*, November 20, 1945; and other statements and accounts cited in chapter 6.

4. For an official review of the impact of the war on the Mexican economy, see Mexico, Secretaría de la Economía Nacional, *El desarrollo de la economía nacional*. The economic effects of the war are also discussed in Niblo, *The Impact of War*; and in Cline, *The United States and Mexico*, 284–91.

5. The impact of inflation on real wages during the war years was widely noted at the time and is documented in Bortz, *Industrial Wages in Mexico City*. The agreement with the United States establishing the bracero program, introduced in 1942, remained in effect until 1964.

6. On the development of the intelligence services, see especially Aguayo, *La charola*; and Navarro, *Political Intelligence*, chap. 4. On conscription, see Rath, "'*Que el cielo*,'" which judges the program to have been a failure. The connection between the war and the 1945–1946 National Campaign Against Illiteracy is discussed in chapter 6 and in Rankin, *¡México, la patria!*, 241–45.

7. For an analysis of the bases of Cárdenas's power, focusing on his coalition-building and political management skills, see Hernández Chávez, *La mecánica cardenista*. For an assessment of the radicalism and (and, in his view, limited) effectiveness of cardenista policies, see Knight, "Cardenismo."

8. On the confrontational relationship between Cárdenas and the country's top industrialists, see Saragoza, *The Monterrey Elite*, chap. 8. On education policy, see Lerner, *La*

educación socialista. Article 3 of the Mexican Constitution, as amended in 1934, mandated the provision of "socialist education." The precise meaning of *socialist* in this context was subject to debate, but it certainly meant that instruction should be secular. Under Ávila Camacho, Article 3 was eventually revised to eliminate the stipulation that education be "socialist." The text introduced in 1945 called for education to be "democratic," "national," "completely removed from any religious doctrine," and "based on the results of scientific progress." See Mexico, Secretaría de Gobernación, *Seis años de actividad nacional*, 104–5.

9. See Schuler, *Mexico Between Hitler and Roosevelt.*

10. On the evolution of and reforms to the PRM under Ávila Camacho, see especially Garrido, *El partido de la Revolución institucionalizada*, chap. 6. On the rise of the middle classes within the ruling party and the establishment of the "popular sector," see Bertaccini, *El regimen priísta.*

11. Recent studies that have illustrated some of the weaknesses of the regime through at least the 1940s include Navarro, *Political Intelligence*; Newcomer, *Reconciling Modernity*; Smith, *Pistoleros and Popular Movements*; and Padilla, *Rural Resistance in the Land of Zapata.* See the following notes for further discussion.

12. Benjamin, "The Leviathan on the Zócalo," 209.

13. Niblo, *Mexico in the 1940s*, xvii.

14. For examples of early works that tended to gloss over the war years and to focus more on the period of the "Mexican miracle," see Cline, *Mexico, Revolution to Evolution*; and Brandenburg, *The Making of Modern Mexico*. In his 1962 book and in *The United States and Mexico*, Cline did acknowledge the economic and political impact of the war, but he focused more on "the Institutional Revolution's increasingly fruitful years" under Alemán and his successors (*Revolution to Evolution*, 34). Brandenburg lumped the war years into a "Cárdenas and Ávila Camacho Epoch," thereby overlooking to some extent the important changes under way as a result of the war during the early 1940s.

15. Knight, "The Rise and Fall of Cardenismo." Other works that explored the political transition under way in the early 1940s in some depth include Medina, *Del cardenismo al avilacamachismo*; Torres, *México en la Segunda Guerra Mundial*; and Medina, *Civilismo y modernización del autoritarianismo*. Though these Colegio de México volumes recognized the importance of the period and of the role played by Ávila Camacho in the political transformation of the early 1940s, the structure of the series was such that international conditions and foreign relations on the one hand and domestic political developments on the other were treated somewhat separately.

16. The 2003 Ley Federal de Transparencia y Acceso a la Información Pública Gubernamental required government agencies to make their records available, and it created the Instituto Federal de Acceso a la Información (IFAI). During this period, the records of internal security agencies such as the Dirección Federal de Seguridad and the Dirección General de Investigaciones Políticas y Sociales

became accessible to researchers at the Archivo General de la Nación.

17. Paz Salinas, *Strategy, Security, and Spies.*

18. Rankin, *¡México, la patria!*; and Niblo, *Mexico in the 1940s*, 115. In a separate work, Niblo addressed the significance of the period for U.S.-Mexican relations; see Niblo, *War, Diplomacy, and Development.*

19. For works on electoral challenges during the 1940s and early 1950s, see, for example, Servín, *Ruptura y oposición*; and Navarro, *Political Intelligence.* For regional studies, see, for example, Newcomer, *Reconciling Modernity*; Smith, *Pistoleros and Popular Movements*; Padilla, *Rural Resistance in the Land of Zapata*; and Gillingham, "Military *Caciquismo* in the PRIísta State."

Chapter One

1. Lázaro Cárdenas statement, September 4, 1939, in Ramo Presidentes, Lázaro Cárdenas del Río (henceforth, "LC"), 550/46-6, Archivo General de la Nación, Mexico City (henceforth, "AGN").

2. Katz, "Mexico, Gilberto Bosques and the Refugees," 6.

3. Sindicato de Trabajadores de la Enseñanza de la República Mexicana to Lázaro Cárdenas, October 9, 1939, LC, 550/46-5, AGN.

4. Juan Negrete López to Lázaro Cárdenas, September 25, 1939, LC, 550/46-5, AGN.

5. Schuler, *Mexico Between Hitler and Roosevelt*, 143.

6. Cámara Nacional de Comercio e Industria, Celaya, Guanajuato, to Lázaro Cárdenas, September 7, 1939, and Asociación de Constituyentes de 1916–1917 to

Lázaro Cárdenas, September 5, 1939, both in LC, 550/46-5, AGN.

7. Ramón Beteta to Lázaro Cárdenas, transmitting message from Eduardo Hay, October 7, 1939, LC, 550/46-6, AGN.

8. Secretaría de Relaciones Exteriores bulletin, October 2, 1939, LC, 550/46-6, AGN.

9. Lázaro Cárdenas statement, "Contra la agresión," May 12, 1940, LC, 550/46-6, AGN; Lázaro Cárdenas to Albert Lebrum, June 11, 1940, LC, 550/46-2, AGN.

10. Lázaro Cárdenas statement, "Contra la agresión," May 12, 1940, LC, 550/46-6, AGN; Lázaro Cárdenas statement, May 22, 1940, reproduced in memorandum by Agustín Leñero, LC, 550/46-6, AGN.

11. Lázaro Cárdenas statement, December 5, 1939, LC, 550/115, AGN; Schuler, *Mexico Between Hitler and Roosevelt*, 143.

12. Lázaro Cárdenas to Elena Vázquez Gómez, June 21, 1940, in Cárdenas, *Epistolario de Lázaro Cárdenas*, 1:416.

13. Paz Salinas, *Strategy, Security, and Spies*, 22.

14. Ibid., 51–60. Castillo Nájera first met with U.S. military officials on June 11, 1940. A series of meetings between a small commission of Mexican military officers and their U.S. counterparts began on July 19, 1940, and continued through the fall and into the following year.

15. Dwyer, *The Agrarian Dispute*, chap. 8, describes how Mexican security cooperation helped to secure a favorable resolution to long-running disputes over agrarian claims.

16. "Resumen de lo que se dijo en la junta celebrada por el Presidente de

la República en el Palacio Nacional, el día 19 de junio de 1940," p. 8, LC, 550/46-8, AGN.

17. See Schuler, *Mexico Between Hitler and Roosevelt*, chap. 8; and Navarro, *Political Intelligence*, chap. 1.

18. "Red Aides Barred by Ávila Camacho," *New York Times*, September 20, 1940.

19. *Novedades*, December 4, 1940, transmitted in Josephus Daniels to Secretary of State, December 5, 1940, State Department Central File, 812.001 Camacho, Manuel A./88, Record Group (henceforth, "RG") 59, National Archives and Records Administration, College Park, Maryland (henceforth, "NARA").

20. "Garrido, lejos de la política," *El Universal*, March 16, 1941; and Buchenau, "Una ventana al más allá," 2.

21. Medina, *Del cardenismo al ávilacamachismo*, 133, 139.

22. "Defensa mutua de México y E. Unidos," *El Universal*, March 5, 1941.

23. "México define claramente su posición internacional," *El Universal*, March 8, 1941. For examples of clearly baseless propaganda asserting that Cárdenas and Ávila Camacho had signed a secret treaty compromising Mexican sovereignty in exchange for U.S. support for the incoming president, see "La venta de la nación," in General de Brigada J. Fernando Ramírez to Mayor Waldo Romo Castro, January 18, 1941, and "El precio del reconocimiento," in Dr. Carlos M. Jiménez Villa to Manuel Ávila Camacho, March 20, 1941, both in Ramo Presidentes, Manuel Ávila Camacho (henceforth, "MAC"), 549.11/4, AGN.

24. "México define claramente su posición internacional," *El Universal*, March 8, 1941.

25. Speech by Enrique Ramírez y Ramírez, February 21, 1941, transcribed in "Mitin celebrado por el Sindicato de Artes Gráficos en el Teatro Hidalgo de la Ciudad de México la noche del 21 de febrero de 1941," MAC, 133.2/12, AGN.

26. Arturo L. Velasco to Manuel Ávila Camacho, March 13, 1941, MAC, 133.2/12, AGN.

27. "La actitud de México ante los EE.UU.," *El Popular*, March 10, 1941. The editor of *El Popular*, Deputy Alejandro Carrillo, shared close ties with Lombardo, and the paper generally reflected the former CTM leader's views.

28. For an editorial in the mainstream press in praise of Padilla's performance, see "México y la lucha por la libertad," *El Universal*, March 10, 1941.

29. "Pacto con Washington sobre bases aereas," *Excélsior*, April 2, 1941; and Paz Salinas, *Strategy, Security, and Spies*, 64–66. For the text of the agreement and diplomatic correspondence concerning the pact, see Archivo Histórico, file III-1962-1, Secretaría de Relaciones Exteriores, Dirección General del Acervo Histórico Diplomático, Mexico City (henceforth, "SRE"). Importantly for Mexico, the terms of the agreement established that the transit of warplanes would be allowed only for the duration of the international emergency and that either country could cancel the accord at any time.

30. "Incaútase México 12 naves del Eje," *Excélsior*, April 9, 1941; "Ocupación y incautación de los barcos extranjeros inmovilizados en puertos mexicanos," in Mexico, Secretaría de Relaciones Exteriores, *Memoria de la Secretaría de Relaciones*

Exteriores, septiembre de 1940–agosto de 1941, 137–47; Cárdenas de la Peña, *Gesta en el Golfo,* 25–28. Cárdenas de la Peña lists the twelve ships seized. In October 1941, after being restricted to the city of Guadalajara for several months, the ships' German and Italian crewmen were briefly allowed freedom of movement, but expressions of concern from the United States and Great Britain prompted the Mexican government to confine the sailors to a facility in Perote. See "Mexico Frees Axis Crews," *New York Times,* October 21, 1941, and "Mexicans Arrest 4 Nazis as Spies," *New York Times,* March 7, 1942.

31. "Protesta por la invasión de Yugoeslavia y la agresión de Grecia," in Mexico, Secretaría de Relaciones Exteriores, *Memoria de la Secretaría de Relaciones Exteriores, septiembre de 1940–agosto de 1941,* 152.

32. Vicente Lombardo Toledano to Manuel Ávila Camacho, May 29, 1941, published in "Lombardo Toledano pide al Señor Presidente se dirija a los pueblos del continente dándoles a conocer el criterio de nuestro país ante los graves problemas internacionales del momento," *El Popular,* May 31, 1941.

33. Manuel Ávila Camacho to Vicente Lombardo Toledano, May 30, 1941, published in "En trascendentales declaraciones, el Señor Presidente Ávila Camacho define su patriótica política internacional," *El Popular,* June 1, 1941; also published in Ávila Camacho, *Igualdad democrática de los pueblos.* It was rumored that Lombardo Toledano's questionnaire and Ávila Camacho's response had been drafted during a secret conference at Cárdenas's ranch in Michoacán. (See George P. Shaw to Secretary of State, June

28, 1941, State Department Central File, 812.00/31715, RG 59, NARA.) In fact, it appears that the response was prepared at the president's request by Undersecretary of Foreign Relations Jaime Torres Bodet. (See Torres Bodet, *Años contra el tiempo,* 64–65.)

34. Manuel Ávila Camacho to Vicente Lombardo Toledano, May 30, 1941, published in "En trascendentales declaraciones, el Señor Presidente Ávila Camacho define su patriótica política internacional," *El Popular,* June 1, 1941.

35. "La política internacional de México," *El Popular,* June 2, 1941.

36. "Movimiento de entusiasta adhesión a la política internacional del Sr. Presidente," *El Popular,* June 3, 1941.

37. "La respuesta de Ávila Camacho es un valioso documento histórico," *El Popular,* June 4, 1941.

38. "Voto de confianza del proletariado al Sr. Presidente de la República," *El Popular,* June 7, 1941.

39. "El dilema histórico del momento actual es: Fascismo o antifascismo," *El Popular,* June 24, 1941.

40. "Sólo hay dos campos: Fascismo o antifascismo," *El Popular,* June 25, 1941.

41. "Declaraciones con motivo de la agresión de Alemania a Rusia," in Mexico, Secretaría de Relaciones Exteriores, *Memoria de la Secretaría de Relaciones Exteriores, septiembre de 1940–agosto de 1941,* 152–53.

42. "Intercambio de notas diplomáticas con la Legación de Alemania, con motivo de las 'Listas Negras,'" in Mexico, Secretaría de Relaciones Exteriores, *Memoria de la Secretaría de Relaciones Exteriores, septiembre de 1940–agosto de 1941,* 148–51.

43. See MAC, 133.2/4, AGN, for dozens of congratulatory messages to Ávila Camacho on his decision to appoint Véjar Vázquez as education minister. The leaders of anticommunist groups such as the Union Nacional Sinarquista, Acción Revolucionaria Mexicanista (known as the Dorados, or Gold Shirts), and the Liga Acción Anticomunista were among those sending telegrams, as was the prominent anticommunist legislator Enrique Carrolla Antuna.

44. Memorandum by William K. Ailshie (U.S. vice consul in Mexico City), October 6, 1941, State Department Central File, 812.00/31792, RG 59, NARA.

45. Santos, *Memorias,* 754–55.

46. Vicente Petrullo to Colonel William J. Donovan, December 22, 1941, Records of the Research and Analysis Branch, Latin American Section, WASH-R+A-INT-6, entry 175, box 1, folder 1, RG 226, NARA.

47. Josephus Daniels (U.S. ambassador to Mexico) to Secretary of State, August 12, 1941, State Department Central File, 812.00/31740, RG 59, NARA. For information on Maximino's April 1941 trip to the United States, see Archivo Histórico, file III-437-20, SRE, and Archivo de la Embajada de México en los Estados Unidos de América, Fondo Embamex II (henceforth, "AEMEUA"), file 73-0/524.3/11, SRE.

48. Military Attaché Report no. 142, by Colonel Gordon McCoy, September 26, 1941, and Office of Naval Intelligence Report no. 481-41-R, by Earl S. Piper, September 29, 1941, both in Military Intelligence Division Regional File, Mexico, 1922–1944, box 2446, classification 2340, RG 165, NARA.

49. "Protesta la C.T.M. por los hechos sangrientos ocurridos ayer tarde," *El Popular,* September 24, 1941.

50. "La masacre del 23 de septiembre," *La Voz de México,* September 26, 1941.

51. See, for example, "¡Unión nacional de todos los mexicanos contra el fascismo!" *La Voz de México,* October 25, 1941.

52. Correa, *El balance de Ávila camachismo,* 81; "Aprueban los diputados las reformas que fijan penas a espias y quintacolumnistas," *Excélsior,* October 11, 1941.

53. "Alcance de las reformas al código penal, aprobadas ayer," *El Popular,* October 11, 1941.

54. "La libertad de expresión," *El Nacional,* October 13, 1941.

55. "Aprobó el Senado ayer la reforma al Código Penal," *Excélsior,* October 25, 1941. The legislation went into effect upon its publication in the government's gazette, the *Diario Oficial,* on November 14, 1941; see Paz Salinas, *Strategy, Security, and Spies,* 129. The "social dissolution" clause was expanded and directed against dissidents on the left during the decades after the war; its repeal was a demand of the student movement of 1968, and the measure was finally rescinded in 1970, when it was replaced with new laws against "terrorism."

56. "Great Britain and Mexico, Normal Relations to Be Resumed," *Times* (London), October 23, 1941. See also, "Mexico and Britain End Diplomatic Rift," *New York Times,* October 23, 1941.

57. Francisco Castillo Nájera memorandum to the Department of State, February 17, 1941, AEMEUA, file 73-0/362(72:73)/1, SRE.

58. Francisco Castillo Nájera to Secretario de Relaciones Exteriores, "Conversación tenida en el Departamento de Estado el día 6 de noviembre de 1941, de las 3:30 a las 4:05 P.M., con el Señor Cordell Hull, secretario de estado de los Estados Unidos," November 6, 1941, AEMEUA, file 73-0/362(72:73)/1, SRE.

59. Francisco Castillo Nájera to Secretario de Relaciones Exteriores, November 26, 1941, AEMEUA, file 73-0/362(72:73)/1, SRE.

60. J. Edgar Hoover to Adolf Berle, November 27, 1941, State Department Central File, 812.00/31835, RG 59, NARA.

61. Vicente Petrullo to Colonel William J. Donovan, December 22, 1941, Records of the Research and Analysis Branch, Latin American Section, WASH-R+A-INT-6, entry 175, box 1, folder 1, RG 226, NARA.

Chapter Two

1. "Tokio declaró la guerra a los E. Unidos y a la Gran Bretaña," *El Universal*, December 8, 1941.

2. "Desde ayer cortó México sus relaciones con Tokio," *El Universal*, December 9, 1941. Again citing the commitments made in Havana, Padilla announced that the government had concluded that "the maintenance of its diplomatic relations with Japan is incompatible with the act of aggression that it committed against the United States of America."

3. "El proletariado mexicano ante la felonía del Japón," *El Popular*, December 8, 1941.

4. "Unidad nacional para defender el país," *El Popular*, December 9, 1941.

5. "Un solo frente nacional de lucha contra el nazifascismo," *El Popular*, December 9, 1941.

6. "Voto de simpatía y adhesión al gobierno," *El Universal*, December 10, 1941; "50,000 burócratas en acto de ayoyo al estado," *Excélsior*, December 10, 1941; and FSTSE manifesto, paid advertisement in *El Popular*, December 9, 1941, 7. *Excélsior* noted that even representatives of the war materials workers' union had marched "in complete order" in the parade in support of Ávila Camacho, despite the fact that several members had been gunned down by soldiers outside the presidential residence just a few weeks earlier.

7. "Tokio declaró la guerra a los E. Unidos y a la Gran Bretaña," *El Universal*, December 8, 1941.

8. "Amplio apoyo al gobierno por su política actual," *Excélsior*, December 9, 1941.

9. "Los senadores condenan la agresión japonesa," *El Universal*, December 9, 1941.

10. "Facultades extraordinarias para el General Manuel Ávila Camacho," *El Popular*, December 9, 1941; and "Facultades extraordinarias al Presidente de la República," *El Universal*, December 10, 1941.

11. See MAC, 550/44-9, AGN, for multiple files containing hundreds of telegrams and letters backing Ávila Camacho's international policy received from around the country between December 1941 and May 1942.

12. Lázaro Cárdenas to Manuel Ávila Camacho, December 8, 1941, MAC, 550/44-9, AGN.

13. Abelardo L. Rodríguez to Manuel Ávila Camacho, December 8, 1941, MAC, 550/44-9, AGN.

14. "Se presentó el Gral. Calles," *El Universal*, December 12, 1941.

15. Raleigh Gibson to Secretary of State, "Resumé of Conditions for December 1941," January 17, 1942, State Department Central File, 812.00/31870, RG 59, NARA.

16. Stephen C. Worster (U.S. vice consul in Coatzacoalcos) to Secretary of State, December 31, 1941, Records of the Research and Analysis Branch, Regular Series, report no. 9591, RG 226, NARA; Stephen Aguirre (U.S. consul in Mexicali) to Secretary of State, ca. December 1941–January 1942, Records of the Research and Analysis Branch, Regular Series, report no. 9679, RG 226, NARA; Raymond Phelan (U.S. vice consul in Agua Prieta) to Secretary of State, December 31, 1941, Records of the Research and Analysis Branch, Regular Series, report no. 12305, RG 226, NARA.

17. "Gran tensión nerviosa ha provocado aquí la guerra," *Últimas Noticias de Excélsior*, primera edición, December 8, 1941.

18. "Encuesta popular sobre la guerra, hecha en la capital," *Últimas Noticias de Excélsior*, primera edición, December 8, 1941.

19. See, for example, "¡Guerra, no! Sino paz con todos los pueblos," *El Sinarquista*, March 20, 1941.

20. See Meyer, *El sinarquismo ¿Un fascismo mexicano?*; and Meyer, *El sinarquismo, el cardenismo y la iglesia*.

21. *El Sinarquista*, December 18, 1941, transmitted in Raleigh Gibson to Secretary of State, December 18, 1941, Records of the Research and Analysis Branch, Regular Series, report no. 9549, RG 226, NARA.

22. Jean Meyer estimates that the UNS had recruited approximately four hundred thousand members by October 1941. The group was especially strong in Querétaro, Guanajuato, Michoacán, Aguascalientes, and San Luis Potosí (Meyer, *El sinarquismo ¿Un fascismo mexicano?*, 46).

23. Manuel Ávila Camacho speech, December 9, 1941, in *La participación de México en la defensa continental* (México: Secretaría de Gobernación, 1941), in MAC, 550/44-1, AGN.

24. Ibid.

25. "Estrecha solidaridad del Senado con el Presidente," *El Universal*, December 11, 1941. Among the senators actively promoting the resolution (which passed unanimously) were Vidal Díaz Muñoz and Celestino Gasca of the CTM.

26. *Excélsior*, December 12, 1941, cited in Raleigh Gibson to Secretary of State, December 12, 1941, State Department Central File, 812.001 Camacho, Manuel A./173, RG 59, NARA.

27. "México está en peligro," *El Popular*, December 10, 1941; and "La voz de México en medio de la tormenta," *El Popular*, December 11, 1941.

28. "El mensaje del Presidente," *Excélsior*, December 10, 1941. The reference to the president's "firmness" was no doubt intended to be read as referring to his strong anti-Axis stance, but the references to his not acting against the "national interests" and the "will of the people" are most easily read as referring to his decision not to take the country officially into the war. For an indication that moderate Mexicans worried about Ávila Camacho's ability to stand up to the left just prior to Pearl Harbor, see J. Edgar Hoover to Adolf Berle, November 27, 1941, State Department

Central File, 812.00/31835, RG 59, NARA, discussed previously.

29. "México ante el conflicto," *El Universal*, December 10, 1941.

30. Miguel Alessio Robles, "La guerra del Pacífico y el mensaje del Presidente de México," *El Universal*, December 15, 1941. Alessio Robles was secretary of industry and commerce under Obregón in 1922.

31. "Los industriales de Monterrey ofrecen su cooperación al General Ávila Camacho," *El Popular*, January 21, 1942.

32. Henry Waterman to Secretary of State, January 29, 1942, State Department Central File, 812.00/31869, RG 59, NARA.

33. *El Sinarquista*, December 18, 1941, transmitted in Raleigh Gibson to Secretary of State, December 18, 1941, Records of the Research and Analysis Branch, Regular Series, report no. 9549, RG 226, NARA. The UNS might also have been well disposed toward Ávila Camacho at this time because he had just agreed to their request for permission to establish a colony of Sinarquista families in Baja California. The first colonists departed en route to the peninsula just after the attack on Pearl Harbor. The president's granting of this authorization on September 11, 1941 (see Abascal, *Mis recuerdos*, 339–40), may well have helped to insulate Ávila Camacho from Sinarquista criticism as he brought Mexico closer to war. And while this acknowledgment of the UNS's legitimacy was among the moves interpreted by leftists as troubling signs of the administration's conservative tendencies, the president knew that he would be able to count on the left's support for his pro-Allied foreign policy regardless of his attitude toward the Sinarquistas.

34. Raleigh Gibson to Secretary of State, December 17, 1941, Records of the Research and Analysis Branch, Regular Series, report no. 9548, RG 226, NARA. Quotation is Gibson's paraphrase of PAN statement.

35. Harold Collins to Secretary of State, January 8, 1942, Records of the Research and Analysis Branch, Regular Series, report no. 12311, RG 226, NARA.

36. "No quiere el jefe del ejecutivo las facultades extraordinarias," *El Universal*, December 13, 1941; and "Declinó el Presidente las facultades extraordinarias," *El Popular*, December 13, 1941.

37. "Perifonemas" (editorial), *Últimas Noticias de Excélsior*, primera edición, December 22, 1941.

38. Raleigh Gibson to Secretary of State, December 16, 1941, State Department Central File, 812.00/31848, RG 59, NARA.

39. "Importantes acuerdos del ejecutivo," *El Universal*, December 11, 1941; and *Excélsior*, December 11, 1941, cited in Raleigh Gibson to Secretary of State, December 11, 1941, State Department Central File, 812.00/31843, RG 59, NARA.

40. "Nuevas reformas quedan aprobadas," *Excélsior*, January 1, 1942; and "Se confieren atribuciones de gran importancia al Estado Mayor Presidencial," *El Popular*, January 3, 1942.

41. "Cesó en sus funciones la Dirección Técnica Militar," *El Popular*, February 2, 1942; and "Se confieren atribuciones de gran importancia al Estado Mayor Presidencial," *El Popular*, January 3, 1942.

42. "Importantes acuerdos del ejecutivo," *El Universal*, December 11, 1941.

43. See Lázaro Cárdenas's message to the inhabitants of the Región Militar del Pacífico, December 31, 1941, published in "Que nadie en México deje de producir, dice Cárdenas," *Excélsior*, January 3, 1942, for a clear, open, public endorsement by Cárdenas of Ávila Camacho's call for unity, production, and discipline.

44. Luis Alamillo Flores, *Memorias*, 550.

45. Naval Intelligence Report no. 104-42, March 10, 1942, Military Intelligence Division Regional File, Mexico, 1922–1944, box 2508, RG 165, NARA, emphasis in original.

46. The details of Cárdenas's resistance as commander of the RMP to U.S. military activities on Mexican territory are outlined in Hermida Ruiz, *Cárdenas*; Carbó, *Ningún compromiso que lesione al país*, 101–45; and Alamillo Flores, *Memorias*, 543–610. Among other U.S. documents demonstrating unhappiness with the level of cooperation provided by Cárdenas, see George S. Messersmith to Secretary of State, May 29, 1942, Geographic File, 1942–1945, file CCS 092, RG 218, NARA, for an account of U.S. frustration with Cárdenas's noncompliance with instructions from Mexico City to allow the installation of radar sets in Baja California.

47. Secretaría de Relaciones Exteriores to Embajada de México en los Estados Unidos, December 10, 1941, Archivo Histórico, file III-914-7, SRE.

48. Sumner Welles to Francisco Castillo Nájera, February 5, 1942, and Francisco Castillo Nájera to the Subsecretario de Relaciones Exteriores, April 20, 1942, Archivo Histórico, file III-914-7, SRE.

49. Fernando Casas Alemán (*subsecretario de gobernación*) to Secretario de Relaciones Exteriores, December 19, 1941, Archivo Histórico, file III-610-25, SRE.

50. "Gobernación vigilará a los extranjeros," *El Popular*, January 1, 1942; and "Control federal de unos delitos," *Excélsior*, January 10, 1942. According to "Un nuevo servicio para la vigilancia de extranjeros, establecerá Gobernación," *El Popular*, January 4, 1942, the new intelligence-gathering section of the interior ministry's investigative bureau would have a budget of thirty million pesos, and it would have the capacity to maintain "a strict vigilance over all foreigners, for it will have agents, technicians, investigators, laboratories, identification [equipment?], etc."

51. Cristóbal Guzmán Cárdenas, "Noveno aniversario del fallecimiento del señor General de División Manuel Ávila Camacho, discurso pronunciado ante su tumba por el señor General de División Cristóbal Guzmán Cárdenas," October 13, 1964, in Instituto Mexicano de Cultura, *Manuel Ávila Camacho*, 86–87.

52. Coronel Cristóbal Guzmán Cárdenas (Mexican military attaché in Washington) to Dirección Técnica Militar, December 8, 1941, Archivo Histórico, file III-919-4, SRE.

53. Brigadier General Sherman Miles (acting assistant chief of staff, U.S. Army) to the Chief of Staff, December 10, 1941, Records of the Joint Mexican–United States Defense Commission, MDC 4120, tab 14-1, RG 218, NARA.

54. Coronel Cristóbal Guzmán Cárdenas to Dirección Técnica Militar, December 9, 1941, Archivo Histórico, file III-919-4, SRE.

55. Brigadier General Sherman Miles to the Chief of Staff, December 10, 1941. This memo refers to a telephone call by one [Lieutenant] Colonel [Lawrence] Higgins to "the President's brother"; this is almost certainly a reference to Maximino, the most politically prominent and internationally connected of the president's several brothers. See also Lieutenant Colonel Henry A. Barber Jr. to Major General S. D. Embick, December 8, 1941, Records of the Joint Mexican–United States Defense Commission, MDC 4120, tab 14-1, RG 218, NARA, for an indication that establishing an aircraft warning system was part of the purpose of the desired reconnaissance patrols; a handwritten note on this memo appears to indicate that Mexican approval for these patrols had been received by December 8, though the specific source of that approval is unclear.

56. Memorandum summarizing a December 9, 1941, report by Anselmo Mena (Mexican consul in San Diego), Archivo Histórico, file III-907-2, SRE.

57. Brigadier General Martin F. Scanlon (assistant chief of the air staff) to the Mexican Military Attaché, [December 10, 1941], Archivo Histórico, file III-919-4, SRE.

58. Coronel Cristóbal Guzmán Cárdenas to General de Brigada J. Salvador S. Sánchez, December 12, 1941, Archivo Histórico, file III-919-4, SRE.

59. Francisco Castillo Nájera to Manuel Ávila Camacho, with copy to Ezequiel Padilla, "Conversación tenida en la Casa Blanca, con el Señor Presidente Roosevelt, el día 16 de diciembre de 1941, de las 13 a las

13:35 horas," [December 16, 1941], Archivo Histórico, file III-2479-10, SRE.

60. General de Brigada J. Salvador S. Sánchez to Coronel Cristóbal Guzmán Cárdenas, December 15, 1941, Archivo Histórico, file III-919-4, SRE.

61. Coronel Cristóbal Guzmán Cárdenas to Major General S. D. Embick, December 16, 1941, Archivo Histórico, file III-919-4, SRE; also in Records of the Joint Mexican–United States Defense Commission, MDC 4120, tab 9-9, RG 218, NARA.

62. Lieutenant Colonel Lawrence Higgins to the Assistant Chief of Staff, G-2, December 16, 1941, Records of the Joint Mexican–United States Defense Commission, MDC 9010, tab 8-4, RG 218, NARA.

63. General J. L. DeWitt of the U.S. Western Defense Command registered his objection to the requirement in a December 18, 1941, phone call to one General Bryden, in which he stated that he thought it would be dangerous to send a party of his men into Mexico on a scouting mission, as planned, if they were not easily identifiable as U.S. soldiers and able to protect themselves; see "Conversation between General Bryden and General DeWitt, 12:40 P.M., December 18, 1941," in Records of the Joint Mexican–United States Defense Commission, MDC 4120, tab 14-1, RG 218, NARA.

64. Francisco Castillo Nájera to Manuel Ávila Camacho, with copy to Ezequiel Padilla, "Conversación tenida en la Casa Blanca, con el Señor Presidente Roosevelt, el día 16 de diciembre de 1941, de las 13 a las 13:35 horas," [December 16, 1941], Archivo Histórico, file III-2479-10, SRE.

65. Francisco Castillo Nájera to Ezequiel Padilla, with copy to Manuel Ávila Camacho, "Conversación tenida con el Señor Subsecretario de Estado, Sumner Welles, el día 17 de diciembre de 1941, de las 11 a las 11:40 horas," [December 17, 1941], Archivo Histórico, file III-2479-10, SRE.

66. Ezequiel Padilla to Francisco Castillo Nájera, December 19, 1941, Archivo Histórico, file III-2479-10, SRE.

67. James W. McGurk to Secretary of State, December 11, 1941, State Department Central File, 740.0011 European War 1939/17376, RG 59, NARA.

68. "Conversación tenida en la Casa Blanca, con el Señor Presidente Roosevelt, el día 16 de diciembre de 1941, de las 13 a las 13:35 horas," Francisco Castillo Nájera to Manuel Ávila Camacho, with copy to Ezequiel Padilla, [December 16, 1941], Archivo Histórico, file III-2479-10, SRE; Ezequiel Padilla to Francisco Castillo Nájera, December 19, 1941, Archivo Histórico, file III-2479-10, SRE; and "México y Edos. Unidos, brazo con brazo frente a cualquier agresor," *Excélsior*, January 13, 1942.

69. "Pide una junta de cancilleres Estados Unidos," *Excélsior*, December 11, 1941; and Francisco Castillo Nájera to Ezequiel Padilla, with copy to Manuel Ávila Camacho, "Conversación tenida con el señor subsecretario de estado, Sumner Welles, el día 17 de diciembre de 1941, de las 11 a las 11:40 horas," [December 17, 1941], Archivo Histórico, file III-2479-10, SRE.

70. See, for example, "Pediráse en Brasil que toda América, como unidad geográfica, declare la guerra a los países del Eje," *Excélsior*, January 5,

1942; "Que América declare guerra al Eje: Tal va a proponer la delegación dominicana," *Excélsior*, January 6, 1942; "Pidese que toda América desde ahora declare la guerra," *Excélsior*, January 11, 1942; and "Argentina lista para separarse de la asamblea: Si no consigue en Río lo que desea, abandonará la junta," *Excélsior*, January 14, 1942.

71. "México encabeza a los delegados de los otros países," *Excélsior*, January 16, 1942. See also, "Despertó interés continental el discurso del Licenciado Padilla," *Excélsior*, January 18, 1942; and "México desempeña brillante papel en la conferencia de cancilleres, que se está celebrando en la ciudad de Río de Janeiro," *El Popular*, January 17, 1942.

72. "Acuerdo unánime sobre la ruptura con el Eje," *El Popular*, January 24, 1942; "Condicionalmente aceptaron romper Chile y Argentina: Transacción aceptada por las 21 repúblicas," *Excélsior*, January 24, 1942.

73. Text of March 27, 1942, accord in AEMEUA, box 130, file 4, classification 583(72:73)/1, SRE.

74. "Welles designó al Lic. E. Padilla como campeón de la democracia," *Excélsior*, April 1, 1942; "Mexico's Padilla," *Time*, April 6, 1942; and "Padilla es tema principal de la revista 'Time,'" *Excélsior*, April 3, 1942.

75. Francisco Castillo Nájera to Subsecretario de Relaciones Exteriores, with copy for Manuel Ávila Camacho, memorandum of meeting between Padilla and Welles, April 1, 1941, AEMEUA, box 130, file 4, classification 583(72:73)/1, SRE.

76. Harold D. Finley to Secretary of State, February 10,

1942, State Department Central File, 812.00/31889, RG 59, NARA.

77. *La Prensa*, February 15, 1942, cited in Harold D. Finley to Secretary of State, February 19, 1942, State Department Central File, 812.00/31896, RG 59, NARA.

78. "Los púlpitos son empleados en Jalisco para realizar propaganda totalitaria," *El Popular*, February 20, 1942; "Unánime respaldo a la denuncia hecha por el Lic. Barba González," *El Popular*, February 24, 1942; Dionisio Encina (PCM secretary general) to Silviano Barba González, in *La Voz de México*, March 5, 1942; and "Vida nacional," *La Nación*, February 28, 1942.

79. "Paro nacional de protesta contra las persecucciones de Jorge Cerdán," *El Popular*, February 11, 1942; and "La CTM organiza una serie de paros en protesta en contra de Jorge Cerdán," *El Popular*, February 14, 1942. As an associate and ally of Maximino Ávila Camacho, Cerdán was a natural enemy of the CTM.

80. "La intervención policiaca hizo terminar, en forma trágica, una ordenada manifestación estudiantil," *El Popular*, March 6, 1942; "Se levanta un clamor popular de respaldo a los estudiantes," *El Popular*, March 7, 1942; "La unidad nacional es imposible si no se castiga a los autores de los atentados," *El Popular*, March 8, 1942; and PS-1 to Jefe de Departamento, March 6, 1942, Ramo Gobernación, Dirección General de Investigaciones Políticas y Sociales (henceforth, "DGIPS"), box 23, file 2-1/061.7/19, AGN.

81. "Padilla realiza una labor de marcado tinte personalista," *El Popular*, April 18, 1942. See "Los gobiernos interpretaron a sus pueblos en Río de Janeiro," *El Popular*, February 8, 1942, for Vicente Lombardo Toledano's congratulatory telegram to Padilla on the occasion of the latter's return from Brazil.

82. *El Hombre Libre*, March 1, 1942, cited in Harold D. Finley to Secretary of State, February 28, 1942, State Department Central File, 812.00/31906, RG 59, NARA; and "Nuestro canciller, 'profeta de Americas,'" *La Nación*, April 18, 1942. Unfortunately for the foreign minister, both ends of the ideological spectrum held his service in the Calles administration in the 1920s against him. By the 1940s, after the falling out between Calles and Cárdenas and the latter's emergence as a champion of redistributive social reforms, many on the left were suspicious of officials who were closely linked with Calles. On the other hand, conservative Catholics had not forgotten the anticlerical stance that Padilla had adopted as Calles's attorney general, especially when he blamed not just a religious fanatic but also the church hierarchy for the 1928 assassination of president-elect Alvaro Obregón.

83. "Unidad nacional," *El Universal*, March 11, 1942.

84. George S. Messersmith to Sumner Welles, March 24, 1942, document 1488, George S. Messersmith Papers, University of Delaware Library, Newark (henceforth, "GSM"); and George S. Messersmith to Cordell Hull, May 6, 1942, document 1501, GSM.

Chapter Three

1. "El torpedeamiento del 'Potrero de Llano' y la indignación de nuestros patrioteros," *El Hombre Libre*, May 17, 1942.

2. "Vida nacional," *La Nación*, May 23, 1942; *El Universal*, May 16, 1942.

3. "Vida nacional," *La Nación*, May 23, 1942; see also "Es unánime la opinión contra el atentado que ha cometido el Eje," *El Universal*, May 17, 1942, for another Lecona statement expressing skepticism about Mexican entry into the war.

4. "Vida nacional," *La Nación*, May 23, 1942; see also "La brutal agresión del Eje contra el 'Potrero del Llano,'" *El Universal*, May 16, 1942, for another Flores M. statement against entering the war.

5. "Vida nacional," *La Nación*, May 23, 1942.

6. "Numerosos sectores secundan la petición de Lombardo Toledano al Señor Presidente de la República," *El Popular*, May 16, 1942.

7. "Todos los mexicanos unidos en torno al Señor Presidente de la República en este supremo trance," *El Popular*, May 16, 1942.

8. Vicente Lombardo Toledano to Manuel Ávila Camacho, May 14, 1942, MAC, 550/44-16, AGN; also published in "Que México declare la guerra a la Alemania nazi, pide la CTAL," *El Popular*, May 15, 1942.

9. "Vida nacional," *La Nación*, May 23, 1942.

10. Narciso Bassols to Manuel Ávila Camacho, ca. May 14, 1942, published in "Vida nacional," *La Nación*, May 23, 1942.

11. Declarations by the Comité Nacional of the Confederación de Trabajadores de México, May 15, 1942, published in "Petición unánime de las organizaciones: Declaración de guerra a los totalitarios," *El Popular*, May 16, 1942. Velázquez was then just

at the beginning of his tenure as head of the official labor bloc, which would continue, with only one brief interruption, for more than half a century, ending only with his death in 1997.

12. See CTM notice in *El Popular*, May 23, 1942, which under the heading "war upon the axis, war," invited "workers, peasants, civil servants, private employees, youths, women, the elderly, Catholics, Protestants, communists, [and] socialists" to a "great popular meeting" to be held the next day as an "act of homage to the victims of the Nazi-fascist aggression and of support for the Government of the Republic."

13. Lázaro Cárdenas to Manuel Ávila Camacho, May 18, 1942, published in Cárdenas, *Epistolario de Lázaro Cárdenas*, 1:486.

14. Cárdenas, *Obras*, 83. Interestingly, in his diary entry for May 18, 1942, Cárdenas referred to "el hundimiento del barco petrolero 'Potrero del Llano,' que *se dice* torpedeó un submarino alemán" (emphasis added), a phrasing that suggested that he was not completely convinced that Germany had been responsible for the attack.

15. Francisco J. Múgica to Manuel Ávila Camacho, May 20, 1942, Fondo Francisco J. Múgica, box 16, vol. CXLIV, document 81, Centro de Estudios de la Revolución Mexicana "Lázaro Cárdenas," Jiquilpan, Michoacán (henceforth, "CERMLC").

16. Francisco J. Múgica to Manuel Ávila Camacho, May 20, 1942, Fondo Francisco J. Múgica, box 16, vol. CXLIV, document 81, CERMLC.

17. These positions of the PAN emerge clearly throughout this period in the pages of its weekly magazine, *La Nación*, which often featured

disapproving reports on Protestant missionary activity and U.S. cultural influences in Mexico.

18. Comité Ejecutivo Nacional of Acción Nacional to Manuel Ávila Camacho, May 21, 1942, Sección Partido Acción Nacional, vol. 40, file 226, Archivo Manuel Gómez Morín, Mexico City (henceforth, "AMGM").

19. Ibid.

20. "Vida nacional," *La Nación*, May 23, 1942.

21. Ibid.

22. George S. Messersmith to Sumner Welles, May 26, 1942, General Records of the U.S. Embassy in Mexico City, 1942, classification 820.02, RG 84, NARA.

23. Ibid.

24. Inspector PS-1 to Jefe del Departamento de Investigación Política y Social, May 21, 1942, DGIPS, box 23, file 2-1/061.7(725.1)/2, AGN.

25. Ibid.

26. "El torpedeamiento del 'Potrero de Llano' y la indignación de nuestros patrioteros," *El Hombre Libre*, May 17, 1942.

27. "El hundimiento del 'Potrero de Llano' visto conforme a derecho internacional," *Omega*, May 18, 1942.

28. "El torpedeamiento del 'Potrero de Llano' y la indignación de nuestros patrioteros," *El Hombre Libre*, May 17, 1942.

29. "Encuesta sobre la guerra," *Tiempo*, May 29, 1942. The question presented to the public was, "Do you believe that Mexico ought to enter the war?" Votes were collected from 4,152 "men on the street" (21.6 percent in favor of entering the war), 2,144 members of "groups of the left" (92.2 percent in favor of entering the

war), 2,686 members of the PRM and unions (31.4 percent in favor of entering the war), 630 "state workers" in government-run factories (67.9 percent in favor of entering the war), and 982 "official employees" in the bureaucracy (36.8 percent in favor of entering the war).

30. Antonio Velázquez Fernández to Manuel Ávila Camacho, May 20, 1942, MAC, 550/44-2, AGN.

31. Luis Cortines to Manuel Ávila Camacho, May 27, 1942, MAC, 550/44-2, AGN.

32. "MJB" [name illegible] to Manuel Ávila Camacho, March 24, 1944, MAC, 161.1/81, AGN.

33. George S. Messersmith to Secretary of State, May 15, 1942, General Records of the U.S. Embassy in Mexico City, 1942, classification 711, RG 84, NARA; and Harold D. Finley circular to fellow officers at the U.S. embassy, June 8, 1942, General Records of the U.S. Embassy in Mexico City, 1942, classification 711, RG 84, NARA.

34. Naval Intelligence Report no. 399-42-R by Major Earl S. Piper, May 28, 1942, Military Intelligence Division Regional File, Mexico, 1922–1944, box 2508, classification 5940-5950, RG 165, NARA.

35. Rufus Lane Jr. to Secretary of State, May 21, 1942, General Records of the U.S. Embassy in Mexico City, 1942, classification 711, RG 84, NARA.

36. Naval Liaison Officer, Mazatlán, to the Office of Naval Intelligence, June 2, 1942, Records of the Office of Naval Intelligence, Latin America Monograph Files, "Mexico" files, classification 601-130, RG 38, NARA.

37. Henry Waterman to Secretary of State, May 22, 1942, General

Records of the U.S. Embassy in Mexico City, 1942, classification 711, RG 84, NARA.

38. Russell White to Raleigh Gibson, May 23, 1942, General Records of the U.S. Embassy in Mexico City, 1942, classification 711, RG 84, NARA.

39. "Muchos padres de familia, que se en cuentran en la desgracia acausa de la mala fe de los Ingratos Gringos . . ." to Manuel Ávila Camacho, no date [ca. May 1942], MAC, 550/44-2, AGN.

40. Ezequiel Martínez to Manuel Ávila Camacho, May 22, 1942, MAC, 550/44-2, AGN.

41. Joaquín Espinosa to Manuel Ávila Camacho, May 15, 1942, MAC, 550/44-2, AGN.

42. Messersmith quotation from George S. Messersmith to Cordell Hull, May 20, 1942, document 1503, GSM.

43. Bernard Gotlieb to George S. Messersmith, May 18, 1942, General Records of the U.S. Embassy in Mexico City, 1942, classification 711, RG 84, NARA.

44. Julian Pinkerton to George S. Messersmith, May 17, 1942, General Records of the U.S. Embassy in Mexico City, 1942, classification 711, RG 84, NARA.

45. Thomas McEnelly to George S. Messersmith, May 25, 1942, Military Intelligence Division Regional File, Mexico, 1922–1944, classification 5940-5950, RG 165, NARA.

46. Henry Waterman to Secretary of State, May 22, 1942, General Records of the U.S. Embassy in Mexico City, 1942, classification 711, RG 84, NARA.

47. "Voluntad unánime para defender el honor e integridad de México," *El Popular*, May 25, 1942.

48. "Unióse ayer todo México en un acto de vigorosa protesta," *Excélsior*, May 25, 1942; "La manifestación de protesta," *El Universal*, May 25, 1942. Estimated attendance figures were not provided. The "Plaza of the Constitution" is the Zócalo's official name.

49. Harold D. Finley to Secretary of State, May 25, 1942, General Records of the U.S. Embassy in Mexico City, 1942, classification 711, RG 84, NARA.

50. Naval Intelligence Report no. 414-42-R, by Major Earl S. Piper, May 28, 1942, Military Intelligence Division Regional File, Mexico, 1922–1944, classification 5940-5950, RG 165, NARA.

51. Kirk, *Covering the Mexican Front*, 93. Kirk interpreted the failure of the event as a sign that the CTM's "force was spent."

52. In notes for his memoirs, Messersmith wrote that shortly after his arrival in Mexico in February 1942 he reached the conclusion that Ávila Camacho "had made up his mind as to what the attitude of Mexico would be" in the event of a provocative act by Germany and that in such a situation Mexico would declare war. If the president had indeed made such a determination, it would explain how he and Padilla were able to move so quickly toward a declaration of war. See document 2000, GSM.

53. Naval Intelligence Report no. 377-42-R, by Major Earl S. Piper, May 16, 1942, Military Intelligence Division Regional File, Mexico, 1922–1944, classification 5940-5950, RG 165, NARA. A U.S. embassy

official later reported that the amount of time allowed for a response had been cut in successive drafts of the note, first from two weeks to ten days, and then from ten days to eight days. See Harold D. Finley to the Secretary of State, June 30, 1942, State Department Central File, 812.00/32001, RG 59, NARA.

54. Naval Intelligence Report no. 377-42-R, by Major Earl S. Piper, May 16, 1942, Military Intelligence Division Regional File, Mexico, 1922–1944, classification 5940-5950, RG 165, NARA.

55. Gaxiola, *Memorias*, 293.

56. Ibid., 294. Gaxiola wrote that Maximino Ávila Camacho "expresó también su conformidad" after Gómez and Suárez spoke, suggesting that he too favored, at most, a limited role for Mexico in the war. It was rumored that the president's authoritarian-minded, staunchly anticommunist older brother was a great admirer of Benito Mussolini, which might help to explain his apparent lack of enthusiasm for active support for the Allied cause.

57. Gaxiola, *Memorias*, 294; George S. Messersmith to Sumner Welles, June 9, 1942, Security-Segregated Records of the U.S. Embassy in Mexico City, 1942, classification 820, RG 84, NARA; and Harold D. Finley to Secretary of State, June 30, 1942, State Department Central File, 812.00/32001, RG 59, NARA. U.S. diplomats suggested that Navy Minister Heriberto Jara and Interior Minister Miguel Alemán might also have hesitated to support Mexican entry into the war. As a leftist who was considered ideologically close to Cárdenas, Jara might well have had reservations about a war policy, and U.S. officials considered Alemán's

loyalties to be suspect because corruption in Gobernación appeared to have allowed some Axis nationals in Mexico to escape surveillance and detention. However, Gaxiola noted that "not all of the attendees [at the cabinet meeting] spoke," and he does not include Jara or Alemán on his list of the officials who did give their views. Agriculture Minister Marte R. Gómez also wrote in a letter that "some kept silent" at the meeting, though he gives no indication as to who spoke and who did not. See Marte R. Gómez to J. Ruben Romero, June 5, 1942, in Gómez, *Vida política contemporánea*, 649.

58. Memorandum of conversation between Guy Ray and José C. Valadés, October 2, 1943, attachment to Guy Ray to Secretary of State, October 2, 1943, General Records of the U.S. Embassy in Mexico City, 1943, classification 710, RG 84, NARA.

59. Marte R. Gómez to J. Ruben Romero, June 5, 1942, in Gómez, *Vida política contemporánea*, 649.

60. Gaxiola, *Memorias*, 293.

61. "Declaración de guerra," *El Popular*, May 23, 1942.

62. Memorandum of conversation between Guy Ray and José C. Valadés, October 2, 1943, General Records of the U.S. Embassy in Mexico City, 1943, classification 710, RG 84, NARA.

63. Ibid.

64. Cárdenas, *Apuntes*, 84.

65. Ávila Camacho informed Cárdenas of his intention to install him in the defense ministry in the May 22, 1942, meeting between the two men. Though the government made no public announcement concerning the appointment until Cárdenas took up his

post in September 1942, the two men agreed that the former president would take over the defense ministry after making a previously planned inspection tour of Baja California. Cárdenas recorded Ávila Camacho's May 22 request that he become defense minister in a handwritten note in the margins of his copy of Lázaro Cárdenas to Manuel Ávila Camacho, June 30, 1942, Archivo Particular de Lázaro Cárdenas, pt. 1, roll 21 [microfilm], AGN.

66. "México no mandará a ningún soldado fuera de nuestro territorio," *El Nacional*, May 22, 1942.

67. "Tranquilidad en la angustia," *Novedades*, May 23, 1942.

68. "Lo que debe saber el pueblo: Que cosa es estado de guerra," *El Universal*, May 24, 1942.

69. "Declaración de guerra," *La Prensa*, May 23, 1942.

70. "Encuesta sobre la guerra," *Tiempo*, May 29, 1942.

71. Ibid.

72. Naval Intelligence Report no. 414-42-R, by Major Earl S. Piper, May 28, 1942, Military Intelligence Division Regional File, Mexico, 1922–1944, classification 5940-5950, RG 165, NARA.

73. Text of May 28, 1942, Manuel Ávila Camacho address to Congress, MAC, 550/44-2, AGN; also in Ávila Camacho, *México en estado de guerra*, and in Mexico City newspapers of May 29, 1942.

74. Statement of Comité Ejecutivo Nacional of Acción Nacional, June 2, 1942, Sección Partido Acción Nacional, vol. 40, file 226, AMGM.

75. José Aguilar y Maya to Manuel Gómez Morín and Roberto Cosío y Cosío, August 4, 1942, Sección Partido Acción Nacional, vol.

40, file 226, AMGM. Further correspondence between Cosío y Cosío and Aguilar y Maya, from June and July 1942, is in the same file.

76. Statement by the Unión Nacional Sinarquista, published in *Novedades*, June 2, 1942.

77. Raleigh Gibson to the Secretary of State, June 2, 1942, General Records of the U.S. Embassy in Mexico City, 1942, classification 820.02, RG 84, NARA.

78. Inspector PS-1 to Jefe de Departamento de Investigación Política y Social, May 26, 1942, DGIPS, box 23, file 2-1/061.7(725.1)/2, AGN.

79. "Suspende sus trabajos el Partido Autonomista Mexicano," *El Universal*, May 27, 1942.

80. Pedro Julio Pedrero to Manuel Ávila Camacho, September 3, 1942, and J. Jesus González Gallo to Pedro Julio Pedrero, September 4, 1942, both in MAC, 559.1/41, AGN.

81. Pedro Julio Pedrero to Manuel Ávila Camacho, January 13, 1943, MAC, 559.1/41, AGN.

82. Pedro Julio Pedrero to J. Jesus González Gallo, April 6, 1943, MAC, 559.1/41, AGN.

83. See MAC, 559.1/41, AGN, for extensive correspondence on Pedrero's placement in a government position. He proposed that he be named a department head of some sort, but he was offered a lowly post as a sales agent for the national oil company in Tepic, Nayarit. He refused that offer but had to settle for the job in Coatzacoalcos, though he sent the president frequent requests for a transfer in the years that followed.

84. Statement by Archbishop Luis María Martínez, published in "El deber de los Católicos ante

la situación actual de México," *El Universal*, May 31, 1942.

85. Raleigh Gibson to Secretary of State, June 2, 1942, State Department Central File, 812.404/2106, hRG 59, NARA.

86. George S. Messersmith to Sumner Welles, August 5, 1942, document 1534, GSM.

87. George S. Messersmith to Sumner Welles, May 21, 1942, document 1503a, GSM. The passages cited are from Messersmith's summary of the views expressed by Martínez.

88. George S. Messersmith to Sumner Welles, August 5, 1942, document 1534, GSM.

89. Statement by the bishop of Chihuahua, published in "Patriótica actitud de otro prelado," *Excélsior*, June 1, 1942; article enclosed in Raleigh Gibson to the Secretary of State, June 2, 1942, State Department Central File, 740.0011 European War 1939/22179, RG 59, NARA.

90. "Pacto de Unidad Obrera," June 1942, Archivo Particular de Ignacio García Tellez, box 19, file 50, Archivo Histórico de El Colegio de México, Mexico City (henceforth, "Colmex").

91. "Los trabajadores, vanguardia de patriotismo," *El Popular*, June 3, 1942.

92. "Pacto de Unidad Obrera," June 1942, Archivo Particular de Ignacio García Tellez, box 19, file 50, Colmex.

93. Harold D. Finley to Secretary of State, June 26, 1942, State Department Central File, 812.504/2087, RG 59, NARA; and Harold D. Finley to the Secretary of State, August 25, 1942, 812.504/2115, RG 59, NARA.

94. U.S. Naval Attaché, Mexico City, to the Office of Naval Intelligence, May 28, 1942, Military Intelligence Division Regional File, Mexico, 1922–1944, box 2509, classification 5940-5950, RG 165, NARA.

95. Harold D. Finley to Secretary of State, June 30, 1942, State Department Central File, 812.00/32001, RG 59, NARA.

96. E. W. Eaton (U.S. vice consul in Durango) to Secretary of State, June 9, 1942, General Records of the U.S. Embassy in Mexico City, 1942, classification 711, RG 84, NARA.

97. Text of Manuel Ávila Camacho speech, June 3, 1942, MAC, 550/44-2, AGN.

98. G. R. Willson to Secretary of State, May 29, 1942, Records of the Research and Analysis Branch, Regular Series, report no. 17078, RG 226, NARA.

99. "Un estado de guerra," *Novedades*, May 30, 1942.

100. Harold D. Finley to Secretary of State, June 30, 1942, State Department Central File, 812.00/32001, RG 59, NARA.

Chapter Four

1. Marte R. Gómez to J. Ruben Romero, June 5, 1942, in Gómez, *Vida política contemporánea*, 649–50.

2. E. W. Eaton to Secretary of State, August 7, 1942, State Department Central File, 812.00/32022, RG 59, NARA.

3. "La mejor manera de sabotear el patriotismo," *La Nación*, August 1, 1942.

4. Harold D. Finley to Secretary of State, August 18, 1942, State Department Central File, 812.00/32029, RG 59, NARA;

and Harold D. Finley to Secretary of State, September 21, 1942, State Department Central File, 812.00/32053, RG 59, NARA.

5. Edward G. Trueblood circular to Guy Ray, Raleigh Gibson, Harold D. Finley, and Joseph W. McGurk, July 29, 1942, General Records of the U.S. Embassy in Mexico City, 1942, classification 711, RG 84, NARA.

6. We do have evidence of more successful events: one dispatch (Harold D. Finley to Secretary of State, August 18, 1942, State Department Central File, 812.00/32029, RG 59, NARA) reported great enthusiasm in a crowd of 150,000 in Monterrey on July 12, 1942, and another (Harold D. Finley to Secretary of State, July 31, 1942, General Records of the U.S. Embassy in Mexico City, 1942, classification 711, RG 84, NARA) stated that based on information available to the embassy, which included consular reports and also, in all likelihood, accounts from the legislators who made the tour, "unhoped for enthusiasm appears to have been aroused in most places."

7. Report by Raleigh Gibson, transcribed in Military Attaché Report no. 609, by Colonel John A. Weeks, May 8, 1942, Military Intelligence Division Regional File, Mexico, 1922–1944, box 2551, RG 165, NARA. The report described Prado and García as "the two men of greatest influence in the Senate" and as "Ávila Camachistas," with García acting and being accepted by his colleagues "as the authorized spokesman for President Ávila Camacho in the Senate."

8. Harold D. Finley to Secretary of State, July 31, 1942, General Records of the U.S. Embassy in Mexico City, 1942, classification 711, RG 84, NARA.

9. Harold D. Finley to Secretary of State, September 21, 1942, State Department Central File, 812.00/32053, RG 59, NARA.

10. "Los estados: Chihuahua, mitín senatorial," *La Nación*, July 25, 1942, emphasis in original.

11. Harold D. Finley to Secretary of State, August 18, 1942, State Department Central File, 812.00/32029, RG 59, NARA.

12. *Jueves de Excélsior*, July 30, 1942, translation enclosed with Harold D. Finley to the Secretary of State, July 31, 1942, General Records of the U.S. Embassy in Mexico City, 1942, classification 711, RG 84, NARA; also filed in State Department Central File, 812.20/365, RG 59, NARA.

13. George S. Messersmith to Franklin D. Roosevelt, July 10, 1942, Security-Segregated Records of the U.S. Embassy in Mexico City, 1942, classification 800.1, RG 84, NARA.

14. Though the revised Lend-Lease contract that superseded the original March 27, 1942, accord was not formally signed until March 18, 1943, U.S. and Mexican officials had agreed by August 1942 that in light of Mexico's new status as a belligerent in the fight against the Axis, the Mexican allocation for military aid would be increased from ten million dollars to seventy million dollars (though this figure was later reduced to forty million dollars) and that the amount that Mexico would eventually have to pay for the equipment would be set at 33 percent of its value rather than 48 percent as had been established in the earlier contract. See Francisco Castillo Nájera to Secretario de Relaciones Exteriores, August 8, 1942, AEMEUA, file 73-0/583(72:73)/1, SRE.

15. Franklin D. Roosevelt to George S. Messersmith, July 23, 1942, Security-Segregated Records of the U.S. Embassy in Mexico City, 1942, classification 800.1, RG 84, NARA.

16. General Handy (assistant chief of staff, U.S. Army) memorandum to Chief of Staff, November 20, 1942, Records of the Office of the Director of Plans and Operations, General Records—Correspondence: Security-Classified General Correspondence, OPD 336.2, case 1, RG 165, NARA.

17. General Joseph T. McNarney (deputy chief of staff, U.S. Army) memorandum to Undersecretary of State, November 20, 1942, Records of the Office of the Director of Plans and Operations, General Records—Correspondence: Security-Classified General Correspondence, OPD 336.2, case 1, RG 165, NARA.

18. General Handy memorandum to Chief of Staff, November 20, 1942, Records of the Office of the Director of Plans and Operations, General Records—Correspondence: Security-Classified General Correspondence, OPD 336.2, case 1, RG 165, NARA.

19. Harold D. Finley to Secretary of State, October 21, 1942, State Department Central File, 812.00/32066, RG 59, NARA.

20. Harold D. Finley to Secretary of State, September 25, 1942, State Department Central File, 812.00/32056, RG 59, NARA.

21. M. J. McDermott (chief of Division of Current Information, Department of State) to Byron Price (director, Office of Censorship), October 12, 1942, State Department Central File, 812.20/399, RG 59, NARA. An investigation by U.S. officials revealed that the article in *El Occidental* was based on a U.S.

wire service story, but that report had been greatly embellished by the Guadalajara newspaper; see John Jacob Meilly to the Department of State, December 2, 1942, State Department Central File, 812.20/409, RG 59, NARA.

22. See, for example, D. R. Ruiz (*comisariado ejidal de La Providencia*, Municipio de Pueblo Nuevo, Chiapas) and other signers to Manuel Ávila Camacho, September 14, 1942, MAC, 545.2/14-6, AGN.

23. José O. Martínez and D. Garbay to Manuel Ávila Camacho, September 17, 1942, MAC, 545.2/14-9, AGN.

24. Harold D. Finley to Secretary of State, November 21, 1942, State Department Central File, 812.00/32080, RG 59, NARA.

25. "Por el ojo de la llave," *El Universal*, December 22, 1942, refers both to Ávila Camacho's statement on the optional nature of attendance at training sessions and to continued draconian enforcement of an attendance requirement, specifically in Nuevo León under Zone Commander Eulogio Ortiz. See also MAC, 545.2/14, AGN, for complaints about forced attendance and abuses.

26. "La gran jornada de 'Acercamiento Nacional,'" *El Popular*, September 9, 1942, refers to the unimpressive results of previous *acercamientos*, and "Bienvenida la guerra, si nos une," *Novedades*, September 16, 1942, calls the 1942 event the *Eighth* Assembly of National Coming-Together. All the major Mexico City newspapers of September 16, 1942, featured extensive coverage of the rally.

27. Cárdenas, *Obras*, 90. *La Prensa*, September 16, 1942, was one of the

newspapers that reported the lack of public interaction between Cárdenas and Calles, and while it seems that the two men did not share an extensive conversation, Cárdenas did later record in his *Obras* (p. 191) that Calles "greeted me with nobility"—probably on this occasion—after his return from exile in the United States.

28. "Seis frases para la historia," *El Universal*, September 16, 1942.

29. "Las rencillas políticas desaparecen," *El Universal*, September 16, 1942.

30. George S. Messersmith to Sumner Welles, September 17, 1942, Security-Segregated Records of the U.S. Embassy in Mexico City, 1942, classification 710, RG 84, NARA; also filed in State Department Central File, 812.20/386, RG 59, NARA.

31. "El ex secretario particular del canciller Padilla dice: México debe pelear las Filipinas!" *Hoy*, October 3, 1942.

32. "Lo que México puede ganar en la guerra," *El Popular*, September 4, 1942.

33. "México cumple su deber más sagrado," *El Popular*, October 17, 1942.

34. "La bandera de México debe ondear en los campos de batalla," *El Popular*, October 20, 1942.

35. See *La Nación*, October 24, October 31, and November 7, 1942, for bitter denunciations of Padilla for having issued instructions to consuls not to interfere in the conscription of Mexicans in the United States. Interestingly, at this time, in response to suggestions that Mexicans should fight only under the Mexican flag, Padilla specifically stated that Mexico was not prepared for an overseas deployment.

36. Ezequiel Padilla statement, October 28, 1942, AEMEUA, file 73-0/311.2(72:47)/1, SRE.

37. Manuel Tello circular to Jefes de Misiones Diplomáticas, November 21, 1942, AEMEUA, file 73-0/311.2(72:47)/1, SRE.

38. Spenser, *The Impossible Triangle*, 165.

39. Harold D. Finley to Secretary of State, November 30, 1942, citing *Excélsior*, November 25, 1942, report on the PCM circular, State Department Central File, 812.00/32082, RG 59, NARA.

40. Harold D. Finley to Secretary of State, July 21, 1942, State Department Central File, 812.00/32006, RG 59, NARA.

41. William Blocker to Secretary of State, August 17, 1942, State Department Central File, 812.00/32027, RG 59, NARA.

42. Memorandum of conversation between Herbert Bursley, MacLean, and Vice Admiral Alfred Johnson, September 23, 1942, State Department Central File, 812.20/396, RG 59, NARA.

43. "Report on Mexican Photographic Mission," by Lieutenant John Reinhardt, no date, but based on ca. September–November 1942 assignment in Mexico, Records of the Washington Radio and Cables and Field Photo Branch, WASH-FIELD-PHOTO-OP 17, box 25, folder 446, RG 226, NARA. For information on the dates of Reinhardt's mission, see Colonel John W. Thomason Jr. to Commander Ford, November 13, 1942, Washington Director's Office Administrative Files, Latin America—Mexico, WASH-DIR-OFF-OP-266: 769, RG 226, NARA.

44. Service record of General de División Cristóbal Guzmán Cárdenas, *hoja de servicios* dated September 19, 1953, Archivo de Cancelados, file XI/111/1-428 (General de División Cristóbal Guzmán Cárdenas), *fojas* 3319 ff., Secretaría de la Defensa Nacional, Dirección General de Archivo e Historia, Mexico City (henceforth, "SDN").

45. Harold D. Finley to Secretary of State, September 25, 1942, State Department Central File, 812.00/32056, RG 59, NARA.

46. George S. Messersmith to Sumner Welles, September 17, 1942, Security-Segregated Records of the U.S. Embassy in Mexico City, 1942, classification 710, RG 84, NARA.

47. Lázaro Cárdenas, *Obras*, 92–93.

48. Circular no. 69, from General de Brigada Tomás Sánchez Hernández, December 5, 1942, Fondo Joaquín Amaro, box 12, Fideicomiso Archivos Plutarco Elías Calles y Fernando Torreblanca, Mexico City (henceforth, "FAPEC").

49. Military Attaché Report no. 1611, by Captain Battles, January 30, 1942, Military Intelligence Division Regional File, Mexico, 1922–1944, classification 6110, RG 165, NARA; and Harold D. Finley to Secretary of State, January 15, 1943, State Department Central File, 812.20/418, RG 59, NARA. Both of these documents note the gradual transfer of functions from the EMP to the new SDN general staff. General de Brigada Tomás Sánchez Hernández to General de División Joaquín Amaro Domínguez, ca. February 15, 1943, Fondo Joaquín Amaro, box 10, FAPEC, transcribes the February 15, 1943, presidential decree through

which the defense ministry's once powerless Estado Mayor del C. Secretario was formally designated as the much more influential Estado Mayor de la Secretaría de la Defensa Nacional.

50. "Invitación al público para que asista a las prácticas de guerra," *Excélsior*, November 19, 1942; and "Magnífico material y buenos artilleros tiene México," *Excélsior*, November 22, 1942.

51. Circular no. 75, from General de División Francisco L. Urquizo, no date [ca. mid- to late December 1942], Fondo Joaquín Amaro, box 7, FAPEC.

52. "Mexico to Send Men Overseas; Mechanized Divisions Prepared," *New York Times*, November 1, 1942; and "Nuestra guerra no es un combate de flores," *La Nación*, November 14, 1942 (translation of *New York Times* article).

53. "Nuestra guerra no es un combate de flores," *La Nación*, November 14, 1942.

54. "Es necesario informar a nuestro pueblo sobre su real participación en la guerra," *Omega*, November 16, 1942.

55. "Defensores de México," *Tiempo*, December 11, 1942.

56. Office of Naval Intelligence Report no. 750-42-R, November 18, 1942, Military Intelligence Division Regional File, Mexico, 1922–1944, classification 2820.03, RG 165, NARA.

57. *Tiempo*, November 13, 1942.

58. "Piden que mexicanos vayan a pelear," *La Prensa*, November 11, 1942; and "Brigadas que vayan a combatir al Eje," *Excélsior*, November 12, 1942. Those listed as supporters of Pamanes Escobedo's suggestion

included left-leaning deputies such as César Garizurieta of Veracruz and Antonio Betancourt Pérez of Yucatán but also more moderate figures such as Juan Gil Preciado of Jalisco. These legislators argued that the suggestion should be taken seriously, inasmuch as Pamanes Escobedo, with his military background, would not have made it lightly.

59. "250,000 mexicanos en una expedición," *La Prensa*, November 15, 1942.

60. "Dávila no tiene autoridad para ofrecer mexicanos," *La Prensa*, November 16, 1942.

61. José María Dávila to J. Jesús Gonález Gallo, November 27, 1942, MAC, 161.1/81, AGN.

62. José María Dávila to Secretario de Relaciones Exteriores, November 18, 1942, Archivo Histórico, file 20-16-10, SRE.

63. "Vida nacional," *La Nación*, November 21, 1942.

64. "Indiscreta declaración de un embajador que sin embargo es alarmante realidad," *Omega*, November 19, 1942.

65. Military Attaché Report no. 1251, by Captain Robert E. Battles, October 12, 1942, Military Intelligence Division Regional File, Mexico, 1922–1944, box 2552, RG 165, NARA.

66. "Cuando las democracias necesiten soldados mexicanos, plantearáse el problema al pueblo," *Excélsior*, November 18, 1942.

67. Ibid.

68. Unsigned report from Mexico City, November 21, 1942, Records of the Research and Analysis Branch, Regular Series, report no. 25036, RG 226, NARA.

69. Harold D. Finley to Secretary of State, December 1, 1942, State Department Central File, 812.20/408, RG 59, NARA.

70. The machinery of the 1940 law was set into motion through an August 3, 1942, decree, according to Ávila Camacho's September 1, 1942, *informe* to the Mexican Congress. See Manuel Ávila Camacho, *Informe que rinde al H. Congreso de la Union*, 29.

71. "Extracto" of Elena Ordaz, Concepción Caldera, and others to Manuel Ávila Camacho, January 3, 1943, MAC, 545.2/14-4, AGN.

72. "La conscripción militar," *El Sinarquista*, November 26, 1942.

73. Ibid.

74. "Pedimos al Señor Presidente que hable con claridad a su pueblo," *El Sinarquista*, November 26, 1942.

75. Lázaro Cárdenas to Manuel Ávila Camacho, December 1, 1942, MAC, 545.2/14, AGN.

76. "No irán a pelear fuera del país," *Excélsior*, December 2, 1942.

77. Second SDN statement cited in "Defensores de México," *Tiempo*, December 11, 1942; and "No saldrán soldados mexicanos a los frentes de guerra extranjeros," *El Sinarquista*, December 10, 1942.

78. "A defender a México," *Novedades*, December 3, 1942.

79. "Página del editor: Homenaje a Lázaro Cárdenas," *Hoy*, December 12, 1942.

80. See "Página del editor: Primero nosotros," *Hoy*, November 28, 1942, for earlier criticism of the foreign minister's efforts to deepen Mexican involvement in the war. *Hoy*'s attacks on Padilla might well have been instigated by Maximino Ávila Camacho, who reportedly

subsidized the magazine's publication; a report to the OSS speculated that the communications minister aspired to succeed his brother as president and that he therefore was seeking to discredit Padilla, whom he saw as a potential rival. See unsigned report from Mexico City, November 7, 1942, Records of the Research and Analysis Branch, Regular Series, report no. 27127, RG 226, NARA.

81. "No saldrán soldados mexicanos a los frentes de guerra extranjeros," *El Sinarquista*, December 10, 1942.

82. "Vida nacional," *La Nación*, December 12, 1942.

83. Urquizo said this had occurred in Mérida, Tampico, "and in other places." "Los conscriptos no saldrán del territorio mexicano para ir a combatir a tierras lejanas," *La Prensa*, December 25, 1942.

84. Ibid.

85. Oficio circular from Lázaro Cárdenas, July 7, 1943, Fondo Joaquin Amaro, box 5, FAPEC. See also "El servicio militar se hará sin distingos," *El Universal*, July 28, 1943. Irregularities in the conscription process and the general lack of effectiveness of the obligatory military service program are discussed in Rath, "Que el cielo un soldado en cada hijo te dio."

86. Mexico, Secretaría de la Defensa Nacional, *Memoria de la Secretaría de la Defensa Nacional, septiembre de 1942–agosto de 1943*, 38–42.

87. Fernando Casas Alemán to Secretario Particular del Presidente de la República, December 24, 1942, MAC, 559.1/49, AGN.

88. E. W. Eaton to Secretary of State, January 6, 1943, State Department Central File, 812.00/32096, RG 59, NARA.

89. Leaflets included as enclosures to Guy Ray to the Secretary of State, January 13, 1943, State Department Central File, 812.20/421, RG 59, NARA.

90. Ibid.

91. "Los conscriptos no saldrán del territorio mexicano para ir a combatir a tierras lejanas," *La Prensa*, December 25, 1942.

92. "Los conscriptos mexicanos no saldrán al extranjero," *La Prensa*, December 27, 1942.

93. *El Universal*, January 1, 1943, 3rd section, 14; also, January 6, 1943, 6; January 10, 1943, 13.

94. *El Universal*, January 3, 1943, 15; also, January 4, 1943, 11.

95. *El Universal*, January 6, 1943, 2nd section, 4; also, January 7, 1943, 2nd section, 1; January 11, 1943, 5.

96. "Interpretación mexicana de la guerra," December 30, 1942, Fondo Incorporado—Félix F. Palavicini, book 13, Archivo Histórico de la Universidad Nacional Autónoma de México, Mexico City (henceforth, AHUNAM).

97. "¡Impedid que se vayan al cerro!" *El Sinarquista*, January 7, 1943.

98. "Quienes son los perturbadores," *El Sinarquista*, January 14, 1943.

99. Herb [Bursley] to Laurence Duggan, January 16, 1943, State Department Central File, 812.20/435, RG 59, NARA.

100. José Lelo de Larrea to Manuel R. Hernández, March 1, 1943, DGIPS, box 775, file 2-1/43/238, AGN.

101. Jorge Mena Baca to José Lelo de Larrea, October 4, 1943, DGIPS, box 775, file 2-1/43/238, AGN.

102. December 31, 1942, speech by Manuel Ávila Camacho, in Archivo Histórico, file III-918-9, SRE. Also published as "Mensaje dirigido a la nación mexicana con motivo del año nuevo," in Ávila Camacho, *La unidad de México*, 13–19.

103. United Press report by Edward Morgan, February 10, 1943, MAC, 708.1/40, AGN.

104. Edward Morgan to Waldo Romo Castro, February 11, 1943, MAC, 708.1/40, AGN.

105. Spanish text of article and quotations from U.S. legislators in MAC, 708.1/40, AGN.

106. Harold D. Finley to Secretary of State, February 24, 1943, citing February 20, 1943, remarks of Ávila Camacho to *La Prensa* correspondent, State Department Central File, 740.0011 European War 1939/28247, RG 59, NARA. Also published in United States, Department of State, *Foreign Relations of the United States, 1943*, 6:397.

107. Simpson, *Many Mexicos*, 298–99; and Mexico, Secretaría de la Economía Nacional, *El desarrollo de la economía nacional bajo la influencia de la guerra*, 11.

108. Harold D. Finley to Secretary of State, May 20, 1943, State Department Central File, 812.00/32155, RG 59, NARA.

109. Presidente Municipal de Siltepec, Chiapas, to Manuel Ávila Camacho, December 26, 1942, DGIPS, box 738, AGN.

110. Presidente Municipal de Rio Blanco, Veracruz, to Secretaría de Gobernación, February 18, 1943, DGIPS, box 745, AGN. Francisco "Pancho" Villa famously incurred the wrath of the United States by carrying out a raid on the town of Columbus, New Mexico, during the Mexican Revolution.

111. Efrén Ramírez Galicia to Manuel Ávila Camacho, March 16, 1943, MAC, 161.1/81, AGN. As president of Mexico in the 1860s, Benito Juárez expelled a French army of occupation.

112. Villaseñor, "La economía de guerra en México," 16–17, 25–30.

113. George S. Messersmith to Laurence Duggan, June 21, 1943, Security-Segregated Records of the U.S. Embassy in Mexico City, 1943, classification 851.6, RG 84, NARA.

114. Sumner Welles to Mr. Summerlin, December 18, 1942, State Department Central File, 711.12/1788, RG 59, NARA; and memorandum by George S. Messersmith, January 14, 1943, Security-Segregated Records of the U.S. Embassy in Mexico City, 1943, classification 800.1, RG 84, NARA.

115. "Mexico to be United States' 'Best Ally,' Observers Predict," *Corpus Christi Times*, no date [April 1943], press clipping in Archivo Histórico, file III-643-1 bis, SRE.

116. "Mexico Willing to Enter Battle," Associated Press report, April 21, 1943, press clipping in Archivo Histórico, file III-643-1 bis, SRE.

117. "La visita del Presidente F. D. Roosevelt causa las más profundas preocupaciones," *Omega*, April 22, 1943; and "Si ya estamos entregando lo que tenemos ¿qué más quiere Roosevelt de nosotros?" *Omega*, April 24, 1943.

118. George S. Messersmith telegram to Department of State, April 28, 1943, State Department Central File, 812.001 Roosevelt Visits/525, RG 59, NARA.

119. Harold D. Finley to Secretary of State, May 20, 1943, State Department Central File, 812.00/32155, RG 59, NARA.

120. George S. Messersmith telegram to Department of State, April 21, 1943, State Department Central File, 811.001 Roosevelt Visits/512, RG 59, NARA.

121. "Roosevelt in Mexico," *Miami Herald*, April 20, 1943, press clipping in Archivo Histórico, file III-643-1 bis, SRE.

122. Military Attaché Report no. 2468, by Brigadier General A. R. Harris, September 20, 1943, Military Intelligence Division Regional File, Mexico, 1922–1944, box 2553, RG 165, NARA.

123. Henry Waterman to Secretary of State, April 24, 1943, State Department Central File, 811.001 Roosevelt Visits/530, RG 59, NARA.

124. Naval Intelligence Report no. 91-43-R, by U.S. Naval Attaché, Mexico City, March 2, 1943, Military Intelligence Division Regional File, Mexico, 1922–1944, classification 5935.01, RG 165, NARA.

125. Major Benjamin Muse (chief, Latin American Section, Foreign Liaison Branch, U.S. Army General Staff) to Lieutenant Colonel O. T. Jamerson (acting foreign liaison officer), May 6, 1943, Records of the Joint United States–Mexican Defense Commission, MDC 9100, tab 8-62, RG 218, NARA.

126. Cárdenas Rodríguez, *Mis dos misiones*, 11–23.

127. "Habla el Gral. Alamillo sobre la misión en Norafica," *El Nacional*, June 7, 1943.

128. Military Intelligence Report no. SI-234, by Major Cantwell C. Brown, July 13, 1943, Records of the Operations Division, classification 350.05, Mexico, RG 165, NARA.

129. *Ultimas Noticias de Excélsior*, April 13, 1943, enclosed in Harold D. Finley to the Secretary of State, April 14, 1943, State Department Central File, 812.001 Cárdenas, Lázaro/287, RG 59, NARA.

130. Harold D. Finley to Secretary of State, May 20, 1943, State Department Central File, 812.00/32155, RG 59, NARA.

131. "28 de mayo," *El Nacional*, May 28, 1943.

132. "Primer año de guerra; El país dará su esfuerzo armado si los acontecimientos lo requiriesen," *El Nacional*, May 29, 1943.

133. "Vida nacional," *La Nación*, June 5, 1943.

134. Harold D. Finley to Secretary of State, June 29, 1943, State Department Central File, 812.00/32171, RG 59, NARA.

135. "250,000 mexicanos pelean en diversos frentes de guerra, dice Flores M.," *Excélsior*, June 3, 1943.

136. Ernesto Hidalgo circular to Miembros del Servicio Exterior Mexicano, January 22, 1943, AEMEUA, file 73-0/524(72:73)/1, SRE.

137. "Vida nacional," *La Nación*, June 12, 1943.

138. Periodic correspondence on troop enlistment totals, e.g., Francisco Castillo Nájera to the Secretario de Relaciones Exteriores, June 15, 1943, AEMEUA, file 73-0/524(72:73)/1, SRE, which gave the most up-to-date total for Mexicans in the U.S. armed forces according to the War Department as 9,061 (as of March 31, 1943); see also "Es necesario proteger a los mexicanos enrolados en los ejércitos extranjeros, *Omega*, June 12, 1943.

139. "Vida nacional," *La Nación*, June 12, 1943.

140. Ibid.

141. "Riña entre 'tarzanes' y marinos," *El Universal*, June 9, 1943.

142. "Tarzanes que son problema," *El Nacional*, June 9, 1943.

143. Alfredo Elías Calles (Mexican consul in Los Angeles) to Mexican Ambassador in Washington, June 9, 1943, and other correspondence, AEMEUA, file 73-0/242.5(73-27)1, SRE.

144. Secretariat of Foreign Relations to Mexican Embassy in Washington, June 15, 1943, AEMEUA, file 73-0/242.5(73-27)1, SRE. This message was reported in "Los incidentes entre 'pachucos' y marinos," *El Universal*, June 16, 1943, and elsewhere.

145. Unsigned report from Mexico City, June 26, 1943, Records of the Research and Analysis Branch, Regular Series, report no. 39198, RG 226, NARA; "Vida nacional," *La Nación*, June 26, 1943; "Han asumido caracteres de salvajismo los ataques a mexicanos en Los Angeles," *Omega*, June 19, 1943; "La opinión pública no está satisfecha," *Omega*, July 5, 1943; and "Que relaciones trate lo de los pachucos, el Senador Flores M. anunció que lo va a solicitar, en breve," *Excélsior*, June 14, 1943.

146. "Los lamentables sucesos ocurridos en Los Angeles," *El Universal*, June 22, 1943.

147. Office of Naval Intelligence Report no. 277-43-R, June 26, 1943, Records of the Research and Analysis Branch, Regular Series, report no. 38715, RG 226, NARA; "Vida nacional," *La Nación*, July 3, 1943.

148. Unsigned report from Mexico City, June 26, 1943, Records of the Research and Analysis Branch, Regular Series, report no. 39198, RG 226, NARA.

149. Harold D. Finley to Secretary of State, August 26, 1942, State Department Central File, 812.00/32036, RG 59, NARA.

150. *La Prensa*, January 5, 1943, enclosed in Harold D. Finley to the Secretary of State, January 5, 1943, State Department Central File, 812.00/32094, RG 59, NARA.

151. Harold D. Finley to Secretary of State, April 13, 1943, State Department Central File, 812.00/32140, RG 59, NARA.

152. "El P.R.M. ya tiene candidatos," *El Nacional*, June 9, 1943; and Knight, "The Rise and Fall of Cardenismo," 308.

153. "30 precandidatos están inconformes: Quienes no fueron escogidos por el P.R.M. jugarán independientemente," *El Universal*, June 10, 1943; and Knight, "The Rise and Fall of Cardenismo," 308. According to Knight, 56 of the 144 PRM candidates were representatives of the new popular sector, which was organized as the Confederación Nacional de Organizaciones Populares (CNOP).

154. The biggest stir within the PRM was caused by former president Abelardo L. Rodríguez, who, as a candidate for the governorship in his native Sonora, suggested that the PRM might no longer be necessary as a bulwark against counterrevolutionary reactionaries and when he later criticized the undemocratic features of the party. See "El Gral. Rodríguez es fiel al PRM," *Excélsior*, June 11, 1943; "Identificado con el P.R.M.," *El Nacional*, June 11, 1943; and "No contra el P.R.M., sino contra sus procedimientos," *El Universal*, July 14, 1943.

155. Benjamin Smith explains that the defeated candidate who killed himself in the Chamber of Deputies, Jorge Meixueiro of Oaxaca, had been the officially designated PRM candidate for his district until shortly before the election, when Ávila Camacho shifted his support to a member of a different party faction in the region. Smith's account shows that especially at the local and state levels, the ruling party was far from being unified or monolithic during this period and that political outcomes were the product of complex interactions between the central government, local political leaders, and popular organizations. Nonetheless, as in this case, the position of the president could be decisive (Smith, *Pistoleros and Popular Movements*, 265–67).

156. "Ni comunistas ni los del PAN en la Cámara," *El Universal*, July 14, 1943.

157. "La reorganización del P.R.M.," *El Universal*, July 14, 1943.

158. Unsigned report from Mexico City, July 9, 1943, Records of the Research and Analysis Branch, Regular Series, report no. 39728, RG 226, NARA.

159. Transcript of conversation dated May 20, 1943, Archivo Particular de Ignacio García Téllez, box 2—Guanajuato, folder 6—Manuel Ávila Camacho, Colmex. After receiving this response from the president, García Téllez announced his intention to retire to private life, whereupon Ávila Camacho assured him of his friendship. Perhaps in recognition of his willingness to put aside his personal interests in the aftermath of the Guanajuato election, García Téllez was invited back into the government in 1944, when he became the head of the new Instituto Mexicano de Seguridad Social.

160. George S. Messersmith to Sumner Welles, July 6, 1943, State Department Central File, 740.0011 European War 1939/31593 1/7, RG 59, NARA, published in United States, Department of State, *Foreign Relations of the United States, 1943*, vol. 6.

Chapter Five

1. George S. Messersmith to Sumner Welles, July 6, 1943, State Department Central File, 740.0011 European War 1939/31593 1/7, RG 59, NARA. Also published in United States, Department of State, *Foreign Relations of the United States, 1943*, 6:404–6.

2. Ibid.

3. Ibid.

4. This possibility is suggested in "Memorandum: Participation of Mexican Forces in the War," by Vice Admiral Alfred W. Johnson, September 7, 1943, Security-Segregated Records of the U.S. Embassy in Mexico City, 1943, classification 711, RG 84, NARA.

5. George S. Messersmith to Sumner Welles, July 6, 1943, State Department Central File, 740.0011 European War 1939/31593 1/7, RG 59, NARA.

6. Ibid.

7. George S. Messersmith to Sumner Welles, August 5, 1943, Security-Segregated Records of the U.S. Embassy in Mexico City, 1943, classification 711, RG 84, NARA.

8. Sumner Welles to George S. Messersmith, August 14, 1943, Security-Segregated Records of the U.S. Embassy in Mexico City, 1943, classification 711, RG 84, NARA.

9. George S. Messersmith to Philip W. Bonsal, chief of the Division of the American Republics,

U.S. Department of State, August 31, 1943, State Department Central File, 740.0011 European War 1939/31593 3/7, RG 59, NARA. Also published in United States, Department of State, *Foreign Relations of the United States, 1943*, 6:408.

10. Major General Guy V. Henry memorandum to the Chief of Staff, September 23, 1943, Records of the Joint Mexican–United States Defense Commission, MDC 9100, tab 8-80, RG 218, NARA.

11. George S. Messersmith to Philip W. Bonsal, November 9, 1943, Security-Segregated Records of the U.S. Embassy in Mexico City, 1943, classification 711, RG 84, NARA. See also George S. Messersmith to Philip W. Bonsal, September 20, 1943, Security-Segregated Records of the U.S. Embassy in Mexico City, 1943, classification 711, RG 84, NARA.

12. George S. Messersmith to Philip W. Bonsal, September 20, 1943, Security-Segregated Records of the U.S. Embassy in Mexico City, 1943, classification 711, RG 84, NARA.

13. George S. Messersmith to Philip W. Bonsal, September 28, 1943, Security-Segregated Records of the U.S. Embassy in Mexico City, 1943, classification 711, RG 84, NARA.

14. Military Attaché Report no. 2426, September 3, 1943, Military Intelligence Division Regional File, Mexico, 1922–1944, box 2553, RG 165, NARA. The report incorrectly gives the date of the rally as August 28; see "Lombardo pide que se envíen mexicanos al frente de guerra," *Excélsior*, August 30, 1943, for the correct date.

15. "No hubo sesión en la Cámara, pero sí hubo comentarios: Sólo un obrero opina que sí deben enviarse mexicanos al frente," *Excélsior*, August 31, 1943.

16. Manuel Torres Blanco (chief of the UNS) to Manuel Ávila Camacho, August 21, 1943, MAC, 161.1/81, AGN. Also published as "Carta al Presidente," *El Sinarquista*, August 26, 1943.

17. "Lombardo sabotea la conscripción de 1925," *El Sinarquista*, September 9, 1943.

18. General de Brigada José Beltrán Moreno to Manuel Ávila Camacho, October 13, 1943, Archivo de Cancelados, file XI/111/1-554 (General de División José Sebastián Beltrán Moreno), SDN.

19. Harold D. Finley to Secretary of State, November 11, 1943, citing *Novedades*, November 2, 1943, State Department Central File, 812.001 Rodríguez, Abelardo/57, RG 59, NARA.

20. Major Robert E. Battles to Chief, American Intelligence Service, October 12, 1943, Military Intelligence Division Regional File, Mexico, 1922–1944, box 2511, classification 6000.04.01, RG 165, NARA.

21. "Antes de medio año México enviará un ejército al extranjero," *Excélsior*, October 14, 1943.

22. Ibid., emphasis added.

23. "Ejército expedicionario," *Excélsior*, October 15, 1943.

24. "México está obligado a pelear en los frentes de guerra," *Excélsior*, October 15, 1943.

25. Ibid.

26. "Senadores pro-envío de tropas al frente," *Excélsior*, October 17, 1943.

27. "México está obligado a pelear en los frentes de guerra," *Excélsior*, October 15, 1943. Other legislators

who were cited as being in favor of participation were Senators Abelardo Reyes (*suplente*, Aguascalientes), Lamberto Elías (suplente, Zacactecas), and Abraham González (Jalisco) and Deputies Gorgonio Quesnel (Veracruz), Adán Velarde (Baja California), Julian Garza Tijerina (Nuevo León), Francisco de P. Jiménez (Michoacán), Octavio Reyes Sindola (Oaxaca), and Salvador Ochoa Rentería (Michoacán).

28. "México está obligado a pelear en los frentes de guerra," *Excélsior*, October 15, 1943.

29. "Ahora sí tiene razón 'Excélsior': Deben ir fuerzas mexicanas a los frentes de guerra," *El Popular*, October 18, 1943.

30. "Condecoraciones y hambre," *Novedades*, October 16, 1943.

31. Military Attaché Report no. 2621, October 22, 1943, Military Intelligence Division Regional File, Mexico, 1922–1944, box 2552, RG 165, NARA.

32. Novo, *La vida en México en el periodo presidencial de Manuel Ávila Camacho*, 36. See also "Ventana, de Salvador Novo: Partes de todo," *Novedades*, October 16, 1943.

33. "Vida nacional: Mexicanos al frente," *La Nación*, October 23, 1943.

34. "Panorama nacional: Mexicanos en los frentes," *Orden*, November 1944; and "Maniobras para deblilitar a la nación," *El Sinarquista*, October 21, 1943.

35. Marcelina M. de González to Manuel Ávila Camacho, October 21, 1943, MAC, 161.1/81, AGN.

36. Harold D. Finley to Secretary of State, October 20, 1943, Security-Segregated Records of the U.S. Embassy in Mexico City, 1943,

classification 711, RG 84, NARA.

37. Military Attaché Report no. 2654, by Lieutenant Colonel Clarence S. Howe, October 29, 1943, Military Intelligence Division Regional File, Mexico, 1922–1944, box 2552, RG 165, NARA.

38. "Mambrú se va a la guerra," *Excélsior*, August 31, 1943.

39. "Ahora sí tiene razón 'Excélsior': Deben ir fuerzas mexicanas a los frentes de guerra," *El Popular*, October 18, 1943.

40. "Condecoraciones y hambre," *Novedades*, October 16, 1943.

41. George S. Messersmith to Philip W. Bonsal, November 23, 1943, Security-Segregated Records of the U.S. Embassy in Mexico City, 1943, classification 711, RG 84, NARA.

42. Ávila Camacho, "Discurso pronunciado en el acto de clausura del Segundo Ciclo de Información para Generales," in *Mensaje a la nación y otros discursos*, 5–8.

43. George S. Messersmith to Philip W. Bonsal, November 23, 1943, Security-Segregated Records of the U.S. Embassy in Mexico City, 1943, classification 711, RG 84, NARA.

44. Ibid.

45. Military Attaché Report no. 2741, by Major Robert E. Battles, November 23, 1943, Military Intelligence Division Regional File, Mexico, 1922–1944, box 2553, classification 5900, RG 165, NARA.

46. Editorials cited in David Thomasson to Secretary of State, November 19, 1943, State Department Central File, 812.001 Camacho, Manuel Ávila/249, RG 59, NARA.

47. Legislators' and PCM comments cited in "México fiel a su tradición," *El Universal*, November 18,

1943. The president of the Senate was Francisco Martínez Peralta (peasant sector, Sonora), and the deputies quoted were Leopoldo Hernández (peasant sector, Federal District) and Octavio Sentíes (México state). Congratulatory letters and telegrams from officials and individuals to Ávila Camacho are found in MAC, 161.1/81, AGN.

48. Juan Silveti to Manuel Ávila Camacho, November 22, 1943, MAC, 161.1/81, AGN.

49. "Apoyo general a lo dicho por el Presidente," *El Nacional*, November 19, 1943.

50. George H. Winters to George S. Messersmith, November 24, 1943, Security-Segregated Records of the U.S. Embassy in Mexico City, 1943, classification 711, RG 84, NARA.

51. Military Attaché Report no. 2808, by Captain Paul B. Miller, December 6, 1943, citing *El Universal*, November 28, 1943, Military Intelligence Division Regional File, Mexico, 1922–1944, box 2553, classification 9900, RG 165, NARA.

52. Captain J. P. Conover (U.S. naval attaché) to George S. Messersmith, December 20, 1943, Security-Segregated Records of the U.S. Embassy in Mexico City, 1943, classification 711, RG 84, NARA.

53. "No es cierta la salida de 150 pilotos," *El Nacional*, December 15, 1943. This denial was specifically in response to a report in *La Prensa*, December 13, 1943.

54. Unsigned report to the Office of Strategic Services, December 17, 1943, Records of the Research and Analysis Branch, Regular Series, report no. 52939, RG 226, NARA.

55. George S. Messersmith to Secretary of State, December 3,

1943, State Department Central File, 812.001 Camacho, Manuel Ávila/250, RG 59, NARA. Also published in United States, Department of State, *Foreign Relations of the United States, 1943*, 6:415.

56. Guy Ray to Secretary of State, December 7, 1943, State Department Central File, 812.00/32229, RG 59, NARA.

57. "Mexico Plans Unit to Fight in Pacific," *New York Times*, December 7, 1943; and Military Attaché Report no. 2821, December 8, 1943, Military Intelligence Division Regional File, Mexico, 1922–1944, box 2553, classification 3600, RG 165, NARA.

58. Guy Ray to Secretary of State, December 7, 1943, State Department Central File, 812.00/32229, RG 59, NARA.

59. "Mexicans Divided on Going to Battle," *New York Times*, December 10, 1943; Guy Ray to Secretary of State, December 9, 1943, State Department Central File, 812.00/32230, RG 59, NARA.

60. David Thomasson to Secretary of State, November 19, 1943, State Department Central File, 812.001 Camacho, Manuel Ávila/249, RG 59, NARA. The leftist legislators suggested as possible members of a "foreign legion" were Senator Nabor Ojeda (peasant sector, Guerrero) and Deputies Salvador Ochoa Renteria (Michoacán) and Graciano Sánchez (peasant sector, Tamaulipas).

61. Guy Ray to Secretary of State, January 6, 1944, State Department Central File, 812.00/32243, RG 59, NARA.

62. "Recibió el Presidente los simbólicos fuegos traídos de todo el país," *Excélsior*, November 20, 1943.

63. Guy Ray to Secretary of State, January 4, 1944, State Department Central File, 812.001 Camacho, Manuel Ávila/253, RG 59, NARA.

64. Guy Ray to Secretary of State, January 6, 1944, State Department Central File, 812.00/32243, RG 59, NARA.

65. "Se restituye a la Villa de Guadalupe Hidalgo, su nombre," *Novedades*, October 27, 1943.

66. "Reforma el ejecutivo el Artículo 31 del Reglamento General de Deberes Militares," *El Nacional*, November 16, 1943; and Naval Attaché Report no. 412-43-R, November 11, 1943, Military Intelligence Division Regional File, Mexico, 1922–1944, box 2448, classification 2600, RG 165, NARA.

67. David Thomasson to Secretary of State, November 16, 1943, State Department Central File, 812.00/32220, RG 59, NARA.

68. David Thomasson to Secretary of State, December 6, 1943, State Department Central File, 812.00/32228, RG 59, NARA. The Catholic union was the Confederación Nacional de Obreros Guadalupanos.

69. George S. Messersmith to Laurence Duggan, February 17, 1944, State Department Central File, 812.20/457, RG 59, NARA.

70. Brigadier General A. R. Harris to Major General Guy V. Henry, February 9, 1943, Records of the Joint Mexican–United States Defense Commission, box 15, MDC 9100-9, tab 8-80, RG 218, NARA.

71. Brigadier General A. R. Harris to Chief, Military Intelligence Service, War Department, February 14, 1944, Records of the Joint Mexican–United States Defense Commission, box 15, MDC 9100-9, tab 8-80, RG 218, NARA.

72. George S. Messersmith to Laurence Duggan, February 17, 1944, State Department Central File, 812.20/457, RG 59, NARA.

73. Military Attaché Report no. 3311, by Major Robert E. Battles, with remark by Brigadier General A. R. Harris, March 7, 1944, Military Intelligence Division Regional File, Mexico, 1922–1944, box 2554, classification 9760, RG 165, NARA.

74. *El Nacional*, March 9, 1944, clipping in MAC, 161.1/81, AGN.

75. "Alocución pronunciada por el Señor Presidente de la República, General de División Manuel Ávila Camacho, en el Casino Militar, el 8 de marzo de 1944, con motivo del banquete ofrecido a la Fuerza Aérea Mexicana," MAC, 161.1/81, AGN.

76. Sargento 1/o de Infantería Jesús Hernández Rivera to Manuel Ávila Camacho, March 30, 1944, Capitán 1/o de Caballería Ramiro Sosa Alvarez to Manuel Ávila Camacho, March 10, 1944, and other telegrams in MAC, 161.1/81, AGN. Also, "Muchos elementos quieren ir al frente," *El Universal*, March 10, 1944; "Abelardo y Amaro piden ir primero," *La Prensa*, March 10, 1944; and "Un alto espíritu de patriotismo de los miembros del Ejército Nacional," *El Popular*, March 10, 1944.

77. "Soldados de México," *El Universal Gráfico*, March 10, 1944.

78. "Nunca tantos . . . ," *Excélsior*, March 10, 1944.

79. "Soldados de México," *El Universal Gráfico*, March 10, 1944.

80. "Nunca tantos . . . ," *Excélsior*, March 10, 1944; "Soldados de México," *El Universal Gráfico*, March 10, 1944;

"Un alto espíritu de patriotismo de los miembros del Ejército Nacional," *El Popular*, March 10, 1944; "México en la guerra," *La Prensa*, March 14, 1944; and "Grandes proporciones adquiere una iniciativa de 'La Prensa,'" *La Prensa*, March 15, 1944.

81. "Oferta suplicante," *El Sinarquista*, March 16, 1944.

82. The strike lasted from March 5 until April 3, 1944; see *Novedades*, April 3, 1944.

83. George S. Messersmith to Franklin D. Roosevelt, March 15, 1944, State Department Central File, 812.20/460, RG 59, NARA.

84. "Memorandum from the Ambassador," George S. Messersmith, for the files [?], March 28, 1944, General Records of the U.S. Embassy in Mexico City, 1944, classification 711, RG 84, NARA; and "Memorandum for the Ambassador," Brigadier General William E. Hall to George S. Messersmith, March 29, 1944, Records of the Joint Mexican–United States Defense Commission, box 15, MDC 9100-9, tab 8-80, RG 218, NARA.

85. "Memorandum for the Ambassador," Brigadier General William E. Hall to George S. Messersmith, April 1, 1944, Records of the Joint Mexican–United States Defense Commission, box 15, MDC 9100-9, tab 8-80, RG 218, NARA.

86. George S. Messersmith to Brigadier General William E. Hall, May 20, 1944, State Department Central File, 812.20/476, RG 59, NARA.

87. George S. Messersmith to Cordell Hull, March 15, 1944, State Department Central File, 812.20/460, RG 59, NARA.

88. Brigadier General A. R. Harris to Assistant Chief of Staff, G-2, War Department, March 31, 1944, Records of the Joint Mexican–United States Defense Commission, MDC 9100-9, tab 8-80, box 15, RG 218, NARA.

89. Major General Guy V. Henry memorandum to Assistant Chief of Staff, Operations Division, War Department, March 17, 1944, and Major General Guy V. Henry to Brigadier General A. R. Harris, March 18, 1944, Records of the Joint Mexican–United States Defense Commission, box 15, MDC 9100-9, tab 8-80, RG 218, NARA.

90. George S. Messersmith to Laurence Duggan, March 23, 1944, General Records of the U.S. Embassy in Mexico City, 1944, classification 711, RG 84, NARA.

91. "Con gran entereza, el Señor Presidente frustró un atentado contra su vida," *Novedades*, April 11, 1944, and other Mexico City newspapers of April 11, 1944; and transcription of April 10, 1944, "Acta de Policía Judicial Militar," in Dr. José Gómez Robleda and Dr. Alfonso Quiroz to General de Brigada Roberto T. Bonilla (*procurador general de justicia militar*), May 2, 1944, Archivo de Cancelados, file 1-55 (General de División Manuel Ávila Camacho), SDN.

92. Guy Ray to Secretary of State, April 11, 1944, State Department Central File, 812.001 Camacho, Manuel Ávila/262, RG 59, NARA.

93. "El atentado al Presidente," *Novedades*, April 11, 1944; and Guy Ray to the Secretary of State, April 11, 1944, State Department Central File, 812.001 Camacho, Manuel Ávila/262, RG 59, NARA. See also *La Nación*, April 15, 1944, and *El Sinarquista*, April 20, 1944, for denunciations of

leftist efforts to blame Catholics and conservative organizations for the assassination attempt.

94. Transcription of April 10, 1944, "Acta de Policía Judicial Militar," in Dr. José Gómez Robleda and Dr. Alfonso Quiroz to General de Brigada Roberto T. Bonilla, May 2, 1944, Archivo de Cancelados, file 1-55, (General de División Manuel Ávila Camacho), SDN.

95. Division of Mexican Affairs memo to Joseph W. McGurk, Philip W. Bonsal, and Laurence Duggan, April 15, 1944, State Department Central File, 812.00/32386, RG 59, NARA. For further references to the relationship between graft and the rise of instability, see also Harold D. Finley to the Secretary of State, August 8, 1943, State Department Central File, 812.00/32180, RG 59, NARA; George S. Messersmith to Cordell Hull, May 30, 1944, State Department Central File, 812.00/32404, RG 59, NARA; and Guy Ray to the Secretary of State, June 9, 1944, State Department Central File, 812.00/32399, RG 59, NARA.

96. "¡Alerta, paro general! El sinarquismo hace un llamado urgente al ejército," *El Sinarquista*, June 22, 1944.

97. See, for example, "Las huelgas políticas son fruto de la debildad del actual régimen," *El Sinarquista*, June 8, 1944; and "Esto no es gobierno," *El Sinarquista*, June 22, 1944.

98. George S. Messersmith to Sumner Welles, May 21, 1942, document 1503a, GSM.

99. "Conclusiones del C. procurador sobre actividades sinarquistas," *El Nacional*, July 6, 1944; and David Thomasson to the Secretary of State, July 7, 1944, State Department Central File, 862.20212/7-744, RG 59, NARA.

100. "El Presidente presenciará hoy el gran acto colectivo en apoyo de nuestro régimen," *El Nacional*, July 9, 1944; "El pueblo mexicano está con el primer magistrado de la nación: Respaldo a su actitud contra el sinarquismo," *El Nacional*, July 10, 1944; and numerous telegrams in MAC, 544.61/39, AGN.

101. Military Attaché Report no. 4227, by Brigadier General A. R. Harris, July 15, 1944, Records of the Research and Analysis Branch, Regular Series, report no. 84467, RG 226, NARA.

102. "Declaración del C. Capitán Segundo de Artillería Benito Castañeda Chavarría," July 12, 1944, Archivo de Cancelados, file XI/111/8-18953 (*ex-capitán* Benito Castañeda Chavarría), SDN.

103. For the president's explanation of his decision to spare Castañeda's life, see Manuel Ávila Camacho to Lázaro Cárdenas, July 12, 1944, published as "Carta del Señor Presidente de la República dando a conocer los motivos que lo impulsaron a conceder al Capitán Castañeda Chavarrría el indulto por gracia," in Ávila Camacho, *Enseñar a leer y escribir a un pueblo es redimirlo*, 9–11.

104. Military Attaché Report no. 4227, by Brigadier General A. R. Harris, July 15, 1944, Records of the Research and Analysis Branch, Regular Series, report no. 84467, RG 226, NARA.

105. Herbert Bursley to Joseph W. McGurk, July 13, 1944, State Department Central File, 812.00/7-1344, RG 59, NARA; and George S. Messersmith to Cordell Hull, July 14, 1944, State Department Central File, 812.00/7-1444, RG 59, NARA.

106. Military Attaché Report no.

4227, by Brigadier General A. R. Harris, July 15, 1944, Records of the Research and Analysis Branch, Regular Series, report no. 84467, RG 226, NARA.

107. George S. Messersmith to Cordell Hull, July 2, 1944, State Department Central File, 812.20/7-244, RG 59, NARA; and George S. Messersmith to Cordell Hull, July 12, 1944, State Department Central File, 812.20/7-1244, RG 59, NARA. A copy of the training plans presented at the foreign ministry can be found in Colonel L. O. Ryan memorandum to George S. Messersmith, July 10, 1944, Archivo Histórico, file III-919-2, SRE.

108. George S. Messersmith to Cordell Hull, June 12, 1944, State Department Central File, 812.20/477, RG 59, NARA.

109. George S. Messersmith to Cordell Hull, July 2, 1944, State Department Central File, 812.20/7-244, RG 59, NARA.

110. "Palabras del Señor Presidente de la República a los CC. jefes, oficiales, clases y tropa del Escuadrón 201 de la Fuerza Aérea Mexicana," July 21, 1944, in Ávila Camacho, *Enseñar a leer y escribir a un pueblo es remidirlo*, 13–14.

111. Ávila Camacho, *Enseñar a leer y escribir a un pueblo es remidirlo*, 13–14.

112. "Tropas mexicanas a la guerra mundial: 4 divisiones saldrán pronto a la contienda," *La Prensa*, July 9, 1944; and "Tendremos que luchar contra los japoneses: México puede poner cuatro divisiones de inmediato en la guerra," *Novedades*, July 9, 1944.

113. David Thomasson to Secretary of State, State Department Central File, 812.20/7-1144, RG 59, NARA.

114. "Padilla ha dicho: 'Irán

mexicanos al frente' . . . y el pueblo opina sobre esta oferta del canciller," *La Nación*, July 15, 1944.

115. "La salida de nuestros pilotos," *Novedades*, July 25, 1944.

116. George S. Messersmith to Joseph W. McGurk, July 29, 1944, State Department Central File, 812.20/7-2944, RG 59, NARA.

117. George S. Messersmith to Joseph W. McGurk, July 26, 1944, General Records of the U.S. Embassy in Mexico City, 1944, classification 711, RG 84, NARA.

Chapter Six

1. Presidential decree of August 21, 1944, in *Ley de emergencia que establece la Campaña Nacional contra el Analfabetismo* (México: Secretaría de Educación Pública, 1944), Archivo Particular de Jaime Torres Bodet, book 66, SRE.

2. Manuel Ávila Camacho to state governors, August 21, 1941, in *Ley de emergencia que establece la Campaña Nacional contra el Analfabetismo*, Archivo Particular de Jaime Torres Bodet, book 66, SRE.

3. Manuel Ávila Camacho speech of August 21, 1944, in *Ley de emergencia que establece la Campaña Nacional contra el Analfabetismo*, Archivo Particular de Jaime Torres Bodet, book 66, SRE.

4. Jaime Torres Bodet speech of August 27, 1944, in *Ley de emergencia que establece la Campaña Nacional contra el Analfabetismo*, Archivo Particular de Jaime Torres Bodet, book 66, SRE.

5. Memorandum by José Aguilar y Maya, August 14, 1944, Archivo Particular de Jaime Torres Bodet, book 66, SRE; and Jaime Torres Bodet, "Observaciones al

memorandum del señor Procurador General de la República respecto al proyecto de ley que establece la Campaña Nacional contra el Analfabetismo," August 14, 1944, Archivo Particular de Jaime Torres Bodet, book 66, SRE.

6. Manuel Ávila Camacho speech of August 21, 1944, in *Ley de emergencia que establece la Campaña Nacional contra el Analfabetismo*, Archivo Particular de Jaime Torres Bodet, book 66, SRE.

7. Bi-Weekly Situation Report, March 6, 1944, Records of the Research and Analysis Branch, Latin America Division, Bi-Weekly Situation Reports, 1944–1945, R. & A. 1306.23, RG 226, NARA.

8. Torres Bodet, *Años contra el tiempo*, 11. In his conversation with Torres Bodet, Ávila Camacho did cite Véjar Vázquez's health as one impediment to his effectiveness at that moment, but he also noted the bitter opposition of many of the teachers to the outgoing minister. It is clear from Torres Bodet's account of his December 21, 1943, meeting with the president that the timing of the teachers' convention determined the timing of the personnel change in the cabinet.

9. Ibid., 35.

10. Torres Bodet, *Educación mexicana*, 11.

11. Guy Ray to the Secretary of State, December 28, 1943, State Department Central File, 812.42/705, RG 59, NARA; and Guy Ray to the Secretary of State, January 6, 1944, State Department Central File, 812.42/707, RG 59, NARA.

12. Victor Manuel Villaseñor to Manuel Ávila Camacho, June 14, 1944, MAC, 433/310, AGN.

13. David Thomasson to the Secretary of State, December 11, 1944, State Department Central File, 812.00/12-1144, RG 59, NARA.

14. William K. Ailshie to the Secretary of State, December 18, 1944, State Department Central File, 812.00/12-1844, RG 59, NARA.

15. J. Jesús González Gallo to Secretario de Gobernación, December 14, 1944, transmitting decree dissolving the Comisión Nacional de Planeación para la Paz, MAC, 433/310, AGN; and memorandum on a "Proyecto de decreto disolviendo la Comisión Nacional de Planeación de [*sic*] la Paz," prepared by the Secretaría Particular, Presidencia de la República, December 13, 1944, MAC, 433/310, AGN.

16. Manuel Ávila Camacho to CC. Secretarios de la H. Cámara de Senadores, December 27, 1944, MAC, 161.1/81, AGN.

17. George S. Messersmith to the Secretary of State, December 30, 1944, General Records of the U.S. Embassy in Mexico City, 1944, classification 711, RG 84, NARA; "Podrán salir tropas y elementos bélicos de México a los frentes," *El Nacional*, December 30, 1944; and "Vida nacional," *La Nación*, January 6, 1945.

18. George S. Messersmith to the Secretary of State, December 29, 1944, State Department Central File, 740.0011 European War 1939/12-2944, RG 59, NARA.

19. "México en la contienda armada," *Novedades*, January 4, 1945.

20. "Vida nacional," *La Nación*, January 6, 1945.

21. "Lo que México ha dado a la guerra en estos años . . . ," *La Nación*, January 6, 1945.

22. "México en la guerra," *El Universal*, January 1, 1945.

23. "¡Al combate!" *El Popular*, January 1, 1945.

24. Francisco Castillo Nájera to Secretary of State, July 24, 1944, State Department Central File, 812.20/7-2944, RG 59, NARA.

25. Colonel Harold R. Maddux to State Department, August 16, 1944, State Department Central File, 812.20/8-1644, RG 59, NARA.

26. General Joseph T. McNarney to Assistant Chief of Staff, Operations Division, August 9, 1944, Records of the Office of the Director of Plans and Operations, General Records—Correspondence, Security-Classified General Correspondence, 1942–1945, OPD 336 Mexico, case 16, RG 165, NARA.

27. Lieutenant Colonel Gregorio Marquez to Assistant Chief of Staff, Operations Division, October 25, 1944, Records of the Joint Mexican–United States Defense Commission, MDC 9100, tab 8-80, RG 218, NARA.

28. Military Attaché Report, by Brigadier General A. R. Harris, August 5, 1944, General Records of the U.S. Embassy in Mexico City, 1944, classification 711, RG 84, NARA.

29. See José Beltrán Moreno to Secretario de la Defensa Nacional, June 27, 1945, Archivo de Cancelados, file XI/111/1-554 (General de División José Sebastián Beltrán Moreno), SDN, for an account of the trip. See Francisco L. Urquizo to Dirección General de Personal, April 14, 1945, Archivo de Cancelados, file XI/111/1-186 (General de División Eulogio Ortiz Reyes), SDN, for the order naming members of the observer mission.

30. Cárdenas Rodríguez, *Mis dos misiones*, 138–39.

31. George S. Messersmith memorandum of conversation with Franklin D. Roosevelt, December 19, 1944, General Records of the U.S. Embassy in Mexico City, 1944, classification 711, RG 84, NARA.

32. See General Brigadier Luis Alamillo Flores to Major General Guy V. Henry, December 11, 1944, Records of the Office of the Director of Plans and Operations, Security-Classified Correspondence, 1942–1945, OPD 336.2 Mexico, case 12, RG 165, NARA, which refers to both the Mexican government's desire to have the squadron go to the Pacific and to the fact that its preference was reinforced by "matters of organization of command" raised by Henry in a conversation on the subject, suggesting that U.S. military authorities found assignment to that theater more convenient. See also George S. Messersmith notes for memoirs, document 2031, GSM, for reference to unwillingness of U.S. command in Europe to accept additional foreign forces.

33. Brigadier General A. R. Harris to Chief, Military Intelligence Service, War Department, December 5, 1944, Records of the Office of the Director of Plans and Operations, Security-Classified Correspondence, 1942–1945, OPD 336.2 Mexico, case 12, RG 165, NARA.

34. "Combatirá el Escuadrón 201 en el frente de la guerra del Pacífico," *El Nacional*, February 20, 1945.

35. "El Escuadrón 201," *El Universal*, February 22, 1945.

36. "El mundo desde México," February 26, 1945, Fondo Incorporado—Félix F. Palavicini, book 27, AHUNAM.

37. George S. Messersmith to Secretary of State, March 5, 1945,

State Department Central File, 812.20/3-545, RG 59, NARA.

38. "El pueblo y la iglesia de México acompañan a los muchachos del Escuadrón 201 y rezan por ellos," *La Nación*, March 10, 1945.

39. "Al frente," *El Universal Gráfico*, February 23, 1945.

40. George S. Messersmith to Secretary of State, March 5, 1945, State Department Central File, 812.20/3-545, RG 59, NARA.

41. "La patria con sus soldados," *Novedades*, February 21, 1945.

42. George S. Messersmith to Joseph W. McGurk, September 5, 1944, State Department Central File, 812.00/9-545, RG 59, NARA.

43. "Pide el Presidente no tocar en un año la sucesión presidencial," *Excélsior*, December 2, 1944.

44. Herbert Bursley to the Secretary of State, December 16, 1944, State Department Central File, 812.00/12-1644, RG 59, NARA.

45. "La política subterránea nulifica la obra constructiva del país," *Excélsior*, January 1, 1945.

46. These charges came from both the left and the right; for his part, the foreign minister defended himself by saying that "not one of my public acts or of my political actions give ground for the belief that I could harbor such insane and foolish ideas" as to aspire to the presidency. See "Padilla realiza una labor de marcado tinte personalista," *El Popular*, April 18, 1942; "Nuesto canciller 'profeta de Américas,'" *La Nación*, April 18, 1942; Harold D. Finley to Secretary of State, May 8, 1942, State Department Central File, 812.00/31977, RG 59, NARA; and George S. Messersmith to Secretary of State, April 18, 1942,

State Department Central File, 812.002/525, RG 59, NARA.

47. George S. Messersmith to Secretary of State, November 11, 1942, State Department Central File, 812.00/32072, RG 59, NARA.

48. On the removal of Romero from his post, see George S. Messersmith to Joseph W. McGurk, November 6, 1944, Security-Segregated Records of the U.S. Embassy in Mexico City, 1944, classification 701.1, RG 84, NARA; "Vida nacional," *La Nación*, November 4, 1944; and "Vida nacional," *La Nación*, November 11, 1944.

49. George S. Messersmith to Edward R. Stettinius Jr. (secretary of state), January 8, 1945, Security-Segregated Records of the U.S. Embassy in Mexico City, 1945, classification 802.1, RG 84, NARA; and "Vida nacional," *La Nación*, January 13, 1945.

50. "News Briefs and Background," November 7, 1942, Records of the Research and Analysis Branch, Regular Series, report no. 27127, RG 226, NARA.

51. See, for example, Robert Wall (civil attaché) memorandum to George S. Messersmith, February 28, 1945, General Records of the U.S. Embassy in Mexico City, 1945, classification 710, RG 84, NARA, for references to efforts of Romero and Castillo Nájera to discredit Padilla during the Chapultepec Conference.

52. Santos, *Memorias*, 647.

53. Guy Ray to Secretary of State, September 24, 1942, State Department Central File, 812.00/32052, RG 59, NARA; Guy Ray to Secretary of State, November 12, 1942, State Department Central File, 812.00/32074, RG 59, NARA; and Harold D. Finley to

Secretary of State, April 13, 1943,
State Department Central File,
812.00/32140, RG 59, NARA.

54. George S. Messersmith
to Sumner Welles, May 3, 1943,
Security-Segregated Records of the
U.S. Embassy in Mexico City, 1943,
classification 802, RG 84, NARA.

55. One such reference by
Maximino to Lombardo and company came in an interview that
appeared in the Mexico City press
on December 8, 1943 (see Guy Ray
to Secretary of State, December
9, 1943, State Department Central
File, 812.00/32230, RG 59, NARA).
Maximino and Lombardo had also
feuded publicly during the spring
of 1942, after reports attributed to
Lombardo a speech in which the
labor leader allegedly denounced
Maximino's accumulation of wealth
as communications minister (see
"Mexico: News Background," January
28, 1943, Records of the Research
and Analysis Branch, Regular Series,
report no. 28204, RG 226, NARA).
Mexican entry into World War II
brought that particular round of snip-
ing to an abrupt end, demonstrating
once again the way in which participation in the war tended to stifle
domestic political strife.

56. George S. Messersmith
to Sumner Welles, April 14, 1943,
Security-Segregated Records of the
U.S. Embassy in Mexico City, 1943,
classification 802, RG 84, NARA.

57. Harold D. Finley to
Secretary of State, April 13, 1943,
State Department Central File,
812.00/32140, RG 59, NARA.

58. Harold D. Finley to
Secretary of State, May 20, 1943,
State Department Central File,
812.00/32154, RG 59, NARA.

59. For conspiracy-minded
Mexicans, the simultaneously timely
(just before the campaigning season
began) and untimely (Maximino
was only fifty-three) nature of the
elder Ávila Camacho brother's death
might have suggested the possibility
that he had been poisoned. However,
Eduardo Suárez recalled in his
memoirs that Maximino had been
told by his doctor early in 1945 that
his health was extremely fragile and
that he would be risking death if he
did not confine himself to his bed (see
Suárez, *Comentarios y recuerdos*, 299).
Moreover, the fact that Manuel later
died at fifty-eight suggests that perhaps Ávila Camacho men were genet-
ically predisposed to have relatively
short life spans. Maximino's death
certificate lists the cause of death as
cardiac arrest (*síncope cardiaco*; see
Archivo de Cancelados, file XI/111/1-
156 [General de División Maximino
Ávila Camacho], SDN). At the time
of his death, Maximino had been
backing Health and Welfare Minister
Gustavo Baz as his preferred candidate for the presidency (see Suárez,
Comentarios y recuerdos, 255).

60. Raleigh Gibson to
Secretary of State, April 7, 1943,
State Department Central File,
812.00/32136, RG 59, NARA; and
Suárez, *Comentarios y recuerdos*, 255.

61. Santos, *Memorias*, 833.

62. Villaseñor, *Memorias-
testimonio*, 191.

63. Alemán Valdés, *Remembranzas
y testimonios*, 199–200.

64. For allegations of Alemán's
connections with Germans early in the
war, see Summary, "Miguel Alemán,
Secretary of Gobernación," March
21, 1942, citing Naval Intelligence
Report no. 209-41, December 15,

1941, Military Intelligence Division Regional File, Mexico, 1922–1944, box 2465, classification 3115 (2), RG 165, NARA. For further allegations that officials at Gobernación regularly received bribes to protect Axis nationals in Mexico, see Military Intelligence Report no. 972, by Major Clarence S. Howe, and Military Intelligence Report no. 1539, by Major Philip S. Greene, both in Military Intelligence Division Regional File, Mexico, 1922–1944, box 2465, classification 3115 (2), RG 165, NARA; these reports refer specifically to the likely involvement of Oficial Mayor Adolfo Ruiz Cortines in receiving bribes, which is striking in light of the anticorruption stand taken by Ruiz Cortines as president (1952–1958).

65. One state-level elected official who benefited from favorable treatment by Alemán was San Luis Potosí governor Gonzalo Santos, who secured a six-year term in office (1943–1949) rather than a four-year mandate as a result of the interior minister's willingness "to torture the Constitution," as Alemán put it when he agreed to allow Santos to take advantage of a new constitutional provision that had not yet gone into effect. See Santos, *Memorias*, 768–69.

66. "El Gral. Enríquez cree extemporánea toda agitación futurista en el país," *Excélsior*, November 15, 1943.

67. George S. Messersmith to Joseph W. McGurk, August 24, 1944, document 1633, GSM.

68. Raleigh A. Gibson to Secretary of State, November 18, 1944, State Department Central File, 812.00/11-1844, RG 59, NARA.

69. Alemán Valdés, *Remembranzas*, 223.

70. Cárdenas, *Obras*, 174.

71. Raleigh Gibson to Secretary of State, June 6, 1945, State Department Central File, 812.00/6-645, RG 59, NARA. A well-connected former Supreme Court judge, Javier Icaza, provided this account of Lombardo Toledano's efforts on behalf of Alemán to the U.S. embassy.

72. Alemán Valdés, *Remembrazas*, 223.

73. Herbert Bursley to Secretary of State, June 6, 1945, State Department Central File, 812.00/6-645, RG 59, NARA.

74. Bi-Weekly Situation Report, June 20, 1945, Records of the Research and Analysis Branch, Latin America Division, Bi-Weekly Situation Reports, 1944–1945, R. & A. 1306.72, RG 226, NARA.

75. Cárdenas, *Obras*, 175; and "Vida nacional," *La Nación*, June 16, 1945.

76. Memorandum of conversation between Guy Ray and Miguel Alemán, September 25, 1945, State Department Central File, 812.00/9-2545, RG 59, NARA, cited in Paz Salinas, *Strategy, Security, and Spies*, 238. While Alemán might have feared that international considerations would prompt the president to throw his support to Padilla, there are in fact indications that Ávila Camacho himself was wary of the foreign minister's close ties with U.S. officials; San Luis Potosí governor Gonzalo N. Santos recalls that Ávila Camacho was angered early in 1945 when he received a letter from U.S. secretary of state "Stetinios" that recommended "in a shameful manner" that Padilla should be "the next president of the Republic." The president supposedly told Santos that he would "save the

letter for history" and that "we are accelerating the resolution of the presidential question . . . in order not to give the gringos time to intervene in this matter." (See Santos, *Memorias*, 827–28.) If the letter to which Santos referred did in fact exist, it has not surfaced, though it is clear that Stettinius made his government's warm feelings for Padilla clear— not necessarily in a diplomatically inappropriate way—in a March 1945 meeting with Ávila Camacho at the end of the Chapultepec Conference. (See Stettinius, *The Diaries of Edward R. Stettinius, Jr.*, 289.)

77. George S. Messersmith to Edward R. Stettinius Jr., June 14, 1945, State Department Central File, 812.00/6-1445, RG 59, NARA. The ambassador reported "on the basis of reliable information" that Lombardo had rallied labor support for Alemán after he "saw Padilla gathering stature" in San Francisco and developed a fear "that Padilla might be a strong candidate." It seems just as likely that Lombardo backed Alemán upon recognizing the strength of his domestic political position, but concern about a possible Padilla candidacy might well have been a factor, too.

78. Cárdenas, *Obras*, 170.

79. Robert Hale to Secretary of State, June 28, 1945, State Department Central File, 812.00/6-2845, RG 59, NARA.

80. Ezequiel Padilla to Manuel Ávila Camacho, July 11, 1945, MAC, 703.6/35, AGN.

81. George S. Messersmith to Nelson A. Rockefeller, April 8, 1945, Security-Segregated Records of the U.S. Embassy in Mexico City, 1945, classification 800, RG 84, NARA.

82. George S. Messersmith to Edward R. Stettinius Jr., June 14,

1944, State Department Central File, 812.00/6-1445, RG 59, NARA.

83. George S. Messersmith to Nelson A. Rockefeller, April 8, 1945, Security-Segregated Records of the U.S. Embassy in Mexico City, 1945, classification 800, RG 84, NARA.

84. George S. Messersmith to John Carrigan, June 1, 1945, State Department Central File, 812.00/6-145, RG 59, NARA.

85. George S. Messersmith to James F. Byrnes (secretary of state), August 23, 1945, State Department Central File, 812.00/8-2345, RG 59, NARA.

86. George S. Messersmith to John Carrigan, July 10, 1945, Confidential Records of the U.S. Embassy in Mexico City, classification 800, RG 84, NARA.

87. John Carrigan memorandum to Butler and Munro, June 6, 1945, State Department Central File, 812.00/6-645, RG 59, NARA.

88. John Carrigan memorandum to Lockwood and Munro, July 2, 1945, State Department Central File, 812.00/7-245, RG 59, NARA.

89. Messersmith: "I assume and hope that we will keep hands off in all of this business of the Mexican elections," in George S. Messersmith to John Carrigan, June 1, 1945, State Department Central File, 812.00/6-145, RG 59, NARA; "My own opinion is that we must keep out of this picture because anything which would make it appear that we are trying to show any interest in a particular candidate would be disastrous for us. If there is one thing on which the Mexicans are sensitive, it is interference by us in their internal affairs," in George S. Messersmith to Nelson A. Rockefeller, April 8, 1945, Security-Segregated Records of the

U.S. Embassy in Mexico City, 1945, classification 800, RG 84, NARA; "Recent events have even made it more abundant [sic] how essential it is for us to keep out of this picture," in George S. Messersmith to Edward R. Stettinius Jr., June 14, 1945, State Department Central File, 812.00/6-1445, RG 59, NARA; and Bureau of Mexican Affairs: "Any such encouragement [to Padilla to run for president] would run counter to our present policy, just as any discouragement woulo.d also run counter to our present policy. I think that this should be the cardinal factor in our attitude," in John Carrigan memorandum to Lockwood and Munro, July 2, 1945, State Department Central File, 812.00/7-245, RG59, NARA.

90. John Carrigan to George S. Messersmith, July 5, 1945, State Department Central File, 812.002/7-545, RG 59, NARA.

91. Guy Ray to Joseph W. McGurk, September 8, 1944, General Records of the U.S. Embassy in Mexico City, classification 710, RG 84, NARA.

92. Guy Ray to Secretary of State, September 26, 1945, State Department Central File, 812.00/9-2645, RG 59, NARA.

93. Guy Ray to Secretary of State, March 29, 1946, State Department Central File, 812.00/3-2946, RG 59, NARA.

94. "Gloria y responsabilidad," El Universal, June 11, 1945.

95. "La primera baja mexicana en oriente," El Nacional, June 13, 1945.

96. Lic. Benito Javier Pérez Verdia, "México y el Escuadrón 201," El Universal, June 28, 1945.

97. "Gran importancia de la tarea que debe realizar el Escadrón

'201,'" El Universal, June 13, 1945; and Military Attaché Report no. R-639-45, by Colonel Loren B. Hillsinger, June 25, 1945, Mexico City Naval Attaché Administrative Files, box 8, A21, RG 38, NARA.

98. Military Attaché Report no. R-761-45, by Colonel Loren B. Hillsinger, August 10, 1945, Mexico City Naval Attaché Administrative Files, box 8, A21, RG 38, NARA. That report noted the loss of pilots Héctor Espinosa Galván, Pablo Luis Rivas Martínez, and Mario López Portillo; news of the death of José Espinosa Fuentes in June had reached Mexico earlier.

99. George S. Messersmith to Secretary of State, July 10, 1945, State Department Central File, 812.00/7-1045, RG 59, NARA.

100. Inspector PS-19 to General Emilio Bai Serra, August 3, 1945, DGIPS, box 132, file 2-1/302.4(011)/2, AGN.

101. George S. Messersmith to Spruille Braden, February 2, 1946, State Department Central File, 812.20/2-246, RG 59, NARA.

102. "Expresa gratitud al 201 el General Ávila Camacho," Excélsior, August 16, 1945.

103. Cárdenas, Obras, 183; and Torres Bodet, Años contra el tiempo, 288.

104. Torres Bodet, Años contra el tiempo, 288.

105. Ibid., 291.

106. Handwritten notes by Francisco Castillo Nájera on a September 17, 1943, meeting with Lázaro Cárdenas and on September 20 and September 21, 1943, meetings with Manuel Ávila Camacho, Archivo Particular de Francisco Castillo Nájera, box 9, file 53, SRE. In expressing his desire to leave the

cabinet, Cárdenas attempted to signal his intention to remain politically inactive by saying that he would be interested in making a long-term official visit to the war fronts in Italy and the USSR. Nonetheless, Ávila Camacho clearly recognized the importance of keeping his predecessor within the ranks of his administration, insisting that Cárdenas remain in his post "for the good of the country."

107. Cárdenas, *Obras*, 132.

108. Francisco J. Múgica to Lázaro Cárdenas, August 29, 1945, Fondo Francisco J. Múgica, box 16, vol. CXLIV, document 26, CERMLC.

109. David Thomasson to Secretary of State, September 5, 1945, State Department Central File, 812.00/9-545, RG 59, NARA.

110. Bi-Weekly Situation Report, September 12, 1945, Records of the Research and Analysis Branch, Latin America Division, Bi-Weekly Situation Reports, 1944–1945, R. & A. 1306.78, RG 226, NARA.

111. Robert Hale to Secretary of State, September 4, 1945, State Department Central File, 812.00/9-445, RG 59, NARA.

112. Bi-Weekly Situation Report, September 12, 1945, Records of the Research and Analysis Branch, Latin America Division, Bi-Weekly Situation Reports, 1944–1945, R. & A. 1306.78, RG 226, NARA. As previously noted, Padilla earned the lasting enmity of many Catholic conservatives as a result of his involvement as attorney general in the 1928 prosecution of José de León Toral, the religious fanatic who shot and killed president-elect Alvaro Obregón. Particularly galling to devout Catholics was the fact that Padilla had

argued that the church hierarchy had backed the assassination.

113. "Vida nacional: Se lanzó," *La Nación*, September 8, 1945.

114. Bi-Weekly Situation Report, October 10, 1945, Records of the Research and Analysis Branch, Latin America Division, Bi-Weekly Situation Reports, 1944–1945, R. & A. 1306.80, RG 226, NARA.

115. Robert Hale to Secretary of State, October 8, 1945, State Department Central File, 812.00/10-845, RG 59, NARA; Santos, *Memorias*, 837.

116. "Gran acogida al homenaje nacional al Escuadrón 201," *La Prensa*, August 13, 1945, and subsequent, almost daily reports over the next two months on the support of movie stars, military men, mothers, teachers, schoolchildren, foreign colonies, and many other groups for the proposed tribute to the squadron.

117. "Las colonias extranjeras tendrán sus 'abanderadas de la victoria," *La Prensa*, September 20, 1945; and "La Liga Central Femenil tiene ya su candidato para abanderada de la victoria," *La Prensa*, September 21, 1945.

118. Victor Hugo Godillo G. (of Comitán, Chiapas) to Manuel Ávila Camacho, August 14, 1945, enclosing the corrido "Al Escuadrón 201," MAC, 550/44-2, AGN; Juan Martínez Morales (of Mexico City), August 20, 1945, enclosing another corrido, MAC, 550/44-2, AGN; and Juan Manuel Márquez (of Mexico City), October 7, 1945, MAC, 550/44-35, AGN.

119. Military Attaché Report no. R-949-45, by Colonel Loren B. Hillsinger, October 25, 1945, Mexico City Naval Attaché Administrative Files, box 8, A21, RG 38, NARA.

120. Francisco L. Urquizo to Ministers of Foreign Relations, the Interior, and the Navy; Chief of the Department of Indigenous Affairs; and Governor of Nayarit (and identical letters to other governors), November 3, 1945, Archivo Histórico, file A/111.0/12, SDN.

121. Francisco L. Urquizo to Javier Rojo Gómez, November 3, 1945, Archivo Histórico, file A/111.0/12, SDN.

122. "Atenta invitación a los habitantes de la ciudad," *El Nacional*, November 16, 1945.

123. Francisco L. Urquizo to Secretario de Educación Pública, November 3, 1945, Archivo Histórico, file A/111.0/12, SDN.

124. General de Brigada Tomás Sánchez Hernández to Secretario de la Defensa Nacional, December 3, 1945, Archivo Histórico, file A/111.0/12, SDN.

125. "Una magna película con las hazañas del E-201," *Novedades*, August 14, 1945; and Carlos Carriedo Galván and Miguel Salkind (of Films Mundiales, SA) to Secretaría de la Defensa Nacional, November 24, 1945, Archivo Histórico, file A/111.0/12, SDN.

126. "La ceremonia en el puente internacional," *El Nacional*, November 17, 1945; and "Recepciones en Saltillo, San Luis Potosí y Querétaro," *El Nacional*, November 18, 1945.

127. Novo, *La vida en México*, 425–26.

128. "Fue emotiva la recepción a los héroes," *El Nacional*, November 19, 1945.

129. Krauze, *El sexenio de Ávila Camacho*, 59.

130. "Brillantemente fue conmemorado el XXXV aniversario de la Revolución," *El Nacional*, November 22, 1945.

131. "El P.R.M. hace un llamado," *El Nacional*, November 20, 1945.

Epilogue

1. Navarro, *Political Intelligence*, chap. 3, provides an account of the election of 1946 acknowledging the likelihood of a degree of fraud but concluding that the polling had generally been orderly and that Padilla had, in any case, lost badly.

2. Gunther, *Inside Latin America*, 34.

3. See "Extraordinaria serenidad del jefe del ejecutivo," *Novedades*, April 11, 1944, for one of many examples of this kind of characterization of Avila Camacho in the Mexican press.

4. Santos, *Memorias*, 827.

5. Lázaro Cárdenas's son, Cuauhtemoc Cárdenas Solórzano, is a former governor of Michoacán (1980–1986), a former mayor (*jefe de gobierno*) of the Federal District (1997–1999), and a three-time candidate for president (1988, 1994, 2000); he was a key figure in the establishment of the Partido de la Revolución Democrática (PRD). The president's grandson, Lázaro Cárdenas Batel, served as the PRD governor of Michoacán from 2004 to 2010. Alemán's son, Miguel Alemán Velasco, has served as governor of Veracruz (1998–2004) and is an influential figure in the PRI. By contrast, the Ávila Camachos seem to disappear from Mexican politics by the end of the 1950s, by which time Manuel and Maximino had died and their brother Rafael had completed his term as governor of Puebla (1951–1957).

6. General de Brigada Antonio Cárdenas Rodríguez to Secretario de

la Defensa Nacional, August 13, 1949; Memorandum from Estado Mayor de la Secretaría de la Defensa Nacional, Sección 3, Mesa 2, September 21, 1949; and Memorandum from Asesoría Judicial, Estado Mayor de la Secretaría de la Defensa Nacional, September 14, 1949, all in Archivo Histórico, file A/111-0/12, SDN. The forcefulness of the general staff's insistence that the FAEM be denied recognition suggests that tensions between the different branches of the armed services may have played some role in this ruling, particularly inasmuch as the Asesoría Judicial's memo reveals that the proposed decree had already won approval from the defense minister; it was subsequently recalled from the president's desk as a result of the general staff's action.

7. Campuzano Rosales, "Los aguiluchos mexicanos," 148–50.

8. "Marcha por última vez el Escuadrón 201," *Reforma*, May 3, 2003.

9. Guy Ray to Joseph W. McGurk, September 8, 1944, General Records of the U.S. Embassy in Mexico City, 1944, classification 710, RG 84, NARA.

10. "Pacto Industrial y de Trabajo," September 27, 1945, cited in Hodges and Gandy, *Mexico Under Siege*, 32.

Archives

MEXICO

Archivo General de la Nación, Mexico City

Archivo Particular de Lázaro Cárdenas

Ramo Gobernación, Dirección General de Gobierno

Ramo Gobernación, Dirección General de Investigaciones Políticas y
Sociales

Ramo Presidentes, Lázaro Cárdenas del Río (1934–1940)

Ramo Presidentes, Manuel Ávila Camacho (1940–1946)

Archivo Histórico de El Colegio de México, Mexico City

Archivo Particular de Eduardo Villaseñor

Archivo Particular de Ignacio García Téllez

Archivo Histórico de la Universidad Nacional Autónoma de México, Mexico City

Fondo Incorporado, Blas Corral Martínez

Fondo Incorporado, Félix F. Palavicini

Fondo Incorporado, Francisco L. Urquizo

Fondo Incorporado, Heriberto Jara

Biblioteca Nacional, Mexico City

Miscelánea Mexicana, Fondo Reservado

Centro de Estudios de la Revolución Mexicana "Lázaro Cárdenas," Jiquilpan, Michoacán
Fondo Francisco J. Múgica
Fondo Lázaro Cárdenas

Fideicomiso Archivos Plutarco Elías Calles y Fernando Torreblanca, Mexico City
Fondo Adolfo de la Huerta
Fondo Joaquín Amaro
Fondo Plutarco Elías Calles

Hemeroteca Nacional, Mexico City

Instituto Nacional de Antropología e Historia, Mexico City
Fototeca

Instituto Tecnológico Autónomo de México, Mexico City
Archivo Manuel Gómez Morín
Biblioteca "Manuel Gómez Morín"

Secretaría de Hacienda y Crédito Público, Biblioteca Miguel Lerdo de Tejada, Mexico City
Archivos Económicos (press clippings)

Secretaría de la Defensa Nacional, Dirección General de Archivo e Historia, Mexico City
Archivo de Cancelados
Archivo Histórico

Secretaría de la Defensa Nacional, Dirección General de Informática, Mexico City
Biblioteca del Ejército

Secretaría de Relaciones Exteriores, Dirección General del Acervo Histórico Diplomático, Mexico City
Archivo de la Embajada de México en los Estados Unidos de América (Fondo Embamex Washington II)
Archivo Histórico "Genaro Estrada"
Archivo Particular de Francisco Castillo Nájera
Archivo Particular de Jaime Torres Bodet
Biblioteca "José María Lafragua"

UNITED STATES

Library of Congress, Washington, D.C.
Prints and Photographs Division

National Archives and Records Administration, College Park, Maryland
    Record Group 38: Records of the Office of the Chief of Naval Operations
    Record Group 43: Records of International Conferences
    Record Group 44: Records of the Office of Government Reports
    Record Group 59: General Records of the Department of State
    Record Group 84: Records of Foreign Service Posts of the Department of State
    Record Group 111: Records of the Office of the Chief Signal Officer
    Record Group 165: Records of the War Department, General and Special Staffs
    Record Group 208: Records of the Office of War Information
    Record Group 218: Records of the Joint Chiefs of Staff
    Record Group 226: Records of the Office of Strategic Services
    Record Group 229: Records of the Office of Inter-American Affairs

University of Delaware, Special Collections Department, Newark, Delaware
    George S. Messersmith Papers

UNITED KINGDOM

National Archives, Kew
    Foreign Office Records, General Correspondence, Political (FO 371)

Newspapers and Magazines
El Hombre Libre
El Nacional
El Popular
El Sinarquista
El Soldado
El Universal
El Universal Gráfico
Excélsior
Hoy
La Nación
La Prensa
La Reacción (?)
La Voz de México
New York Times

Novedades

Omega

Orden

Revista del Ejército

Tiempo

Time

Últimas Noticias de Excélsior

Books, Pamphlets, and Articles

PRIMARY SOURCES

Abascal, Salvador. *Mis recuerdos: Sinarquismo y Colonia María Auxiliadora (1935–1944)*. Mexico City: Editorial Tradición, 1980.

Alamillo Flores, Luis. *Memorias: Luchadores ignorados al lado de los grandes jefes de la Revolución Mexicana*. Mexico City: Ediciones Extemporáneos, 1976.

Alemán, Miguel. *Programa de gobierno*. Mexico City, 1945.

Alemán Valdés, Miguel. *Discursos de Alemán, 11 de septiembre a 30 de diciembre de 1945*. Mexico City, [1946].

———. *Discursos de Alemán, julio–septiembre, 1945*. Mexico City, [1945].

———. *Miguel Alemán contesta*. Austin: University of Texas at Austin, Institute of Latin American Studies, 1975.

———. *Remembranzas y testimonios*. Mexico City: Editorial Grijalbo, 1987.

Angulo, Humberto G. "El costo de la vida, los salarios medios nominales y el salario real." *Revista de Economía* 8, no. 12 (December 15, 1945): 23–26.

Ávila Camacho, Manuel. *Address on the Day of the Americas, April 14th, 1942*. Mexico City: Department of State for Foreign Affairs (SRE), Bureau of International News Service, 1942.

———. *Buenos vecinos, buenos amigos: Discursos pronunciados por los presidentes de México y de los Estados Unidos de América, en Monterrey, N.L., el 20 de abril de 1943*. Mexico City: Secretaría de Gobernación, 1943.

———. *Conceptos del Señor Presidente de la República sobre temas vitales para México, vertidos ante varios congresos y agrupaciones representativas de las fuerzas activas de la nación*. Mexico City: Secretaría de Gobernación, 1942.

———. *El progreso y la abundancia dependen del hombre mismo, no de las instituciones públicas*. Mexico City: Secretaría de Gobernación, 1942.

———. *Enseñar a leer y escribir a un pueblo es redimirlo*. Mexico City: Secretaría de Gobernación, 1944.

————. *Ideario de la nación mexicana*. Mexico City: Ediciones de la Comisión "Editorial de Izquierda" de la Cámara de Diputados del Congreso de la Unión, 1942.

————. *Igualdad democrática de los pueblos: México ante el conflicto mundial*. Mexico City: Secretaría de Gobernación, 1941.

————. *Informe que rinde al H. Congreso de la Unión*. Mexico City: Secretaría de Gobernación, 1942.

————. *The International Policy of Mexico*. Mexico City: Department of State for Foreign Affairs (SRE), Bureau of International News Service, 1941.

————. *La política internacional (1943–44)*. Mexico City: Secretaría de Relaciones Exteriores, Departamento de Información para el Extranjero, 1944.

————. *La unidad de México es la mejor comprobación de que México existe*. Mexico City: Secretaría de Gobernación, 1942.

————. *Los problemas de la guerra y la preparación de la paz: Una América libre, fuerte y culta, inestimable promesa para el mundo*. Mexico City: Secretaría de Gobernación, 1945.

————. *Mensaje a la nación y otros discursos*. Mexico City: Secretaría de Gobernación, 1943.

————. *The Mexican Soldier and the Destiny of the Americas: Speech*. Mexico City: Department of State for Foreign Affairs (SRE), Bureau of International News Service, 1941.

————. *Mexico and the War in the Pacific*. Mexico City: Department of State for Foreign Affairs (SRE), Bureau of International News Service, 1941.

————. *Mexico in a State of War*. Mexico City: Department of State for Foreign Affairs (SRE), Bureau of International News Service, 1942.

————. *Nuestra política exterior (1944–1945)*. Mexico City: Secretaría de Relaciones Exteriores, Departamento de Información para el Extranjero, 1945.

————. *To the Second National Congress of the C.T.M., To the 1941 Graduating Class of Teachers: Speeches*. Mexico City: Department of State for Foreign Affairs (SRE), Bureau of International News Service, 1941.

————. *Un año de política internacional mexicana, 1941–42*. Mexico City: Secretaría de Relaciones Exteriores, Departamento de Información para el Extranjero, 1942.

————. *Una patria más alta y más luminosa*. Mexico City: Secretaría de Gobernación, 1943.

————. *Un nuevo capítulo de la expresión del gobernante mexicano*. Mexico City: Secretaría de Gobernación, 1942.

————, Alberto Lleras Camargo, and Ezequiel Padilla. *Nuestra adhesión a la causa de América*. Mexico City: Secretaría de Relaciones Exteriores, Departamento de Información para el Extranjero, 1945.

———, and Ezequiel Padilla. *Hacia la organización de la nueva paz*. Mexico City: Secretaría de Relaciones Exteriores, Departamento de Información para el Extranjero, 1945.

———, Ezequiel Padilla, Josephus Daniels, Luis Sánchez Ponton, and Jaime Torres Bodet. *Panamerican Day Addresses in Mexico, April 14th, 1941*. Mexico City: Department of State for Foreign Affairs (SRE), Bureau of International News Service, 1941.

Bassols, Narciso. *Debates y propuestas: Antología*. Compiled by Angel Albíter Barrueta. Toluca: Gobierno del Estado de México, 1986.

Benítez, Carlos H. "Mexico Looks Forward." *Inter-American* (May 1944): 10–13.

Braden, Spruille. *Diplomats and Demagogues: The Memoirs of Spruille Braden*. New Rochelle, New York: Arlington House, 1971.

Brenner, Anita. *The Wind That Swept Mexico: The History of the Mexican Revolution, 1910–1942*. New York: Harper and Brothers, 1943.

Campa S., Valentín. *Mi testimonio: Memorias de un comunista mexicano*. 2nd ed. Mexico City: Ediciones de Cultura Popular, 1985.

Cárdenas, Lázaro. *Epistolario de Lázaro Cárdenas*. 2 vols. Mexico City: Siglo Veintiuno Editores, 1975.

———. *Obras: Apuntes, 1941–1956*. Mexico City: Universidad Nacional Autónoma de México, 1973.

Cárdenas Rodríguez, Antonio. *Mis dos misiones*. Mexico City, 1949.

Castillo Nájera, Francisco. *Discurso pronunciado en la ciudad de Los Angeles el 15 de diciembre de 1945*. Mexico City: Secretaría de Relaciones Exteriores, Departamento de Información para el Extranjero, 1945.

Comité Nacional Antinazifascista. *Homenaje del pueblo mexicano a la Unión Soviética: Documentos para la historia*. Mexico City: Imprenta de la Cámara de Diputados, 1944.

Confederación de Trabajadores de México. *C.T.M., 1937–1941*. Mexico City: Confederación de Trabajadores de México, 1942.

Corona del Rosal, Alfonso. *Mis memorias políticas*. Mexico City: Editorial Grijalbo, 1995.

Correa, Eduardo J. *El balance del Ávila Camachismo*. Mexico City: El Autor, 1946.

Daniels, Josephus. *Shirt Sleeve Diplomat*. Chapel Hill: University of North Carolina Press, 1947.

Gaxiola, Francisco Javier. *Memorias*. Mexico City: Editorial Porrúa, 1975.

Gómez, Marte R. *Vida política contemoránea: Cartas de Marte R. Gómez.* 2 vols. Mexico City: Fondo de Cultura Económica, 1978.

Gómez Morín, Manuel. *Diez años de México: Informes del jefe de Acción Nacional.* Mexico City: Editorial Jus, 1950.

Gunther, John. *Inside Latin America.* New York: Harper and Brothers, 1941.

Hediger, Ernest S. "Impact of War on Mexico's Economy." *Foreign Policy Reports* 19, no. 7 (June 15, 1943): 78–84.

Hull, Cordell. *The Memoirs of Cordell Hull.* 2 vols. New York: Macmillan, 1948.

Kirk, Betty. *Covering the Mexican Front: The Battle of Europe versus America.* Norman: University of Oklahoma Press, 1942.

Lombardo Toledano, Vicente. *Obra histórico-cronológica.* 19 vols. (1940–1946). Mexico City: Centro de Estudios Filosóficos, Políticos y Sociales "Vicente Lombardo Toledano," 1994.

———. *Obras completas.* 25 vols. Puebla: Gobierno del Estado de Puebla, 1990.

[Messersmith, George S., and Francisco Castillo Nájera.] *Cordialidad entre México y Estados Unidos.* Mexico City: Secretaría de Relaciones Exteriores, Departamento de Información para el Extranjero, 1946.

Mexico, Departamento del Distrito Federal, Dirección de Acción Social. *México en la postguerra (Primer Ciclo de Conferencias).* Mexico City, 1944.

Mexico, Junta de Administración y Vigilancia de la Propiedad Extranjera. *Breve memoria de su actuación durante el período comprendido entre el 15 de junio de 1942 y el 15 de junio de 1943.* Mexico City, [1943].

Mexico, Secretaría de Economía, Dirección de Estudios Económicos. *Desarrollo de la economía nacional, 1939–1947.* Mexico City, 1947.

Mexico, Secretaría de Gobernación. *Seis años de actividad nacional.* Mexico City, 1946.

Mexico, Secretaría de la Defensa Nacional. *Memoria de la Secretaría de la Defensa Nacional, septiembre de 1940–agosto de 1941.* Mexico City, 1941.

———. *Memoria de la Secretaría de la Defensa Nacional, septiembre de 1941–agosto de 1942.* Mexico City, 1942.

———. *Memoria de la Secretaría de la Defensa Nacional, septiembre de 1942–agosto de 1943.* Mexico City, 1943.

———. *Memoria de la Secretaría de la Defensa Nacional, septiembre de 1943–agosto de 1944.* Mexico City, 1944.

———. *Memoria de la Secretaría de la Defensa Nacional, septiembre de 1944–agosto de 1945.* Mexico City, 1945.

Mexico, Secretaría de la Economía Nacional, Oficina de Barómetros Económicos. *El desarrollo de la economía nacional bajo la influencia de la guerra, 1939–1945.* Mexico City, 1945.

Mexico, Secretaría de Relaciones Exteriores. *Memoria de la Secretaría de Relaciones Exteriores, septiembre de 1939–agosto de 1940*. Mexico City, 1941.

———. *Memoria de la Secretaría de Relaciones Exteriores, septiembre de 1940–agosto de 1941*. Mexico City, 1941.

———. *Memoria de la Secretaría de Relaciones Exteriores, septiembre de 1941–agosto de 1942*. 2 vols. Mexico City, 1942.

———. *Memoria de la Secretaría de Relaciones Exteriores, septiembre de 1942–agosto de 1943*. 2 vols. Mexico City, 1943.

———. *Memoria de la Secretaría de Relaciones Exteriores, septiembre de 1943–agosto de 1944*. Mexico City, 1944.

———. *Memoria de la Secretaría de Relaciones Exteriores, septiembre de 1944–agosto de 1945*. 2 vols. Mexico City, 1945.

———. *Memoria de la Secretaría de Relaciones Exteriores, septiembre de 1945–agosto de 1946*. Mexico City, 1946.

Millan, Verna Carleton. "Inflation Merry-Go-Round." *Inter-American* (April 1944): 29–31, 48.

Novo, Salvador. *La vida en México en el periodo presidencial de Manuel Ávila Camacho*. Mexico City: Consejo Nacional para la Cultura y las Artes, 1994.

Ortiz Garza, Nazario S. *Remembranzas: Visiones de un luchador*. Mexico City: Fundación de Invertigaciones Sociales, A.C., 1991.

Padilla, Ezequiel. *The Agreements with the United States before the Mexican Senate*. Mexico City: Department of State for Foreign Affairs (SRE), Bureau of International News Service, 1941.

———. *América después de la victoria*. Mexico City: Secretaría de Relaciones Exteriores, Departamento de Información para el Extranjero, 1944.

[———]. *The Continental Doctrine in the Mexican Senate*. Mexico City: Department of State for Foreign Affairs (SRE), Bureau of International News Service, 1941.

———. *En la tribuna de la Revolución: Discursos*. Mexico City: Editorial Cultura, 1929.

———. *Nuestra política internacional*. Mexico City: Secretaría de Relaciones Exteriores, Departamento de Información para el Extranjero, 1945.

———. *Seguridad económica y régimen democrático en la post-guerra*. Mexico City: Secretaría de Relaciones Exteriores, Departamento de Información para el Extranjero, 1943.

———. *Three Speeches at Rio de Janeiro*. Mexico City: Department of State for Foreign Affairs (SRE), Bureau of International News Service, 1942.

[————]. *Words That Made History: Three Addresses by Ezequiel Padilla*. New York: Consulate General of Mexico, 1942.

————, Mario de Pimentel Brandao, and José L. Chouhy Terra. *La defensa política de América*. Mexico City: Secretaría de Relaciones Exteriores, Departamento de Información para el Extranjero, 1943.

Padilla, José Ignacio. *Sinarquismo: Contrarrevolución*. Mexico City: Editorial Polis, 1948.

Partido de la Revolución Mexicana. *Ávila Camacho y su ideología, ¡La Revolución en marcha!: Jira electoral*. Mexico City: [PRM], 1940.

————. *Memoria del Partido de la Revolución Mexicana, 1943–1944*. Mexico City: Departamento de Prensa y Propaganda del PRM, [1944].

————. *¡México en guerra!* Mexico City: PRM, 1942.

————. *33 meses al servicio de la Revolución, Memoria del Partido de la Revolución Mexicana, 1940–1943*. Mexico City: Departamento de Prensa y Propaganda del PRM, [1943].

Partido Revolucionario Institucional. *Historia documental del partido de la Revolución*. 14 vols. Mexico City: Partido Revolucionario Institucional, Instituto de Capacitación Política, 1981.

Prewett, Virginia. "The Mexican Army." *Foreign Affairs* 19, no. 3 (April 1941): 609–20.

Sandoval Castarrica, Enrique. *Historia oficial de la Fuerza Aérea Expedicionaria Mexicana*. Mexico City: Secretaría de la Defensa Nacional, 1946.

Santos, Gonzalo N. *Memorias*. Mexico City: Grijalbo, 1986.

Silva Herzog, Jesús. *La Revolución Mexicana en crisis*. Mexico City: Ediciones Cuadernos Americanos, 1944.

————. *Una vida en la vida de México*. Mexico City: Siglo Veintiuno Editores, 1986.

————. *Un ensayo sobre la Revolución Mexicana*. Mexico City: Cuadernos Americanos, 1946.

Simpson, Lesley Byrd. *Many Mexicos*. 2nd ed. New York: G. P. Putnam's Sons, 1946.

Sindicato Nacional de Trabajadores de Hacienda. *Conferencias de orientación nacional*. Mexico City: Biblioteca de Publicaciones Sindicales, [1942].

Stettinius, Edward R., Jr. *The Diaries of Edward R. Stettinius, Jr., 1943–1946*. Edited by Thomas M. Campbell and George C. Herring. New York: New Viewpoints, 1975.

Stevenson, Coke R., and Ezequiel Padilla. *La política del buen vecino y los mexicanos en Texas*. Mexico City: Secretaría de Relaciones Exteriores, Departamento de Información para el Extranjero, 1943.

Suárez, Eduardo. *Comentarios y recuerdos (1926–1946)*. Mexico City: Editorial Porrúa, 1977.

Tannenbaum, Frank. *Mexico: The Struggle for Peace and Bread*. New York: Alfred A. Knopf, 1950.

Taracena, Alfonso. *La vida en México bajo Ávila Camacho*. 2 vols. Mexico City: Editorial Jus, 1976.

Torres Bodet, Jaime. *Años contra el tiempo*. Mexico City: Editorial Porrúa, 1969.

———. *Educación mexicana: Discursos, entrevistas, mensajes*. Mexico City: Ediciones de la Secretaría de Educación Pública, 1944.

United States, Department of State. *Foreign Relations of the United States*. Multiple volumes covering 1940–1945. Washington, D.C., 1963–1965.

Urquizo, Francisco L. *3 de Diana*. Mexico City: Publicaciones Mundiales, 1947.

Valadés, José C. *La unidad nacional*. Vol. 10 of *Historia general de la Revolución Mexicana*. Mexico City: Ediciones Gernika, 1985.

Véjar Vázquez, Octavio. *Hacia una escuela de unidad nacional: Discursos*. Mexico City: Ediciones de la Secretaría de Educación Pública, 1944.

Villaseñor, Eduardo. "La economía de guerra en México." *Investigación Económica* 3, no. 1 (January–March 1943): 7–33.

———. *Memorias-testimonio*. Mexico City: Fondo de Cultura Económica, 1974.

Villaseñor, Victor Manuel. *Memorias de un hombre de izquierda*. 2 vols. 2nd ed. Mexico City: Biografias Gandesa, Editorial Grijalbo, 1977.

Wallace, Henry A., Ezequiel Padilla, and Eduardo Salazar. *Panamerican Friendship: Speeches*. Mexico City: Department of State for Foreign Affairs (SRE), Bureau of International News Service, 1941.

Wilkie, James W. *Frente a la Revolución Mexicana: 17 protagonistas de la etapa constructiva; Entrevistas de historia oral*. 3 vols. Mexico City: Universidad Autónoma Metropolitana, 1995.

SECONDARY SOURCES

Aboites Aguilar, Luis. *Excepciones y privilegios: Modernización tributaria y centralización en México, 1922–1972*. Mexico City: El Colegio de México, 2003.

Aguayo, Sergio. *La charola: Una historia de los servicios de inteligencia en México*. Mexico City: Grijalbo, 2001.

Aguilar Camín, Héctor, and Lorenzo Meyer. *In the Shadow of the Mexican Revolution: Contemporary Mexican History, 1910–1989*. Translated by Luis Alberto Fierro. Austin: University of Texas Press, 1993.

Benjamin, Thomas. "The Leviathan on the Zócalo: Recent Historiography of the Postrevolutionary Mexican State." *Latin American Research Review* 20, no. 3 (1985): 195–217.

Bertaccini, Tiziana. *El regimen prísta frente a las clases medias, 1943–1964*. Mexico City: Consejo Nacional para la Cultura y las Artes, 2009.

Bethell, Leslie. "From the Second World War to the Cold War: 1944–1954." In *Exporting Democracy: The United States and Latin America*, edited by Abraham F. Lowenthal, 41–70. Baltimore, MD: Johns Hopkins University Press, 1991.

———, and Ian Roxborough. "Latin America between the Second World War and the Cold War: Some Reflections on the 1945–1948 Conjuncture." *Journal of Latin American Studies* 20 (1988): 167–89.

———, and Ian Roxborough, eds. *Latin America between the Second World War and the Cold War, 1944–1948*. Cambridge: Cambridge University Press, 1992.

Boils, Guillermo. *Los militares y la política en México, 1815–1974*. Mexico City: Ediciones "El Caballito," 1975.

Bortz, Jeffrey L. *Industrial Wages in Mexico City, 1939–1975*. New York: Garland, 1987.

Brandenburg, Frank. *The Making of Modern Mexico*. Englewood Cliffs, NJ: Prentice-Hall, 1964.

Brown, Lyle C. "Mexican Church-State Relations, 1933–1940." *Journal of Church and State* 6 (1964): 202–22.

Buchenau, Jürgen. "Una ventana al más allá: Los últimos años de Plutarco Elías Calles, 1941–1945." *Boletín, Fideicomiso Archivos Plutarco Elías Calles y Fernando Torreblanca* 46 (May–August 2004): 1–32.

Calvo, Dana. "The Saga of the Aztec Eagles." *Los Angeles Times Magazine* (July 25, 2004): 12–15, 29.

Camp, Roderic Ai. *Generals in the Palacio: The Military in Modern Mexico*. New York: Oxford University Press, 1992.

———. *Mexican Political Biographies, 1935–1993*. Austin: University of Texas Press, 1995.

———. *Mexico's Leaders: Their Education and Recruitment*. Tucson: University of Arizona Press, 1980.

Campbell, Hugh G. *La derecha radical en México, 1929–1949*. Translated by Pilar Martínez Negrete. Mexico City: Secretaría de Educación Pública, 1976.

Carbó, Margarita. *Ningún compromiso que lesione al país: Lázaro Cárdenas y la defensa de la soberanía*. Mexico City: Plaza y Valdés, 2002.

Cárdenas, Héctor. *Historia de las relaciones entre México y Rusia*. Mexico City: Secretaría de Relaciones Exteriores, 1993.

Cárdenas de la Peña, Enrique. *Gesta en el Golfo: La Segunda Guerra Mundial y México*. Mexico City: Editorial Primacias, 1966.

Carr, Barry. *Marxism and Communism in Twentieth-Century Mexico*. Lincoln: University of Nebraska Press, 1992.

Cline, Howard F. *Mexico: Revolution to Evolution, 1940–1960*. London: Oxford University Press, 1962.

————. *The United States and Mexico*. Rev. ed. New York: Atheneum, 1963.

Conn, Stetson, and Byron Fairchild. *The Framework of Hemisphere Defense*. Washington, D.C.: Department of the Army, Office of the Chief of Military History, 1960.

Contreras, Ariel José. *México 1940: Industrialización y crisis política*. Mexico City: Siglo Veintiuno Editores, 1977.

Cuellar Ponce de León, Alfonso. *¿Qué fue y que es el Escuadrón 201?* [Mexico City]: ISSSTE, 1995.

Dwyer, John J. *The Agrarian Dispute: The Expropriation of American-Owned Rural Land in Postrevolutionary Mexico*. Durham, NC: Duke University Press, 2008.

————. "Diplomatic Weapons of the Weak: Mexican Policymaking during the U.S.-Mexican Agrarian Dispute, 1934–1941." *Diplomatic History* 26, no. 3 (Summer 2002): 375–95.

Garfias Magaña, Luis. "El General Joaquin Amaro, el Istmo de Tehuantepec y la soberanía nacional." *Boletín, Fideicomiso Archivos Plutarco Elías Calles y Fernando Torreblanca* 38 (September–December 2001): 1–32.

Garrido, Luis Javier. *El partido de la Revolución institucionalizada: La formación del nuevo estado en México (1928–1945)*. Mexico City: Secretaría de Educación Pública, 1986.

Gauss, Susan M. *Made in Mexico: Regions, Nation, and the State in the Rise of Mexican Industrialism, 1920s–1940s*. University Park: Pennsylvania State University Press, 2010.

Gellman, Irwin F. *Good Neighbor Diplomacy: United States Policies in Latin America, 1933–1945*. Baltimore, MD: Johns Hopkins University Press, 1979.

Gillingham, Paul. "Maximino's Bulls: Popular Protest after the Mexican Revolution, 1940–1952." *Past and Present* 206 (February 2010): 175–211.

————. "Military *Caciquismo* in the PRIísta State: General Mange's Command in Veracruz." In *Forced Marches: Soldiers and Military Caciques in Modern Mexico*, edited by Ben Fallaw and Terry Rugeley, 210–37. Tucson: University of Arizona Press, 2012.

González y González, Luis. *Los días del Presidente Cárdenas*. Vol. 15 of *Historia de la Revolución Mexicana*. Mexico City: El Colegio de México, 1981.

Haber, Stephen H. *Industry and Underdevelopment: The Industrialization of Mexico, 1890–1940*. Stanford, CA: Stanford University Press, 1989.

Hamilton, Nora. *The Limits of State Autonomy: Post-Revolutionary Mexico.* Princeton, NJ: Princeton University Press, 1982.

Hart, John Mason. *The Coming and the Process of the Mexican Revolution.* Berkeley: University of California Press, 1987.

Hermida Ruiz, Angel J. *Cárdenas: Comandante del Pacífico.* Mexico City: Ediciones El Caballito, 1982.

Hernández Chávez, Alicia. *La mecánica cardenista.* Vol. 16 of *Historia de la Revolución Mexicana.* Mexico City: El Colegio de México, 1979.

Hernández Enríquez, Gustavo Abel, and Armando Rojas Trujillo. *Manuel Ávila Camacho: Biografía de un revolucionario con historia.* 2 vols. Mexico City: Ediciones del Gobierno del Estado de Puebla, 1986.

Hodges, Donald C. *Mexican Anarchism after the Revolution.* Austin: University of Texas Press, 1995.

———, and Ross Gandy. *Mexico 1910–1982: Reform or Revolution?* London: Zed Press, 1983.

———. *Mexico under Siege: Popular Resistance to Presidential Despotism.* London: Zed Books, 2002.

Instituto Mexicano de Cultura. *Manuel Ávila Camacho.* Mexico City: Talleres del SEI, 1981.

Joseph, Gilbert M., Anne Rubenstein, and Eric Zolov, eds. *Fragments of a Golden Age: The Politics of Culture in Mexico since 1940.* Durham, NC: Duke University Press, 2001.

Katz, Friedrich. "Gilberto Bosques and the Refugees." *Americas* 57, no. 1 (July 2000): 1–12.

———. *The Secret War in Mexico: Europe, the United States, and the Mexican Revolution.* Chicago, IL: University of Chicago Press, 1981.

Knight, Alan. "Cardenismo: Juggernaut or Jalopy?" *Journal of Latin American Studies* 26, no. 1 (February 1994): 73–107.

———. "The Rise and Fall of Cardenismo, c. 1930–c. 1946." In *Mexico since Independence*, edited by Leslie Bethell, 241–320. Cambridge: Cambridge University Press, 1991.

Krauze, Enrique. *El sexenio de Ávila Camacho.* Mexico City: Editorial Clio, 1999.

———. *Mexico, Biography of Power: A History of Modern Mexico, 1810–1996.* Translated by Hank Heifetz. New York: Harper-Collins, 1997.

Lajous, Alejandra. *Los orígenes del partido único en México.* Mexico City: Universidad Nacional Autónoma de México, 1979.

Lerner, Victoria. *La educación socialista.* Vol. 17 of *Historia de la Revolución Mexicana.* Mexico City: El Colegio de México, 1979.

Lieuwen, Edwin. *Mexican Militarism: The Political Rise and Fall of the*

Revolutionary Army, 1910–1940. Westport, CT: Greenwood Press, 1981.

Loaeza, Soledad. *El Partido Acción Nacional: La larga marcha, 1939–1994; Oposición leal y partido de protesta.* Mexico City: Fondo de Cultura Económica, 1999.

Loyo Camacho, Martha Beatriz. *Joaquín Amaro y el proceso del institucionalización del Ejército Mexicano, 1917–1931.* Mexico City: Universidad Nacional Autónoma de México et al., 2003.

Loyola, Rafael, ed. *Entre la guerra y la estabilidad política: El México de los 40.* Mexico City: Editorial Grijalbo, 1990.

Loyola Díaz, Rafael. "La influencia de las 'democracias' durante la Segunda Guerra Mundial en México." *Reportes de Investigación, Universidad Autónoma Metropolitana (División de Ciencias Sociales y Humanidades)* 20 [1980]: 1–21.

Lozoya, Jorge Alberto. *El ejército mexicano (1911–1965).* Mexico City: El Colegio de México, Centro de Estudios Internacionales, 1970. [Published as *Jornadas 65.*]

Martínez Assad, Carlos, ed. *La sucesión presidencial en México, 1928–1988.* Mexico City: Nueva Imagen, 1992.

Martínez Valle, Adolfo. *El Partido Acción Nacional: Una historia política.* Mexico City: Editorial Porrúa, 2000.

Medin, Tzvi. *El sexenio alemanista: Ideología y praxis política de Miguel Alemán.* Mexico City: Ediciones Era, 1990.

Medina, Luis. *Civilismo y modernización del autoritarismo.* Vol. 20 of *Historia de la Revolución Mexicana.* Mexico City: El Colegio de México, 1979.

———. *Del cardenismo al Ávilacamachismo.* Vol. 18 of *Historia de la Revolución Mexicana.* Mexico City: El Colegio de México, 1978.

Meyer, Jean. *El sinarquismo, el cardenismo y la iglesia, 1937–1947.* Mexico City: Tusquets Editores, 2003.

———. *El sinarquismo ¿Un fascismo mexicano? 1937–1947.* Mexico City: Editorial Joaquín Mortiz, 1979.

———. "Revolution and Reconstruction in the 1920s." In *Mexico since Independence*, edited by Leslie Bethell, 201–40. Cambridge: Cambridge University Press, 1991.

Meyer, Lorenzo. *México y los Estados Unidos en el conflicto petrolero (1917–1942).* Mexico City: El Colegio de México, 1972.

Meyer, Michael C., and William L. Sherman. *The Course of Mexican History.* 5th ed. New York: Oxford University Press, 1995.

Middlebrook, Kevin J. *The Paradox of Revolution: Labor, the State, and*

Authoritarianism in Mexico. Baltimore, MD: Johns Hopkins University Press, 1995.

Miller, Michael Nelson. *Red, White, and Green: The Maturing of Mexicanidad, 1940–1946*. Southwestern Studies 107. El Paso: Texas Western Press, 1998.

Moreno, Daniel. *Los partidos políticos del México contemporáneo*. 8th ed. Mexico City: Costa-Amic Editores, 1982.

Mosk, Sanford A. *Industrial Revolution in Mexico*. Berkeley: University of California Press, 1954.

Moya Palencia, Mario. *1942 ¡Mexicanos al grito de guerra!* Mexico City: Grupo Editorial Miguel Ángel Porrúa, 1992.

Navarro, Aaron W. "La fusión fracasada: Almazán y Amaro en la campaña presidencial de 1940." *Boletín, Fideicomiso Archivos Plutarco Elías Calles y Fernando Torreblanca* 49 (May–August 2005): 1–32.

———. *Political Intelligence and the Creation of Modern Mexico, 1938–1954*. University Park: Pennsylania State University Press, 2010.

Newcomer, Daniel. *Reconciling Modernity: Urban State Formation in 1940s León, Mexico*. Lincoln: University of Nebraska Press, 2004.

Newell G., Roberto, and Luis Rubio F. *Mexico's Dilemma: The Political Origins of Economic Crisis*. Boulder, CO: Westview Press, 1984.

Niblo, Stephen R. *The Impact of War: Mexico and World War II*. La Trobe University Institute of Latin American Studies Occasional Paper 10. Melbourne: La Trobe University Institute of Latin American Studies, 1988.

———. *Mexico in the 1940s: Modernity, Politics, and Corruption*. Wilmington, DE: Scholarly Resources, 1999.

———. *War, Diplomacy, and Development: The United States and Mexico, 1938–1954*. Wilmington, DE: Scholarly Resources, 1995.

Obregón Pagán, Eduardo. *Murder at the Sleepy Lagoon: Zoot Suits, Race, and Riot in Wartime L.A.* Chapel Hill: University of North Carolina Press, 2003.

Oikión Solano, Verónica. *Michoacán en la vía de la unidad nacional, 1940–1944*. Mexico City: Instituto Nacional de Estudios Históricos de la Revolución Mexicana, 1995.

Ortiz Garza, José Luis. *México en guerra: La historia secreta de los negocios entre empresarios mexicanos de la comunicación, los Nazis y E.U.A.* Mexico City: Planeta, 1989.

Padilla, Tanalís. *Rural Resistance in the Land of Zapata: The Jaramillista Movement and the Myth of the Pax-Priísta, 1940–1962*. Durham, NC: Duke University Press, 2008.

Paz Salinas, María Emilia. *Strategy, Security, and Spies: Mexico and the U.S. as Allies in World War II*. University Park: Pennsylvania State University Press, 1997.

Piñeyro Piñeyro, José Luis. "The Mexican Army and the State: Historical and Political Perspective." *Revue Internionale de Sociologie* 14 (April–August 1978): 111–57.

Plasencia de la Parra, Enrique. "Las infanterías invisibles: Mexicanos en la Segunda Guerra Mundial." *Historia Mexicana* 52, no. 4 (April–June 2003): 1021–71.

Ramírez Melgarejo, Ramón. "La bola chiquita, un movimiento campesino." In *Adaptación, cambio y rebelión*. Tlalpan, D.F.: Centro de Investigaciones Superiores, Instituto Nacional de Antropología e Historia, 1974.

Rankin, Monica A. *¡México, la patria!: Propaganda and Production during World War II*. Lincoln: University of Nebraska Press, 2009.

Rath, Thomas. "'*Que el cielo un soldado en cada hijo te dio . . .*': Conscription, Recalcitrance and Resistance in Mexico in the 1940s." *Journal of Latin American Studies* 37, no. 3 (2005): 507–31.

Reich, Cary. *The Life of Nelson A. Rockefeller: Worlds to Conquer, 1908–1958*. New York: Doubleday, 1996.

Reynolds, Clark W. *The Mexican Economy: Twentieth-Century Structure and Growth*. New Haven, CT: Yale University Press, 1970.

Rock, David, ed. *Latin America in the 1940s: War and Postwar Transitions*. Berkeley: University of California Press, 1994.

Ross, Stanley, ed. *Is the Mexican Revolution Dead?* New York: Alfred A. Knopf, 1966.

Saragoza, Alex M. *The Monterrey Elite and the Mexican State*. Austin: University of Texas Press, 1988.

Schuler, Friedrich E. *Mexico Between Hitler and Roosevelt: Mexican Foreign Relations in the Age of Lázaro Cárdenas, 1934–1940*. Albuquerque: University of New Mexico Press, 1998.

Schwab, Stephen I. "The Role of the Mexican Expeditionary Air Force in World War II: Late, Limited, but Symbolically Significant." *Journal of Military History* 66, no. 4 (October 2002): 1115–40.

Servín, Elisa. *Ruptura y oposición: El movimiento henriquista, 1945–1954*. Mexico City: Cal y Arena, 2001.

———, ed. *Del nacionalismo al neoliberalismo, 1940–1994*. Mexico City: CIDE, FCE, Conaculta, INEHRM, Fundación Cultural de la Ciudad de México, 2010.

Smith, Benjamin T. *Pistoleros and Popular Movements: The Politics of State Formation in Postrevolutionary Oaxaca*. Lincoln: University of Nebraska Press, 2009.

Smith, Peter H. "Mexico since 1946: Dynamics of an Authoritarian Regime." In *Mexico since Independence*, edited by Leslie Bethell, 321–96. Cambridge: Cambridge University Press, 1991.

Smith, Robert Freeman. *The United States and Revolutionary Nationalism in Mexico, 1916–1932*. Chicago, IL: University of Chicago Press, 1972.

Solís, Leopoldo. *La realidad económica mexicana: Retrovisión y perspectivas*. Mexico City: Siglo Veintiuno Editores, 1970.

Sosenski D., Gregorio. *La cuarta frontera de Baja California y el gobierno surpeninsular del general Francisco J. Múgica*. Mexico City: Instituto Nacional de Estudios Históricos de la Revolución Mexicana, 2001.

Spenser, Daniela. *The Impossible Triangle: Mexico, Soviet Russia, and the United States in the 1920s*. Durham, NC: Duke University Press, 1999.

Stiller, Jesse H. *George S. Messersmith: Diplomat of Democracy*. Chapel Hill: University of North Carolina Press, 1987.

Torres, Blanca. *Hacia la utopía industrial*. Vol. 21 of *Historia de la Revolución Mexicana*. Mexico City: El Colegio de México, 1984.

———. *México en la Segunda Guerra Mundial*. Vol. 19 of *Historia de la Revolución Mexicana*. Mexico City: El Colegio de México, 1979.

Wilkie, James W. *The Mexican Revolution: Federal Expenditure and Social Change since 1910*. Berkeley: University of California Press, 1967.

Womack, John, Jr. "The Mexican Revolution, 1910–1920." In *Mexico since Independence*, edited by Leslie Bethell, 125–200. Cambridge: Cambridge University Press, 1991.

———. *Zapata and the Mexican Revolution*. New York: Alfred A. Knopf, 1969.

Wood, Bryce. *The Making of the Good Neighbor Policy*. New York: Columbia University Press, 1961.

UNPUBLISHED MANUSCRIPTS

Campuzano Rosales, Antonio. "Los aguiluchos mexicanos: El Escuadrón 201, una historia olvidada." *Licenciatura* thesis, Escuela Nacional de Estudios Profesionales "Acatlán," Universidad Nacional Autónoma de México, 1995.

Chacón, Susana. "El conflicto de la cooperación: México–Estados Unidos (1940–1955)." Thesis in the possession of the author, n.d.

Ezeta Benavides, Leopoldo. "La dependencia informativa ante el hundimiento del buque tanque 'Potrero del Llano,' mayo 13 de 1942." Licenciatura thesis, Universidad Nacional Autónoma de México, 1988.

Fein, Seth. "Hollywood and United States–Mexican Relations in the Golden Age of Mexican Cinema." PhD diss., University of Texas, 1996.

Gauss, Susan Marie. "Made in Mexico: The Rise of Mexican Industrialism,

1938–1952." PhD diss., State University of New York–Stony Brook, 2002.

Guevara, María de la Luz. "*Por la Nacion*: U.S.-México Collaboration during World War II and the Mexican Fighter Squadron 201." Paper presented at ILASSA Student Conference on Latin America, University of Texas, Austin, 2004.

Harrison, Donald Fisher. "United States–Mexican Military Collaboration during World War II." PhD diss., Georgetown University, 1976.

Katz, Friedrich. "International Wars, Mexico, and U.S. Hegemony." Paper presented at the Boston Area Latin American History Workshop, Harvard University, Cambridge, MA, October 10, 2005.

Navarro, Aaron. "Opposition and Dominance in the Mexican Presidential Election of 1940: The Challenge of Almazanismo." Paper presented at the Graduate Student Workshop on Latin American History, Harvard University, Cambridge, MA, March 5, 2003.

———. "Pillar of the State: The Formation of Mexican Intelligence, 1938–1954." Paper presented at the Latin American Studies Association Congress, Las Vegas, NV, October 7–9, 2004.

———. "Political Intelligence: Opposition, Parties and the Military in Mexico, 1938–1954." PhD diss., Harvard University, 2004.

Padilla, Tanalís. "From Agraristas to Guerrilleros: The Jaramillista Movement and the Myth of the Pax Priísta." PhD diss., University of California–San Diego, 2001.

Quiroz Carranza, Roxana. "La propaganda antibélica en Mexico desde los antecedentes de la Segunda Guerra Mundial hasta el termino de la Guerra Fría." Licenciatura thesis, Universidad Nacional Autónoma de México, 1991.

Rankin, Monica Ann. "¡México, la Patria! Modernity, National Unity, and Propaganda during World War II." PhD diss., University of Arizona, 2004.

———. "Selling the Peace: Revolution and Industrialization in Mexico's World War II Propaganda." Paper presented at the Latin American Studies Association Congress, Las Vegas, NV, October 7–9, 2004.

Rath, Thomas. "Que el cielo un soldado en cada hijo te dió . . . ; Conscription, Recalcitrance, and Resistance in Mexico in the 1940s." M.Phil. thesis, Oxford University, 2003.

Rivera Torres, Beatriz Martha. "Industrialización y movimiento obrero en México durante el período de la Segunda Guerra Mundial." Licenciatura thesis, Universidad Nacional Autónoma de México, 1980.

Samano Iturria, Claudia. "Notas sobre la frontera norte de México durante la Segunda Guerra Mundial." Licenciatura thesis, Universidad Nacional Autónoma de México, 1992.

Sanders, Nichole Marie. "Gender, Welfare and the 'Mexican Miracle': The Politics of Modernization in Postrevolutionary Mexico." PhD diss., University of California–Irvine, 2003.

Tudor, William G. "Flight of Eagles: The Mexican Expeditionary Air Force *Escuadrón 201* in World War II." PhD diss., Texas Christian University, 1997.

Velázquez Flores, Rafael. "Factores, bases y fundamentos de la política exterior de México durante la Segunda Guerra Mundial." Licenciatura thesis, Universidad Nacional Autónoma de México, 1988.

Wager, Stephen Joseph. "The Mexican Army, 1940–1982: The Country Comes First." PhD diss., Stanford University, 1992.

Walker, Phyllis Greene. "The Modern Mexican Military: Political Influence and Institutional Interests in the 1980s." MA thesis, American University, 1987.

Zavala Pérez, Oscar. "La participación de México en la Segunda Guerra Mundial." Licenciatura thesis, Universidad Nacional Autónoma de México, 1995.